European Anti-Discrimination and the
Politics of Citizenship

European Anti-Discrimination and the Politics of Citizenship

Britain and France

Edited by

Christophe Bertossi
Senior Research Fellow
Institut Français des Relations Internationales (IFRI)

First published in 2007 by
PALGRAVE MACMILLAN
Houndmills, Basingstoke, Hampshire RG21 6XS and
175 Fifth Avenue, New York, N.Y. 10010
Companies and representatives throughout the world.

PALGRAVE MACMILLAN is the global academic imprint of the Palgrave Macmillan division of St. Martin's Press, LLC and of Palgrave Macmillan Ltd. Macmillan® is a registered trademark in the United States, United Kingdom and other countries. Palgrave is a registered trademark in the European Union and other countries.

ISBN-13: 978-1-4039-9361-8
ISBN-10: 1-4039-9361-0

This book is printed on paper suitable for recycling and made from fully managed and sustained forest sources.

A catalogue record for this book is available from the British Library.

Library of Congress Cataloging-in-Publication Data
    European anti-discrimination and the politics of citizenship : Britain and France / edited by Christophe Bertossi.
        p. cm.
    Includes bibliographical references and index.
    ISBN 1-4039-9361-0 (cloth)
        1. Citizenship – Great Britain. 2. Citizenship – France. 3. Discrimination – Government policy – Great Britain. 4. Discrimination – Government policy – France. 5. Multiculturalism – Great Britain. 6. Multiculturalism – France. I. Bertossi, Christophe.

JN906.E97 2007
323.60941—dc22   2006049475

10 9 8 7 6 5 4 3 2 1
16 15 14 13 12 11 10 09 08 07

To Z.

Contents

Part III   Discriminations in French and British Contexts

Acknowledgments

This book is the outcome of my stay at the Centre for Research in Ethnic Relations (CRER), University of Warwick (UK) between 2001 and 2003. It would never have existed without the constant encouragements of its Director, Professor Danièle Joly, and my colleagues and friends at CRER: Professor John Rex, Dr Khursheed Wadia, Edgar Hassan, Mike McLeod, Dr Bob Carter, Sam Hundal, and Caroline Oakman. Professor Catherine Wihtol de Wenden from the Centre d'Etudes et de Recherches Internationales (Sciences Po in Paris) and Dr Khadija Mohsen-Finan from the French Institute of International Relations (IFRI) further supported me, and provided me with thoughtful and always useful comments. In this process, I crossed paths with many others with whom my initial propositions were discussed, reformulated, and clarified, notably Professor Hideki Tarumoto (Hokkaido University), Professor Mats Andren (Göteborg University), Professor Gunther Dietz (Grenada University), Professor Jean Baubérot (Ecole Pratique des Hautes Etudes), and Jean-Michel Belorgey (Conseil d'Etat).

As editor of the book, I am much indebted to all the contributors for their friendly willingness to participate in this project.

I would also like to thank Rania Nader, Ziad Bou Akl, and Katharine Hoagland for helping with the final manuscript. Please forgive me if I have missed you out: I thank each and every one of you for conversations and assistance.

Finally, when I began this project, I found in Rémy Leveau's writings a vivid inspiration, although I had not met him. When I eventually had the chance to work with him at IFRI, this encounter became an even more illuminating experience. He finally left us all suddenly, but he left us with his inspiration. I hope this book will meet his expectations.

Notes on Contributors

Valérie Amiraux is Senior Research Fellow at the French CNRS and affiliated with the CURAPP (University fo Amiens). She currently holds a Marie Curie Fellowship and is based at the Robert Schuman Center for Advanced Studies of the European University Institute in Florence (Italy). She is the author of many books, including (with Gerdien Jonker) *Politics of Visiblity. Young Muslims in European Public Spaces* (Bielefeld, Transcript Verlag, 2006).

Etienne Balibar is currently Emeritus Professor of Moral and Political Philosophy at Nanterre, and Distinguished Professor of Humanities at the University of California, Irvine. He has given courses and seminars in various countries, including Italy, the Netherlands, Mexico, Chile, Argentina, Germany, and the United States of America. He has published extensively, including *Race, Nation, Class* (1988) (with Immanuel Wallerstein), *Les frontières de la démocratie* (1992), *Droit de cité. Culture et politique en dèmocratie* (1998), *Nous, citoyens d'Europe? Les frontières, l'Etat, le peuple* (*We, the People of Europe?*) (2001). Forthcoming is *Extreme Violence and the Problem of Civility* (The Wellek Library Lectures 1996).

Jim Beckford FBA, Professor of Sociology at the University of Warwick, is author of *Social Theory and Religion* (2003) and of many other works on sociological aspects of controversial religion.

Christophe Bertossi is Senior Research Fellow and head of the "Migrations, Identities, Citizenship" programme at the Institut français des relations internationales (Ifri) in Paris. He is Associate Research Fellow at the Centre for Research in Ethnic Relations at the University of Warwick, where he was a Marie Curie Research Fellow during 2001–2003. He is also Research Associate at the Center for Comparative Immigration Studies, University of California in San Diego. He has extensively published on migrations, citizenship, and multicultural societies in Europe.

Stephen Castles is Professor of Migration and Refugee Studies at the International Migration Institute (IMI), University of Oxford. From 2002 to 2006, he was Director of the Refugee Studies Centre at Oxford University. He has carried out research on migration and multicultural societies in Europe, Australia, and Asia for many years, and is the author of many books.

Estelle Ferrarese is currently Research Fellow at the CERSES (Center for Research of Meaning, Ethics and Society), CNRS – University of Paris V. She was a post-doctoral Research Fellow at the New School for Social Research in New York and an Alexander von Humboldt-Foundation Research Fellow at the Humboldt University in Berlin. Her main research interests concern theory of recognition, theories of democracy and citizenship, nineteenth- and twentieth-century German political thought, and feminist theories.

Andrew Geddes is Professor of Politics at the University of Sheffield and author of many works on immigration, including *Immigration and European Integration: Towards Fortress Europe?* (2000) and *The Politics of Migration and Immigration in Europe* (2003).

Virginie Guiraudon is Marie Curie Professor in Social and Political Sciences at the European University institute, Florence Italy, on leave from the National Center for Scientific Research in France (CNRS) where she holds a permanent research position. She is the author of *Les politiques d'immigration en Europe* (2000) and co-editor of *Controlling a New Migration World* (2001) and *Immigration Policy in Europe: The Politics of Control* (2006). Her current research focuses on the Europeanization of anti-discrimination and immigration policy.

Danièle Joly is Director of the Centre for Research in Ethnic Relations and Professor at the University of Warwick. She has published extensively on ethnicity, Islam, and migrations with a particular focus on refugees, including *Blacks and Britannity* (2001), *Haven or Hell: Asylum Policy and Refugees in Europe* (1996), *Britannia's Crescent: Making a Place for Muslims in British Society* (1995).

John Rex is Professor Emeritus at the University of Warwick. His long and distinguished career has included posts at the University of Leeds, Birmingham, Durham, Warwick, Aston, Toronto, Capetown, and New York. He has been a member of UNESCO International Experts Committee on Racism and Race Prejudice. He has extensively published, including *Key Problems of Sociological Theory, Race Community and Conflict, Colonial Immigrants in a British City, Race Relations in Sociological Theory, Race and Ethnicity.*

Anja Rudiger is a research consultant specializing in equality, diversity, and migration issues. She set up and led the British Refugee Council's research unit (2004–2006), provided policy advice to the chairperson of the European Monitoring Centre on Racism and Xenophobia (2000–2004), and managed an international gender mainstreaming service (1998–2000). Consultancies have included systematic reviews for the UK Home Office and the European Commission.

Carl-Ulrik Schierup is Professor at The National Institute for Working Life (NIWL) and the University of Linköping (Campus Norrköping), Department of Ethnic Studies (Sweden). He is Director of the research area "Work, Migration and Citizenship" at NIWL and Director of CEUS (The Centre for Ethnic and Urban Studies), Norrköping. He is the author of many books and articles in English and the Scandinavian languages.

Khursheed Wadia is Senior Research Fellow at the Centre for Research in Ethnic Relations, at the University of Warwick. She has written extensively on gender, politics, and society and is author (with Gill Allwood) of *Women and Politics in France: 1958–2000* (Routledge, 2000) and of *Refugee Women in Britain and France* (Manchester University Press, forthcoming 2006).

1
Introduction

Christophe Bertossi

1.1   The news: a brief preamble

On 27 October 2005, in Clichy-sous-Bois, a Parisian suburb: two teenagers of North-African and Sub-Saharan origin, 15 and 17 years old respectively, died when they were electrocuted after seeking refuge from the police in a power station. Two days later in the same city, police fired tear-gas at the entrance of a mosque. That was the start of three weeks of riots affecting almost all the regions in France. On 7 November, a curfew was imposed by the government, reactivating a 1955 law originally aimed at stemming insurrection during the Algerian war of independence. Three thousand youngsters were arrested by the police, half of whom were under the age of 18. Pictures of the 9000 burning cars were broadcast around the world for a month. These images symbolized the limits of French republican integration and citizenship.

The immediate policy response to these events pointed to the so-called anti-integration attitudes of migrants to explain the crisis, whose identities were highlighted as the core problem facing their social, cultural, and political integration into French society. As a matter of fact, however, these 'migrants' were French citizens. What's more, as far as their identities were concerned, they did not mobilize on any cultural or religious claims. A police report to the Interior Minister concluded that the main factor behind the crisis in the suburbs was discrimination (*Le Monde*, 7 December 2005). The issue was actually about equality of opportunities and chances of access to social mobility, as well as spatial segregation connected to ethnic and religious identity (see Fitoussi, Laurent and Maurice, 2004). The youngsters involved in the three-week riots fought against the symbols of their relegation into territories where republican equality did not reach, notably the institutional symbols of

French society (police forces, firemen, schools, and so on). They did not contest the principles of French citizenship. They claimed their legitimate place within it.

This gap between the policy understanding of the crisis, and the social and economic roots of the riots belongs to a particular context: in recent years, French identity politics have been marked by the institutionalization of Islam under the auspices of the Interior Minister; a debate on French secularism (*laïcité*) leading to the ban of Muslim headscarves in public schools;[1] the negative referendum on the European constitutional treaty in May 2005, partly connected to attitudes against the accession of Turkey to the European Union and the fear of being 'swamped' by Eastern Europeans; the vote and then withdrawal of a law celebrating the positive contributions of French colonialism overseas;[2] and the presence of the leader of the extreme right-wing party in the second round of the 2002 presidential election.

On the other side of the Channel, Britain went through its own crisis in identity and integration politics after the 2001 riots in the Northern England industrial towns of Burnley, Bradford, and Oldham. In the aftermath of similar disturbances from the late 1950s onwards, British policies had developed a peculiar definition of integration, strikingly conducive to accepting ethnic and cultural pluralism. However, the post-2001 context showed something different. The Community Cohesion agenda developed by the Home Office emphasized a new perspective whereby social disadvantage was less a result of discrimination against minority groups than the consequence of ethnic and religious communities living 'parallel lives', and rejecting integration into 'Britishness' (Cantle, 2001). The chairman of the Commission for Racial Equality – the gatekeeper of the British Race Relations agenda – concluded in 2004 that 'multiculturalism implies separateness and division' and called for the promotion of an active and common citizenship.

In other words, with the arrival of the new millennium, universal French citizenship and multiculturalism-friendly British Race Relations policies reached similar limits: neither actually succeeded in making ethnicity an ordinary characteristic of fully fledged citizenship. What is even more striking, both philosophical models, which had thus far been mutually exclusive, apparently converged toward a similar reading of the 'irreconcilable relationship' between membership of an ethnic and religious minority, and full integration into citizenship. At the same time, French integration policies tried to take an anti-discrimination approach, traditionally absent from the republican model based on concepts of the uniqueness of the individual and the abstract citizen.

Since 2005, a new independent authority, whose design was inspired by the British Commission for Racial Equality, has been in charge of the fight against discrimination in France. While this is an attempt to recognize the weight of everyday discrimination against French citizens of migrant origin, there is no real evidence of there being the political will that could pave the way for a 'liberal hour' in France on the ethnicity issue.[3] Debates in France and in Britain focus more enthusiastically on 'encumbering identities' (Miller, 2001) in general, and Islam in particular.

As a result, the situation is strikingly contradictory today. How is it possible to comprehend the limits of both the French and British national frameworks for the integration of minority groups into the social and political rights of citizenship? How can we read the apparent blurring of the opposition between French and British models of integration?

1.2 Dilemmas of citizenship in Europe

Our understanding of the transformations and limits of the French and British models of integration and citizenship is incomplete if we focus only on the way each situation is embedded in a coherent set of principles, what Adrian Favell calls 'philosophies of integration' (Favell, 1998). Emphasizing either the correspondence or the distance between these public philosophies and the recent developments of identity politics in both countries is far from satisfying. A full analysis must also address these contradictions as part of the construction of citizenship in contemporary France and Britain.

What is more, limiting analysis to the national level fails to inform us about the current context in which these transformations and limits in citizenship-building take place. There is a supplementary dimension that must be added to a comparison between France and Britain. Europe itself constitutes this additional dimension, for at least two main reasons.

First, French and British integration crises echo similar developments in other European Community (EU) countries, most notably in the Netherlands in the aftermath of the murders of Pim Fortuyn in May 2002 and Theo Van Gogh in November 2004. The traditional 'philosophy' of liberal tolerance yielded ground to perceptions of Islam as a threat to Dutch liberal norms and values. This perception is now shared by public opinion in most EU countries, especially after the bombings in Madrid on 11 March 2004 and in London on 7 July 2005.

Second, European integration has deeply transformed both the notion of citizenship and the very relationship between identity, rights, and sovereignty, out of which modern democracy emerged in the aftermath of the American and French revolutions in the late eighteenth century. With EU integration, elements of sovereignty have been transferred to European supranational institutions. Whereas citizenship had become an old-fashioned notion, from the mid-1980s onwards it started to attract important attention from academics and policy makers, under the twofold process of the durable settlement of migrants in Europe and progress toward the further political integration of European communities. This contributed to a reformulation of the very relationship between identity and rights, that is, between nationality and active citizenship.

In this context, a global dilemma emerged from within the usual conception of citizenship and blurred the traditional markers of what it meant to be a member of a European polity. This citizenship dilemma concerns at least three different levels: the relevance of nationality as a social, political, and cultural closure of the citizens' community; the possible dissociation between citizenship rights and national belonging; and the case of discrimination as a structural challenge to national citizenship. The point here is to emphasize the interdependence between these different levels of the citizenship question in Europe today.

1.3   A citizenship beyond the national?

In the early 1990s, the renewal of citizenship studies emerged from proposals focused on the revision of national modern citizenship. Authors suggested new post-national (Ferry, 1991; Soysal, 1994; Habermas, 1998), cosmopolitan (Linklater, 1998), multicultural (Kastoryano, 1998), and transnational (Bauböck, 1994) theoretical frameworks aimed at a reform of the notion of citizenship. All these developments found in European integration the resource and impetus for such a renewal. European integration was perceived as an opportunity for by-passing internal contradictions of national democracy, while these national contradictions were underscored by the presence of migrants and claims made by ethnic minorities for equal access to citizenship rights. In this context, the fate of migrants in their new countries of settlement became a question of political and social justice that challenged the legitimacy of national principles (Bertossi, 2001). Meanwhile, Europe presented itself as a new horizon for redefining post-national citizenship coupled with a strengthened multicultural democracy.[4]

The reading of this process considered citizenship as the result of a progressive dialectic in which Europe constituted a new step after the nation state. Citizenship resulted from the progressive inclusion of excluded segments of national populations (such as women, youngsters, non-property owning working classes, people with a disability or an illness, and so on) through an increasingly developed set of civil, political, and social rights (Marshall, 1950; Leca, 1990). This process seemed to come to a standstill as far as the place of migrants within the homogeneous conception of national democracy was concerned. The issue then turned into a debate about the problematic integration of populations originating from postcolonial immigration. This debate defined national identity as either a necessary resource for such integration or, on the contrary, an inadequate constraint preventing incorporation of new citizens into their receiving polity.

These academic developments thus paralleled a new policy focus on the notion of nationality as a condition for incorporating new citizens. Between 1980 and 2000, all Western European countries reformed their nationality legislation.[5] There was a European convergence toward the generalization of the principle of birth-rights to citizenship and the progressive suppression of blood-rights-based citizenship legislations, such as in Germany in 1999. This liberalization of nationality regimes in Europe did not prevent the rise of anti-immigration politics, illustrated by the electoral successes of far-right parties in European countries in the 2000s.

Using nationality as a method for migrants' integration resulted in a kind of consensus according to which an equality-based society had the right to limit rights (compare Arendt's 'rights to have rights') as far as this was articulated by the political principle grounding the modern state's legitimacy and moral order: the nation. Another trend in these reforms concerned the progressive abandonment of colonial heritages that entitled some migrants to rights that non-postcolonial migrants were not. Following these reforms, the former were increasingly treated as the latter and lost most of their privileges.

Such nationality policies, however, failed to fully address the European and migratory challenge to national citizenship. National entitlement to citizenship could not answer the issue of what Tomas Hammar defined as denizenship: individuals who had not accessed formal citizenship but who, as foreigners, participated substantially in their country of installation, notably through associations in the voluntary sector, and who were subject to citizenship obligations (paying taxes, for example) without being entitled to citizenship rights (Hammar, 1990).

This called for a new mode for incorporating non-citizens into a polity of which they were already 'acting citizens'. This echoed a theme that had mobilized migrants and populations from migrant origins since the 1980s, focusing on the necessary dissociation between nationality and citizenship, particularly in France and the 1983–85 *Beur* civic movements, albeit without success.[6]

What such mobilizations failed to start was finally initiated by European integration. Article 8 of the 1992 Maastricht Treaty defined a citizenship of the EU disconnected from nationality. But this separation was constrained in two ways: only nationals of an EU Member State were entitled to it and the national vote was excluded from its scope. Some authors highlighted how far this twofold limitation further reinforced the problem of nationality as an ambiguous principle for distributing citizenship rights, as Europeans were provided with more rights from which third-country nationals were excluded (Martiniello, 1994; Weil and Hansen, 1999). The 1999 European Summit in Tampere called for a removal of the nationality condition from the definition of EU citizenship, but nothing changed. At the end of the day, there remained as before only those few EU countries which had given third-country nationals local political rights, from the end of the 1960s onwards, and thus far before the issue entered the EU agenda.[7]

This is at the heart of the sharp contradiction in European integration's by-passing of national limits: it generalized the distinction between being a member of a polity and of being a national, but failed to address the real issue of including third-country nationals, or to reconcile citizenship as an institutional and sociological fabric of equality-based societies with globalization, including the globalization of human mobility.

1.4   Anti-discrimination as a citizenship issue

A European perspective on citizenship also emerged at a less institutionalized level, challenging the formalism of national citizenship as an actual source of empowerment. In other words, being a national was not a sufficient guarantee for accessing substantial equality of opportunity and membership. Some formal citizens were still treated as if they were not 'genuine citizens' because they were identified as members of minority groups. This paved the way for discrimination to take center stage in the politics of citizenship. Some authors used Myrdal's argument about an 'American dilemma', and applied it to the European situation (Schierup, Hansen and Castles, 2004).

As early as the mid-1960s, Jim Rose used the notion for post-war Britain, revealing a critical gap between the common creed of equality on which British citizenship policies were based, and the reality of ethnic minorities being systematically discriminated against (Rose, 1969). It was a first landmark in the public recognition of discrimination as a policy problem (Brown, 1984; Daniel, 1968; Smith, 1977), leading progressively to the progressive implementation of the current Race Relations framework.

This discrimination line reversed existing nationality politics, inspired more by a republican conception of citizenship than by a liberal one. As Rainer Bauböck puts it, 'for a liberal conception, in contrast with the republican tradition of Aristotle, Rousseau or Hannah Arendt, the inclusion of the inactive or even the incompetent as equal members in the polity is a basic achievement of contemporary democracy' (Bauböck, 1994: 202). If nationality reforms had swung the pendulum from a liberal to a republican understanding of inclusion in European countries, the anti-discrimination perspective swung it back and complemented it with multicultural and multi-faith issues as constitutive elements of citizenship. Consequently, it led to recognition that the fact of being a national could not prevent members of ethnic or religious minorities from being discriminated against, from experiencing a lack of civil, social, or economic resources, or an inequality of opportunity in education, employment, or even leisure. These became the main challenges to the relevance of citizenship as an institution of common belonging in an equality-based society.

Of course, this attempt to de-republicanize citizenship found variable political opportunities in the EU countries. A less favorable country from that perspective was France, as French normative citizenship could not recognize ethnic factors as an explanation of why some citizens were less equal than others. In contrast, British integration policies were based on this very fight against racial discrimination, springing from the development of Race Relations legislation in 1965, 1968, and 1976. The latter conception found an attentive ear at the European level. European institutions had based their approach to integration (albeit outside of EU competence) on an emphasis on equality of opportunities rather than abstract individual equality (often used as a means toward assimilation).

European integration moved forward in 1997 with the Amsterdam Treaty. Article 13 of the Treaty addressed discriminations on the grounds of race and ethnic origins, religion and belief, gender, disability, age, and sexual orientation. Two EU Council Directives were adopted pursuant to this article: one addressing racial discrimination at large, the other targeting all forms of discrimination at the workplace. EU Member States had to adopt these Directives before July 2003 and December 2005 respectively. This has contributed to the Europeanization of anti-discrimination as an element of citizenship policies. It has had an impact on the legislation of individual EU countries. The way EU policy tended to merge anti-discrimination as a mainstream strategy challenged the British public apparatus, which was based on the separation of racial and ethnic (1976 Race Relations Act and its 2000 Amendment), gender (1976), and disability (1995) discrimination, while failing to take account of religious discrimination (with the exception of Northern Ireland).

Similarly, this EU agenda also impacted French integration policies. In 1996, the Council of State assessed that 'being the basis of the juridical order of our society, the principle of equality is threatened when new and serious inequalities extend in the society. ... Equality of rights seems to be a mere formal petition. Thus, the credibility of the equality principle is definitely at stake in the field of equality of opportunities' (Conseil d'Etat, 1998: 45). This constituted an apparently striking reversal of the policy approach to integration (for a detailed description of this shift to anti-discrimination in France, see Bertossi, 2003).

1.5 Challenges to diversity

Less than a decade after the Amsterdam Treaty, the situation seems to be back at square one. The European constitutional crisis pursuant to the negative referendums in France and the Netherlands has rung the death-knell for a qualitative transformation of European integration from the economic to the political. This, in turn, prevented further development toward an EU citizenship. Also, the post-Cold War international context has been marked by fears concerning Islam, particularly after 9/11. These fears have grown in Europe and have nurtured the politics of integration's rediscovering of the value of national identity as a reservoir of common belonging. Subsequent developments in popular discourse indifferently equated and mixed the terms Islam, Muslims, ethnic minorities, migrants, Islamists, and international terrorism. This has influenced social attitudes which have, in turn, reinforced the production of racial and religious discriminations.

As a result, the principle of multiculturalism has been attacked on several sides: the European project that supported ethno-cultural and religious diversity dramatically weakened; the crisis of national integration frameworks stigmatized so-called anti-integration attitudes among ethnic and religious groups; no resolutions of how it is possible to reconcile the fabric of equality in globalized societies were provided. At the policy level, a critical approach to integration is no longer made, and the issue of integration is only assessed against the so-called ethnic and religious identities of members of minority groups, without really taking into account the wider context of a crisis in national welfare and high levels of unemployment. At an academic level, attacks on the idea of multi-culturalism have found a new legitimacy, as illustrated by Brian Barry's book *Culture and Equality* (Barry, 2001).

Thus, the questions are the following ones: whither citizenship in a context of ethno-cultural and religious diversity, after the emergence of an anti-discrimination agenda in the European Union but at a time of increasing social and policy challenges to diversity itself? What can the issue of discrimination help us to understand about the limits of national citizenship, illustrated by what happened in the French sub-urbs or in Bradford and Oldham, when integration is seen as an issue of cultural and religious confrontation? This book aims at addressing these questions through a comparison between France and Britain. It looks for resolutions of the apparent contradictions between equality and diver-sity from a perspective that situates the anti-discrimination agenda at the center of the necessary renewals of citizenship in Europe today.

1.6 Outline of the book

Part I of this book addresses contradictions of citizenship from a theo-retical perspective, as part of the dilemma between equality and diver-sity, and shows the extent to which discrimination is center stage in these contradictions. The section opens with a contribution by Steven Castles focusing on the way globalization reinforces internal contradic-tions of citizenship (between inclusion and exclusion, the citizen and the national, the active and the passive citizen, identity and cohesion). Castles argues that the post-Cold War era substituted a North–South divide for the East–West divide, paving the way for a hierarchical nation-state system and a subsequent hierarchical citizenship system: if the majority of the world's people are defined as citizens, their citizenship is characterized by a gradation in real rights and freedom, and by transna-tional racism as exemplified by anti-immigration politics.

Echoing Castles's conclusions, Anja Rudiger analyzes in Chapter 3 the citizenship dilemmas from an EU perspective, with particular attention to the Amsterdam Treaty provisions on anti-discrimination and the two 2000 EU Council Directives. She identifies key constraints to the development of an equality-*cum*-diversity policy approach (e.g., national identity, republicanism, and the uniqueness of the individual citizen). Rudiger concludes that a group-based approach to citizenship could resolve Europe's citizenship dilemmas. She shows, however, how such a group-based approach is still a long way from informing the national integration policies of EU Member States. Rudiger's comments on the relationship between a human rights-based perspective on the issue of racial and religious discrimination on the one hand, and a minority group-based approach to citizenship on the other, leads to the following question: to what extent can an EU anti-discrimination policy be linked to 'policies of recognition' in the perspective developed by Charles Taylor and multiculturalists in the 1990s? In Chapter 4, Estelle Ferrarese outlines the distinction between anti-discrimination policies and policies of recognition as well as their overlapping characteristics.

The first section's final chapter deals with the way members of minority groups can mobilize in favor of access to equal opportunities (and outcomes) in Europe. In Chapter 5, John Rex explains that the 'discrimination versus equality dilemma' must be linked to the tradition of the welfare state. Starting from T. H. Marshall's definition of citizenship, Rex argues that while some authors have celebrated multiculturalism without any reference to class struggles and access to social rights, this is not an adequate approach. Issues of incorporating members of minority groups into equality of opportunity and membership are directly linked to the forms of conflict, mobilization, and discussion that members of a polity, including ethnic and religious groups, may arrange within the welfare state.

Part II of the book focuses on the development of EU anti-discrimination policies in the aftermath of the Amsterdam Treaty. In Chapter 6, Carl-Ulrik Schierup analyzes the emergence of the EU anti-discrimination agenda in relation to EU policies against social exclusion. Schierup looks at the welfare crisis in Europe and the shift from a social inclusion policy aimed at equality to a new approach based on economic efficiency. This transformation has resulted in the stigmatization of migrants and ethnic minority members out of the workplace, and has had racializing effects in labor market deregulation. Consequently, the issue is about the disconnection between the fight against social exclusion, the issue of racial and religious discrimination, and the more general question of citizenship.

Virginie Guiraudon and Andrew Geddes's Chapter 7 addresses the emergence of anti-discrimination at the top of the EU policy agenda in the mid-1990s. They highlight how the 1996 Inter-Governmental Conference – and the subsequent incorporation of anti-discrimination provisions within the EU Treaty – exceeded anti-discrimination provisions in the national laws of all Member States but the UK and the Netherlands. Guiraudon and Geddes analyze why France agreed to this agenda and why Britain was a reluctant partner in the negotiations. They identify key frames that explain this paradoxical context, namely a traditional anti-fascist agenda, the role of social networks including NGOs and academic activists, and the functioning of EU institutions, most notably the Commission and the Parliament.

Chapter 8 turns to the question of how EU anti-discrimination policies – and their implementation at a national level in France and Britain – can successfully address the specific issue of religious discrimination as distinct from traditional discriminatory factors such as race and ethnicity. Valérie Amiraux highlights the complex relationship between the different grounds on which minority members are discriminated against (i.e., gender, ethnicity, race, etc.), and reflects on the need for a better understanding of individuals' membership in a religious group from the EU anti-discrimination perspective.

The third and last part of the book looks at the situation of minority group members in France and Britain, and the sociological and institutional context in which they are discriminated against. In Chapter 9, Danièle Joly and Jim Beckford address the situation of Muslims in French and British prisons, and explore the wide range of contexts that bring issues about Islam and prison to the forefront in both countries. In doing so, they also show how discrimination can be an issue particularly at stake in the relationship between members of minority groups and institutions of the dominant society.

What is true of the prison institutions is also true of the military. In Chapter 10, Christophe Bertossi shows how ethnicity and Islam have become critical issues in the French armed forces, after a shift from conscription to the professionalization of the French military in 1996–97. French servicemen of ethnic origin volunteer for the military because they want to escape the racial and religious discrimination they face in French civil society; they also volunteer because most of them endorse the values and principles of the Republic. But they still confront discrimination, and racial and religious prejudice within the military, because of the ethnic identity attributed to them by their peers and their hierarchy. Seeking integration and recognition as ordinary soldiers and equal citizens, they are made 'ethnic' by an institution of the Republic. Finally, in Chapter 11, Khursheed Wadia emphasizes the gender dimension of discrimination. Wadia's leftist-feminist approach to citizenship highlights how much citizenship, as 'action' and a means toward collective mobilization among minority groups, could resolve the discrimination dilemma in Europe. This perspective is used to analyze the situation of women refugees and asylum seekers in France and Britain. Wadia concludes that if citizenship can be perceived as a way of becoming part of an active political and social community, as much as it is a way to achieve a status tied to the possession of rights, then refugee women's associations are citizenship-builders for some of the most disadvantaged groups in Europe.

The last chapter of the book presents Etienne Balibar's reaction to the different contributions, in which he draws conclusions about how well European anti-discrimination policies and citizenship, as an equality- and cohesion-generating institution, can face the crisis of multiculturalist principles in this peculiar context in which ethno-cultural and religious identities are seen as a challenge to European values and principles. Whither citizenship in this context?

Notes

1. The law 'in application of the principle of *laïcité*' forbidding 'all signs or clothes obviously demonstrating a religious belonging' in public schools was voted on 15 March 2004. It was implemented in metropolitan France and in the departments and territories overseas, but with some exceptions in Neo-Caledonia. At the start of the following school year, school officers negotiated with 600 Muslim school girls, 47 of whom were finally excluded.
2. The Constitutional Council declared that the content of Article 4 of the law of 23 February 2005 came within the competence of administrative rules and not of the law. This article stipulated that 'History syllabi recognize in particular French presence overseas, notably in Northern Africa, and afford the eminent attention they deserve to the history and sacrifices of French military combatants originating from these territories' (my translation).
3. Adlai Stevenson defined this notion of a 'liberal hour' as a context in which politics converge on a consensus about the need of a political change related to a specific social issue. This notion was used by Jim Rose and his team for explaining changes in British integration politics in the 1960s towards a political consensus related to the fight against racial discriminations (Rose, 1969).
4. This issue concerned integration of populations from migrant origins but the successive EU enlargements also contributed to the reinforcement of this problematic, notably within normative frameworks developed by the Council of Europe in the mid-1990s with regard to regional minorities in Eastern Europe (see Rouland, Pierré-Caps and Poumarède, 1996).

5. Reforms of nationality legislation were voted in Sweden (1980), the UK and Portugal (1981), the Netherlands, Finland and Greece (1984), Austria (1984), Luxembourg (1985), Germany (1990, 1999), Spain and Denmark (1991), Belgium (1991 and 2000), Italy (1992), France (1993, 1998).
6. 'Beurs' refers to Arab populations in French slang. It was used by French new citizens from North-African origins when they mobilized in the 1980s and claimed equality of membership during the debates on the reform of French nationality legislation (see Catherine Wihtol de Wenden and Rémy Leveau, 2001).
7. The countries who implemented a local right to vote to non-European migrants are Ireland (1963), Sweden (1968), Denmark (1977), Norway (1978), Finland (1981), and the Netherlands (1983). Similar reforms had been discussed at the end of the 1990s in other countries: some failed (e.g., in France), others succeeded (e.g., the 2004 reform in Belgium).

References

Bauböck, R., 'Changing the Boundaries of Citizenship', in Bauböck, R. (ed.), *From Alien to Citizens: Redefining the Status of Immigrants in Europe* (Aldershot: Avebury, 1994).

Barry, B., *Culture and Equality: An Egalitarian Critique of Multiculturalism* (Cambridge: Polity, 2001).

Bertossi, C., *Les frontières de la citoyenneté en Europe. Nationalité, résidence, appartenance* (Paris: L'Harmattan, 2001).

Bertossi, C., 'Politics and Policies of French Citizenship, Ethnic Minorities and the European Agenda', in Ruspini, R., and Gorny, A., (eds), *Migration in the New Europe: East-West Revisited* (Basingstoke: Palgrave, 2003).

Bertossi, C., 'The Migrant's Vote', in Deloye, Y. (ed.), *Encyclopedia of European Elections* (Basingstoke: Palgrave, 2006).

Brown, C., *Black and White Britain: The Third PSI Survey* (London: Heinemann, 1984).

Cantle, T., *Community Cohesion* (London: Home Office Publications, 2001).

Conseil d'Etat, *Sur le principe d'égalité* (Paris: La Documentation française, 1998).

Daniel, W. W., *Racial Discrimination in England: Based on the PEP Report* (Harmondsworth: Penguin, 1968).

Favell, A., *Philosophies of Integration. Immigration and the Idea of Citizenship in France and Britain* (Basingstoke: Macmillan – now Palgrave, 1998).

Ferry, J.-M., 'Pertinence du national', *Esprit*, 11 (November 1991): 80–93.

Fitoussi, J.-P., Laurent, E., and Maurice, J., *Ségrégation urbaine et intégration sociale* (Paris: La Documentation française, Rapport du Conseil d'Analyse Economique, 2004).

Habermas, J., *The Inclusion of the Other: Studies in Political Theory* (Cambridge, MA: MIT Press, 1998).

Hammar, T., *Democracy and the Nation State: Aliens, Denizens and Citizens in a World of International Migration* (Aldershot: Avebury, 1990).

Kastoryano, R. (ed), *Quelle identité pour l'Europe? Le multiculturalisme à l'épreuve* (Paris: Presses de Sciences Po, 1998).

Le Monde, 'Selon les RG, les émeutes en banlieues n'étaient pas le fait de bandes organisées' (7 December 2005).

Leca, J., 'Individualism and Citizenship', in Leca, J., and Birnbaum, P. (eds), *Individualism: Theories and Methods* (Oxford: Clarendon Press, 1990).

Linklater, A., 'Cosmopolitan Citizenship', *Citizenship Studies*, 2:1 (Carfax Publishing: February 1998): 23–41

Marshall, T. H., *Citizenship and Social Class: And Other Essays* (Cambridge: Cambridge University Press, 1950).

Martiniello, M., 'Citizenship of the European Union: A Critical View', in Bauböck, R. (ed.), *From Alien to Citizens: Redefining the Status of Immigrants in Europe* (Aldershot: Avebury, 1994).

Miller, D., *Citizenship and National Identity* (Cambridge: Polity Press, 2001).

Rose, E. J. B. (in association with Deakins, N.), *Colour and Citizenship: A Report on British Race Relations* (London: Oxford University Press, 1969).

Rouland, N., Pierré-Caps, S., and Poumarède, J., *Droits des minorités et des peuples autochtones* (Paris: Presses Universitaires de France, 1996).

Schierup, C.-U., Hansen, P., and Castles, S., *Migration, Citizenship and the European Welfare State: A European Dilemma* (Oxford: Oxford University Press, 2004).

Smith, D. J., *Racial Disadvantage in Britain* (London: Penguin, 1977).

Soysal, Y. N., *Limits of Citizenshi: Migrants and Postnational Membership in Europe* (Chicago, IL: Chicago University Press, 1994).

Weil, P., and Hansen, R. (eds), *Nationalité et citoyenneté en Europe* (Paris: La Découverte, 1999).

Wihtol de Wenden, C., and Leveau, R., *La Beurgeoisie. Les trois âges de la vie associative issue de l'immigration* (Paris: CNRS Editions, 2001).

Part I

From Citizenship to Discrimination: The Limits of Inclusion

2

Nation and Empire: Hierarchies of Citizenship in the New Global Order

Stephen Castles

2.1 Introduction

In our book *Citizenship and Migration* (Castles and Davidson, 2000), Alastair Davidson and I argued that the nation-state and citizenship were becoming global norms. For the first time in history, the great majority of the world's people lived in countries with the constitutional forms and institutional structures of democratic nation-states. This also meant that most people in the world were legally defined as citizens – rather than as subjects of monarchs or dictators. Of course, many of these nation-states were democracies in name only. Nonetheless, the rapid proliferation of the nation-state model was a significant development both for national politics and international relations. We went on to examine the serious challenges to nation-state citizenship posed by globalization and international population mobility.

However, more recent trends make it necessary to take the analysis further. Following the end of the Cold War, the East–West divide with its two superpowers has been replaced by a division between the North and South, in which both are dominated by a single superpower: the United States. Some analysts suggest that we are entering an epoch of a 'new empire', analogous to ancient Rome or the British Empire. However, the situation seems more complex. The North–South division is far from absolute, with areas of social exclusion in the North and of prosperity in the South. Nor is domination by the superpower absolute. The emerging global order is new in character. I suggest that this order can usefully be characterized as *the hierarchical nation-state system*. Furthermore, I argue that the varying power of states at the different levels leads to a similar hierarchy of rights and freedom of their peoples, which I refer to as *hierarchical citizenship*.

This chapter starts by looking at some of the inherent contradictions of nation-state citizenship and how these contradictions have been sharpened by globalization and international migration. Some responses to these challenges are discussed, such as changes in citizenship rules and the rise of multiculturalism. The chapter then examines the hierarchical nation-state system and hierarchical citizenship, and looks at some of the contradictions in current discourses on global governance, again focusing on international migration as a key site of differentiation. Finally, I discuss perspectives for countering hierarchical citizenship by working toward transnational democracy.[1]

2.2 Differentiated and contradictory citizenship in the nation-state

Being a citizen is part of the 'common sense' of the modern nation-state. It designates membership in the national community. Citizens possess a range of civil, political, and social rights. Such rights are balanced by obligations: to obey the laws, pay taxes, and to defend the country in the case of war. In principle, each citizen is meant to belong to only one nation-state, and that nation-state is meant to include as citizens all people who permanently live on its territory. Everybody in the country is meant to belong, while the rest of the world is excluded: foreigners cannot belong.[2]

However, these neat principles are far from reality. In Western Europe, some 13 million residents from outside the European Community (EU) have been unable to become citizens for legal or social reasons. In Japan, the exclusion of the descendants of Korean forced laborers now goes into the fourth and fifth generations. In the United States, whole sectors of the economy are based on the labor of undocumented Mexican and other foreign workers, while African Americans experience high rates of segregation in 'black ghettoes', chronic unemployment, and high rates of imprisonment and execution. Australia and Canada pride themselves on their capacity to integrate immigrants, but many of their aboriginal people are excluded from most of the real benefits of citizenship. In Britain, the percentage of children from the lowest socio-economic group entering university is lower than a generation ago. Class origin and gender remain predictors of life chances, occupation, and income throughout the Western world. Citizenship in nation-states is deeply *differentiated*.

Such differentiation has always been a characteristic of citizenship. Even in the earliest democracy, the Greek *polis*, slaves, foreigners, and women were excluded from citizenship. In the emerging democracies of the eighteenth and nineteenth centuries, the right to vote was based on the idea of the capacity of the male property owner to represent the people dependent on him: women, children, servants, and employees. Universal suffrage was the result of bitter struggles, and was not achieved until well into the twentieth century.

In the modern nation-state, therefore, citizenship is highly ambiguous. The main *contradictions* can be summed up as those

- between inclusion and exclusion
- between the citizen and the national
- between the active and the passive citizen
- between the citizen as political sovereign and the warrior-citizen.

The first has already been discussed: the inclusion of some people as full citizens is based on the partial or full exclusion of many others.

The second contradiction – between the citizen and the national – is closely linked. In liberal theory, all citizens are meant to be free and equal persons, who as citizens are homogeneous individuals (Rawls, 1985: 2324). This requires a separation between a person's political rights and obligations, and their membership in specific groups, based on ethnicity, religion, social class, or regional location. The political sphere is one of universalism, and difference is to be restricted to the 'non-public identity' (Rawls, 1985). But this conflict with the reality of nation-state formation, in which becoming a citizen has generally depended on membership in a national community. The nation-state is the combination of a political unit, which controls a bounded territory (the state), with a national community (the nation or people), which has the power to impose its political will within those boundaries. A *citizen* is always also a member of a nation, a *national*. Historically, this tension has been expressed in measures to incorporate minority groups into the 'national culture'. As Ernest Renan pointed out in 1882 in his famous discourse, *What is a Nation* (Renan, 1992), forgetting the history of ethnic distinctiveness and the process of obliterating it is vital to national identity. This fundamental contradiction between citizen and national is at the root of some of the divisions which tore Europe apart in the nineteenth and twentieth centuries, such as anti-Semitism, racism, and nationalism.

The third contradiction – that between the active and the passive citizen – refers to a fundamental conflict between radical-democratic and conservative theory on the relative importance of *rights* and *obligations*. The concept of popular sovereignty, which developed in the French Revolution, was based on the ideal of active citizens, whose most important right was participation in the processes of law making and government. By contrast, earlier social contract theory involved *passive citizens*, who had rights to protection from unlawful activity, but were obliged to obey state authority. This struggle remains crucial. Active citizenship implies not only extending political rights to include everybody, but also – as Marshall (1964) emphasized in post-1945 Britain – creating social and economic conditions that allow members of the working class and other disadvantaged groups to fully participate. Starting with Thatcher and Reagan, neo-conservative ideologies have returned to the idea of a passive citizen defined through obligations to 'the community' – especially the duties to work and to obey the law (Mead, 1986). The notion of 'the third way' (Giddens, 1998) is a social-democratic response to the difficulty of defending the welfare state in the context of globalization. The third way abandons ideas of class equality in favor of policies of 'social inclusion' in a national community.

The fourth contradiction of citizenship is that between the citizen as the political sovereign and the warrior-citizen. This is evident in the close link between universal suffrage and conscription until recently. The right to vote was tied to the duty to lay down one's life for the nation if necessary. In the late 1990s, the abolition of universal military service in France was seen by many – on both the Right and Left – as a threat to civic consciousness. Military service was regarded as crucial in forming a 'community of citizens' (Schnapper, 1994: 49). The ideal of the warrior-citizen originated in the mass mobilization needed for democratic revolutions, but became highly problematic in the era of nationalism and total warfare. It implied that democratic nations could only be consolidated internally by hostility to external groups, thus justifying imperialism and racism. The ideal was also sexist: the duty of the young man to die for the nation was matched by the duty of the young woman to bear children for future wars (Yuval-Davis and Anthias, 1989).

2.3   How globalization and migration challenge nation-state citizenship

The contradictions inherent in nation-state citizenship have been sharpened by globalization. First, globalization undermines the relative autonomy of the nation-state by breaking the nexus between power and place, upon which the 'national industrial societies' of the nineteenth and early twentieth centuries were based (Wieviorka, 1994). The dynamics of economic life now transcend national borders, and cannot be fully controlled by national governments. The nation-state is still the basic unit for welfare systems, but no government can pursue welfare policies which ignore the pressures of global markets. What does it mean to be a citizen, if one's vote cannot influence key political decisions, because they are no longer made by national parliaments?

Second, globalization has undermined the ideology of distinct national cultures, which was crucial to the nationalist project. Rapid improvements in transport and communications have led to an unprecedented degree of cultural interchange. The industrialization of media production and the dominance of global cultural factories, mean the diffusion of specific value systems, connected with consumerism, individualism, and American lifestyles.

Third, globalization means rapidly increasing mobility of people across national borders. The period since 1980 has been marked by migrations of all kinds: temporary and permanent movements; economic migrations and refugee exoduses; individual and family flows; highly skilled specialists and manual workers (Castles and Miller, 2003). Today, at least 175 million people live outside their countries of birth (United Nations Population Division, 2002). Often, cultural difference and social marginalization are linked, creating disadvantaged ethnic minorities. The effects of migration are felt most in areas already undergoing rapid change. Economic and social transformation in poor countries lead to emigration, while the destinations may be global cities with burgeoning service economies, or new industrial countries undergoing rapid urbanization.

Fourth, globalization changes the meaning of social space. Improvements in transport and communication make it easier for migrants to maintain links with their areas of origin, and to carry out circulatory or repeated mobility. This has led to the emergence of *transnational communities*: groups with regular and significant activities in two or more countries – people who live across national boundaries. Sociologists distinguish between transnationalism from above – activities 'conducted by powerful institutional actors, such as multinational corporations and states' – and transnationalism from below – activities 'that are the result of grassroots initiatives by immigrants and their home country counterparts' (Portes, Guarnizo and Landolt, 1999: 221). Transnational communities are not new: the diaspora concept goes back to ancient times (Cohen, 1997; Van Hear, 1998). New is the rapid proliferation of transnational communities wherever there are migrants, leading to significant changes in behavior and consciousness (Vertovec, 1999).

Immigration and growing cultural diversity poses a dual challenge to nation-states. First, admitting the 'Other' into the national community through citizenship appears as a threat to national cohesion and identity. The process of immigration has become so rapid that there is no time to obliterate difference, let alone to forget it. Second, sharing a shrinking social cake with new groups appears as a threat to the conditions of local workers. The social polarization brought about by economic restructuring and policies of privatization and deregulation leaves little room for minority rights. It is much easier to turn these groups into scapegoats for the social crisis, by blaming them not only for their own marginality, but also for the decline in general standards. Migration is therefore seen as a central aspect of the North–South conflict, and migrants may be perceived as infiltrators who will drag the rich countries down to Third World poverty.

2.4   The rise and fall of multiculturalism

In response to such dilemmas, nearly all countries of immigration have changed their immigration and citizenship laws, and even their constitutions.[3] Following the 1973 'Oil Crisis', Western European governments adopted 'zero immigration' policies, but found themselves unable to stop family reunion and community formation. With the upsurge in migration following the collapse of the Soviet Bloc, states adopted a range of measures to restrict immigration, sometimes characterized as the construction of a 'fortress Europe'. At the supranational level, the 1985 Schengen Convention created an area of free internal flows but tight external boundaries. The 1997 Amsterdam Treaty provided for the introduction of joint European Union (EU) rules on immigration and asylum by May 2004 – which have proved difficult to implement in practice, due to member state governments' fears over losing sovereignty.

The move toward multiculturalism addresses the dilemmas of ethnically diverse societies more directly. In the past, governments believed that immigration would not bring about significant cultural change. Either the migrants could be kept separate from the host population and denied citizenship rights under the 'guest worker' model (in Germany, Switzerland, and others) or they would be assimilated fully into the host community, as in the 'classical immigration countries' (USA, Canada, and Australia). By the 1970s, it was becoming clear that both these approaches were failing. Migrants were everywhere doing the least desirable and worst paid jobs, leading to processes of labor market segmentation. Similarly, low income, discrimination, and racism led to residential segregation. Migrants responded by developing ethnic communities with their own cultural, social, economic, and political infrastructure.

In Canada and Australia, where immigrants rapidly became citizens and voters, politicians and officials found they had to take account of the needs and values of ethnic communities. The result was the rise of multiculturalism as a government strategy combining the principles of cultural diversity and social equality. The state recognized the legitimacy of distinct communities with their own languages, religions, and cultural practices, while at the same time adopting measures to ensure that members of these communities had equal access to government services and education, and protection against discrimination. In Europe, multicultural models were adopted in Sweden in 1975 and in the Netherlands in 1979. The United Kingdom also moved toward defining itself as a multicultural society. In France and Germany, however, policy makers saw multiculturalism as a recipe for cultural fragmentation. Even here, local educational and social service agencies often tacitly adopted multicultural measures.

By the early 1990s, the key problem in Western Europe was how to include immigrants and their descendents as citizens. Several Western European countries (Germany, Switzerland, and Austria) had highly restrictive naturalization rules. The *ius sanguinis* principle (citizenship by descent) meant that even children born within the country to immigrant parents had no right to citizenship. Virtually all the countries of immigration have found it necessary to modify their citizenship laws. The new rules are a combination of *ius sanguinis* with *ius soli* (citizenship by birth in the country) and *ius domicilii* (citizenship on the basis of long-term residence) (Castles and Davidson, 2000: ch. 4). The most dramatic milestone was the German citizenship law of 1999. It represented an historical shift from a 'folk' or 'ethnic' model of citizenship to a more modern and inclusive type.[4]

Dual citizenship is important for immigrants, as an appropriate way of managing the multiple identities which arise from globalization. But it is anathema to nationalists, who insist on undivided loyalty to just one nation-state. Countries of emigration have begun to see dual citizenship as a way of maintaining links with emigrants, and to encourage remittances and skills transfers. The adoption of dual nationality by Mexico has led to a large increase in the number of dual nationals in the

United States. The classical immigration countries have all accepted dual citizenship, as have some European countries like the United Kingdom and Sweden. Other countries still formally reject dual citizenship, but often accept it in practice. For instance, 45 percent of naturalizations in Germany in 2000 led to dual or multiple citizenship (Beauftragte der Bundesregierung für Ausländerfragen, 2002: 414).

Finally, regional supranational models can lead to new models of citizenship. The 1992 Maastricht Treaty established Citizenship of the European Union, embracing freedom of movement and residence in member states; the right to vote and to stand for office in local and European Parliament elections in any EU country; diplomatic protection by diplomats of any EU state in a third country; the right to petition the European Parliament and to appeal to an ombudsman (Martiniello, 1994: 31). However, an 'EU passport' is legally still a passport of one of the member countries. So far, EU citizenship has done little for immigrants from outside the EU, although current debates in the EU point to the extension of some rights to third country nationals (Geddes, 2003). Other regional organizations, such as the North American Free Trade Agreement (NAFTA), have thus far not attempted to create transnational citizenship rights.

Overall, it is clear that many countries of immigration have moved away from older exclusionary or assimilationist ideas of national belonging, and toward more inclusive multicultural models. Since the mid-1990s, however, there has been a backlash. The Canadian government has moved away from an open commitment to multiculturalism, and now speaks instead of 'Canadian heritage and citizenship' – although actual policies seem to have changed little. The conservative government in power in Australia since 1996 has rejected measures in favor of minorities (both immigrants and Aboriginal people) and has abolished many multicultural services. In Europe, both Sweden and the Netherlands have changed their emphasis from recognition of cultural diversity to policies designed to achieve educational and occupational integration.

These changes have taken place in a climate of increasing public hostility to immigrants and asylum seekers. Right-wing parties and certain sections of the media have portrayed immigration and multiculturalism as threats to social cohesion and national identity. Immigration restrictions have been tightened, in order to stop the entry of asylum seekers and undocumented workers from the South. Policies in favor of minorities have been abolished or restricted in many places. Since 11 September 2001, immigrants and asylum seekers have been portrayed as potential terrorists and as a threat to national security. A new racism against outsiders threatens existing minorities with increased intolerance and social exclusion.

2.5 The rise of the hierarchical nation-state system

From the late 1940s until about 1990, global power relations were based on a bipolar system arising from the ideological, military, political, and economic competition between two superpowers, the United States and the Soviet Union, together with their allies or satellites. This East–West conflict was a main determining factor for all other major trends of the epoch, such as decolonization, the growing significance of the nation-state, the emergence of the Third World, proxy wars, the technological and informational revolution, the development of welfare states, and the growth of supranational governance. Obviously, the end of that struggle and the apparent victory of the liberal-democratic model must have fundamental consequences for citizenship.

When the Soviet Bloc collapsed in the early 1990s, many people hoped that this would lead to a more unified world. The resulting 'peace dividend' would make it possible to divert resources from military expenditure and use them for development, democratization, and peace-building. One observer actually proclaimed the 'end of history', in the sense that major ideological conflicts would be replaced by gradual change within a universal liberal-democratic value system (Fukuyama, 1992). However, it has become clear that the East–West divide has simply been replaced by a North–South divide. This concept expresses not a geographical configuration, but a political and social one. The main division is between the powerful and prosperous post-industrial nations (including North America, Western Europe, Japan, Australia, and New Zealand), and the less powerful and poorer countries of Africa, Asia, and Latin America. However, the North includes areas and groups subject to social exclusion, while the South has elites which enjoy considerable prosperity. There are also important regions and groups in intermediate or transitional positions.

A key difference between the old East–West bipolar world and the new North–South division is that a single superpower now dominates both parts. This has led some analysts to suggest that the United States is now the 'new Empire' (Hardt and Negri, 2000): a global imperial power that rules the whole world, in the same way that Rome used to rule much of the Mediterranean world and Western Europe, or that Britain ruled its far-flung Empire before 1914. Although the notion of empire does seem to describe some aspects of the new reality – including the United States's aggressive use of military and economic power, and its claim to a universal and superior set of values – it does not fit well in other respects. For instance, conflicts between the United States and its allies over the use of force against Iraq and other 'rogue states' do not indicate a total imperial hegemony. Nor can the United States simply appoint the leaders of subordinate states, as Rome appointed governors or Britain viceroys.

The post-Cold War order seems therefore to be new in character. It is based on a single dominant superpower at its center, but this center is surrounded not by powerless vassals, but by a hierarchy of states with varying levels of dependence on the center and varying levels of power toward other states. This can be conceptualized as a set of concentric circles of states, defined in terms of power (not geography). I suggest that this order can usefully be labeled as *the hierarchical nation-state system*. Furthermore, I suggest that the varying power (in political, military, economic, and cultural terms) of states in these circles leads to a similar hierarchy of rights and freedoms of their peoples, which I refer to as *hierarchical citizenship*.

This notion of hierarchies of power and rights should be contrasted with the claims to universalism inherent in dominant discourses on global governance. Fukuyama's assertion of the end of history had a short life: it expired in the early 1990s on the battlefields of former Yugoslavia, Kuwait, and Somalia. Yet it is clear that the United States and the 'international community' (essentially the Northern nations and the powerful intergovernmental agencies) believe that there is only one acceptable model for economics, politics, international relations, and human rights. All other approaches are backward and really supported only by fundamentalists, terrorists, and rogue states. This is the basis for a claim of global political legitimacy, giving the North the right to impose structural adjustment policies, to intervene militarily in conflicts, and to bring about regime change where it so desires. Thus, Fukuyama's optimistic view has been superseded by a much darker prognosis also formulated in the early 1990s: Huntington's view of the inevitable 'clash of civilizations' (Huntington, 1993).

2.6   Models of international relations in modernity

It is important to put this new global order in historical perspective: it is the latest in a series of systems of international relations since the dawn of modernity. The *Westphalian System* was established in 1648 following the Thirty Years War (Held, McGrew, Goldblatt and Perraton, 1999). International relations were based on the idea of a world of sovereign states. Rulers had sovereignty over their territory and could reign over their subjects as they saw fit, but were supposed to follow certain rules – such as non-interference in internal affairs – in relations with each other. This world was conceptualized as a European one, and conquest and colonialism of states and peoples outside Europe was accepted. There was no notion of cultural community between rulers and subjects in this model: it was held together by power and the divine right of kings. Warfare did not require mass mobilization, but was largely a matter for gentlemen commanding armies of regular soldiers and mercenaries.

Following the American and French Revolutions of the late eighteenth century, a new *democratic-nationalist order* emerged. The idea of popular sovereignty made it necessary to define who belonged to the people, through the institution of citizenship. The state became a nation-state, dependent on popular legitimacy and myths of cultural homogeneity. Ethnic identity and racial exclusion of minorities were integral features of nationalism. The principle of the warrior-citizen and universal conscription meant that inter-state conflict now took on the characteristics of total warfare described by Clausewitz (Kaldor, 2001). War became evermore destructive, leading to large-scale slaughter and mass refugee flows.

The *bipolar world system*, based on the ideological confrontation between two competing superpowers in the Cold War, tamed the destructive potential of the democratic-nationalist order – but only by threatening even greater destruction through nuclear war. The resulting stalemate was appropriately labeled as MAD – Mutually Assured Destruction. At the same time, the superpowers fought proxy wars in less developed areas, often in the form of struggles over colonial liberation and state building (Zolberg, Suhrke and Aguayo, 1989). The Cold War helped provide the impetus for positive developments like full employment and the emergence of the welfare state. But these were bought at the price of bloody wars – for instance, in Vietnam and Angola – and massive refugee flows. Refugees fleeing communist domination in Hungary, Czechoslovakia, Vietnam, or Cuba were welcomed as Cold War heroes, but those trying to escape massive violence in new states in Africa, Asia, and Latin America were not welcomed in the North (Chimni, 1998).

The fourth and current world order following the collapse of the bipolar system is the *hierarchical nation-state system*. Its contours are becoming clearer with each new international conflict. In the course of the 1990s there were seven major military operations designed (at least in part) to prevent mass refugee flows. Six were under the auspices of the United Nations Security Council (in Northern Iraq, Bosnia and Herzogovina, Somalia, Rwanda, Haiti, and East Timor) (Roberts, 1998), while a seventh (in Kosovo) was led by NATO. In each of these, Northern military, political, and economic superiority was used in an attempt to impose certain interests and values on less developed countries. Where Northern material interests were only marginally affected, and intervention was mainly driven by human rights values, as in Somalia and Rwanda, the action was half-hearted and belated, failing to restore order in the former and to prevent genocide in the latter. The more recent military actions in Afghanistan and Iraq have followed more traditional great power interests, although again using human rights for legitimacy.

2.7   Contradictions of the hierarchical nation-state system

The most distinctive feature of the new global order is that the overwhelming majority of polities now define themselves as sovereign nation-states. The number of members of the United Nations has grown from 50 when the world body was established in 1945 to 191 in 2002 (when Switzerland joined). Theorists of globalization sometimes argue that the nation-state is set to disappear, but this argument is difficult to sustain: not only are there more states than ever, but the great majority of them have adopted the institutional structures of democratic nation-states, including constitutions, elections, and the rule of law. Of course, in many cases these institutions are mere facades for authoritarian regimes, but the ideological hegemony of the nation-state model is obvious.

In international legal terms, all nation-states are equal. In reality however, there is a marked hierarchy in which power flows from the center through a number of intermediate level states, to be imposed on the weakest countries of the South. This is not a simple process in which the superpower can pass out orders which have to be obeyed. The principle of nation-state sovereignty means that complicated incentives and pressures are used to obtain compliance.

The following hierarchy is apparent:

Tier 1   The USA – the globally dominant power in military, economic, political, and cultural affairs.

Tier 2   Highly developed countries like the EU Member States, Japan, Canada, and Australia.

Tier 3   Transitional countries like Russia, and newly industrializing countries like Brazil or Malaysia.

Tier 4   The less developed countries of the South.

Tier 5   'Failed states' like Afghanistan or Somalia; countries defined as 'rogue states' by the USA, such as Iraq and North Korea; and peoples without states like the Palestinians and Kurds.

Positions in the hierarchy are not permanently fixed. Central and Eastern European countries are moving from Tier 3 to 2, through the political and economic reforms needed for EU membership. The intermediate countries of East Asia and Latin America also strive to become modern developed countries, although political reform often trails behind economic growth, and there is always the threat of being pushed backwards by financial crisis, as Argentina experienced in 2002.

The hierarchy can be seen in various types of international interaction. For instance, *international law* is supposed to apply equally to all states and people. Yet the United States made strenuous efforts to ensure that the International Criminal Court would not be able to try US citizens accused of crimes against humanity. Similarly, the United States has refused to apply the Geneva Convention on the rights of combatants to those accused of being terrorists. Prisoners have been detained under conditions that do not comply with the requirements for prisoners of war. They have been detained without charge and denied the right to a hearing before a court of law. These cases also show the limitations of US hegemony: in 2004, the United States had to drop its claims to exemption to the jurisdiction of the International Criminal Court, after revelations on the treatment of prisoners in Iraq. In the case of the Guantanamo Bay detainees, some British citizens were released, although those from states lower in the international hierarchy were unable to gain such privileges.

The same applies to *rules on international trade*. The World Trade Organization (WTO) is designed to free up world trade by creating a system of fair and universal rules. However, the United States continues to subsidize and protect its own producers against competition from both developed and less developed countries. For instance, US subsidies to 25,000 cotton farmers so depress cotton prices that millions of peasant farmers in Africa lose more than $350 million a year. The resulting losses to some of Africa's poorest countries exceed the entire US aid budget for these areas (Stiglitz, 2002: 269). Some West African farmers are likely to abandon cotton production and may well emigrate to Europe, due to historical links between cotton-producing areas like Mali and France.

However, Europeans should not point the finger at the United States, for the EU Common Agricultural Policy is a major factor in ruining the livelihoods of many farmers in Africa.

Since the beginning of the Westphalian system, the state has claimed a monopoly over the means of violence. In the hierarchical nation-state system, this has been redefined as a *monopoly over weapons of mass destruction and the means of their delivery* by a select group of Northern powers. The United States – the only country to have used both nuclear weapons and chemical weapons (Agent Orange in Vietnam) – classifies less developed countries which try to break this monopoly as rogue states that may be destroyed. This was the legitimation for the attack on Iraq, and now neo-conservative elements in Washington seem to be cooking up similar plans for Iran.

Finally, we can observe the hierarchy of power in the organs of *global governance*. Each state is supposed to have equal voting rights in such bodies as the United Nations and the World Trade Organization (WTO). In reality, states that vote against Northern interests are put under considerable pressure. Financial incentives and threats of denial of foreign investment and aid are used to secure the outcomes wanted by the more powerful states. The pressure put on small states with seats in the UN Security Council to support US and British policies on Iraq was instructive, for it showed both the mechanisms involved and their limitations in a situation in which intermediate powers questioned US and British objectives. However, in the World Bank and the International Monetary Fund (IMF), there is no pretense of equality. Here, the 'shareholders' – the rich nations – dominate openly. Former World Bank Vice-President Joseph Stiglitz has shown how free market ideologies and narrow financial interests prevailed in the IMF, leading to policies which exacerbated the crises in East Asia and Russia in the 1990s (Stiglitz, 2002).

2.8   Hierarchical citizenship

The other major innovation in today's global order is that – for the first time in history – the majority of the world's people are defined as citizens. Nation-state citizenship as a global norm implies the possession of a set of civil, political, and social rights, but this legal principle once again masks a steep gradation in real rights and freedoms.

Tier 1

US citizens enjoy a high level of formal rights, while democratic structures and a strong legal system ensure that most Americans can successfully claim these rights. But even here there are exceptions: Native Americans, African Americans, and other ethnic or religious minorities may experience de facto exclusion from political, economic, and social participation. The same applies to stigmatized groups like welfare recipients and single mothers. For such minorities, formal equality as citizens is not enough. They need differentiated rights that take account of their special needs and identities: self-government rights for Native Americans, public recognition and equal opportunities measures for ethnic and religious minorities, and a stronger welfare state for socially excluded groups.[5]

Tier 2

The citizens of other highly developed countries also enjoy strong rights and the rule of law. Rights may be somewhat weaker than in the United States in some areas, such as legal protection, but stronger in others, especially welfare. Here, too, some minorities lack the social power to effectively claim their rights, and need special measures to secure genuine participation.

Tier 3

Citizens of transitional and intermediate countries have lower standards of rights and legal protection. Official corruption and ineffective or biased policing can reduce personal security. Elections may be less fair. Social protection may be less developed and health services less effective. In the new industrial countries of Asia, discourses on community responsibility versus individual rights can reduce personal freedom.

Tier 4

The people of the poorer countries of the South may be citizens in name but not in reality. Elections are often mere facades for dictatorial regimes. Police and armed forces may oppress the people rather than protect them, and welfare systems may be almost nonexistent. Sometimes, the poor quality of social services may be a result of structural adjustment policies imposed by the North.

Tier 5

The worst thing to be in a world of nation-states is a 'non-citizen'. This category includes people living in a country where the state has disintegrated and there is no protection from rival armed fractions. Many states in the South, such as Somalia, Sierra Leone, the Democratic Republic of the Congo, Afghanistan, and Azerbaijan, have passed through or are in such conditions. It is just as bad to live in a country defined as a 'rogue state' by the United States, because this can mean not only oppression by the local ruler, but the threat of bombardment or even invasion by the mighty US military machine. Refugees may be deprived of their original citizenship when they flee, but refused citizenship or even the right of abode by the state where they seek refuge. In a world of nation-states, statelessness equals social death. Australian law has coined the evocative term 'unlawful person' to designate such people.

Thus, the absolute equality of human rights laid down in the instruments of international law, like the UN Charter or various conventions, does not exist in social reality, where hierarchy and relativism prevail. All people may have certain rights on paper, but many lack the opportunities and resources to actually enjoy these rights.

2.9 Transnational racism

The relativity of rights is particularly clear when we look at the right to migrate. Zygmunt Bauman has argued that, in the globalized world, 'mobility has become the most powerful and most coveted stratifying factor'. The new global economic and political elites are able to cross borders at will, while the poor are meant to stay at home: 'the riches are global, the misery is local' (Bauman, 1998: 9 and 74). Northern states compete with each other to attract highly skilled workers, such as Indian information technology specialists. The British National Health Service (NHS) is heavily dependent on African and Asian doctors and nurses. But the same countries are taking drastic measures to exclude lower-skilled workers – even though they urgently need them. The NHS also employs migrant workers as cleaners and cooks. Often these are undocumented workers, employed illegally through sub-contractors. US agriculture and services rely on undocumented migrant workers. Japan urgently needs low-skilled workers, not just for industry and construction, but also to look after its ageing population. Malaysian plantations and factories would close down without undocumented Indonesian laborers. In all these cases, illegal workers may actually be preferred because their lack of rights makes them easier to exploit. The hierarchy of citizenship helps to construct a *differentiated global labor force*.

In a world of nation-states, most people can get a passport, but not all passports are equal. Citizens of the United States can go everywhere and enjoy unrivalled protection. Passports of other highly developed countries give the right to cross most borders. Citizens of third-tier countries may find their rights to mobility quite constrained, while those of the fourth and fifth tiers often have no internationally recognized passport at all. As Bertold Brecht wrote many years ago, as a refugee in Helsinki: 'The passport is the most noble part of a person … that is why it is recognized if it is good, but a person may not be recognized, however good he is' (Brecht, 1961: 7–8, my translation).

Globalization essentially means flows across borders – flows of capital, commodities, ideas, and people. States welcome the first two types, but are suspicious of the others. However, globalization also creates strong pressures to move. Global media beam idealized images of First World lifestyles into the poorest villages. Electronic communications facilitate the dissemination of knowledge of migration routes and work opportunities. Many of the world's excluded perceive that mobility brings the chance of prosperity, and are desperate to migrate. This helps explain the upsurge in asylum seekers and undocumented migrants since about 1990. Thus, globalization creates the cultural capital needed for mobility.

It also creates the necessary social capital, for another key characteristic of globalization is that power is diffused through networks (Castells, 1996). Network organization characterizes the 'globalization from above' of transnational corporations and global governance, as well as the 'globalization from below' of migrants and their communities. Their informal networks facilitate movements even when official policies try to stop them (Castles, 2004). At the same time, some of these networks take on institutionalized forms in the 'migration industry' – one of the fastest growing forms of international business. This term embraces the many people who earn their livelihoods by organizing migration as travel agents, people smugglers, bankers, lawyers, labor recruiters, and housing agents. It is such networks which help to reconnect the South and the North at a time when many areas of the South have become economically irrelevant to the globalized economy (Duffield, 2001).

The hierarchization of the right to migrate can be seen as a new form of *transnational racism*. Its intellectual basis lies in discourses on the 'naturalness' of violence in less developed regions and the cultural incompatibility of their peoples with Western-Christian civilization. This is the background to Huntington's 'clash of civilizations'. Such discourses developed during the wars accompanying the break-up of Yugoslavia and the Soviet Union. These conflicts were portrayed as the re-emergence of 'age-old ethnic hatreds'. The implication was that groups with different cultures and histories could not share a single territory (Gallagher, 1997; Turton, 1997). This led to the idea of a new 'tribalism' in which people in less developed areas retreat from universalist to localist outlooks, and chaos dominates much of the world (Global

Commission, 1995: 16–17). Some analysts spoke of a massive increase in violence, crime, war, and drug addiction, and the development of a new barbarism in which torture, rape, and cannibalism were becoming commonplace (Kaplan, 1996a). Such ideas have been further reinforced by fears of terrorism and fundamentalism since 11 September 2001.

In the South, the defense of local or sectional interests against Northern domination may be based on religious and cultural symbols of dignity and identity. Resistance movements may appear particularistic and backward looking, because discourses of universalism have been monopolized by globalizing forces. These discourses legitimate such measures as restrictive immigration rules, deportation of 'unwanted' migrants, or military attacks on 'rogue states'. Some Northern intellectuals now argue that democracy was just a passing phase in world history, and not suitable for certain cultures (Kaplan, 1996b). Others, however, see democracy as something that can and should be imposed by force, especially where political and economic interests demand it.

2.10   National and international hierarchies of citizenship

The hierarchies of nation-states and citizenship are among the factors which perpetuate underdevelopment and conflict in the South. Inequality, impoverishment, and violence drive migration. These interlinked causes lead to a blurring of the distinction between forced migration and economic migration. Failed economies generally also mean weak states, predatory ruling cliques, and human rights abuse. This leads to the 'asylum-migration nexus': many migrants and asylum seekers have multiple reasons for mobility, and it is impossible to completely separate economic and human rights motivations – which is a challenge to the neat categories that bureaucracies seek to impose. The international hierarchies of citizenship have not replaced the national hierarchies (referred to above as differentiated citizenship). Rather they complement them and interact with them in complex ways. The weakening of national boundaries inherent in globalization means that the rights and conditions of citizens are shaped by both national and transnational factors. These hierarchies are summed up in the two tables which follow. Table 1 shows typical forms of differentiation of citizenship within nation-states. Of course, not all forms exist in all countries. However, it would be hard to find any country where there were not some types of inequality, which contradict the inclusive and universalist principles of citizenship theory.

Table 1 Hierarchies of citizenship within nation-states

Types	Characteristics
Full citizens	People born in the country plus naturalized immigrants – but excluding certain minority groups
Denizens	Immigrants who have obtained some citizenship rights on the basis of long-term residence
Undocumented migrants	Lack nearly all rights except those guaranteed by international human rights instruments
Asylum seekers	Very limited rights under special regimes
Ethnic, religious, and social minorities	Formally enjoy all legal rights, but may not be able to claim them due to discrimination or social exclusion
Indigenous peoples	Mainly in white settler societies (USA, Canada, Australia, New Zealand, Latin America). Subject to historical processes of dispossession, legal discrimination, and social exclusion
Gender divisions	Legal discrimination against women now rare in Northern countries, though still common in the South. Institutional and informal discrimination persists

Table 2 does not represent a single hierarchy, but rather lists a number of mechanisms, which have been explained in the course of this article. It is important to analyze the ways in which the national and international hierarchies interact. Clearly, origin in a country which is high in the international citizenship hierarchy is likely to lead to a high position in national hierarchies: few migrants from highly developed countries end up as undocumented migrants or asylum seekers. People from Tiers 4 and 5 of the international hierarchy are most likely to end up with a low position in the national scale. The importance of the discourses on the naturalness of violence and chaos in assigning groups to subordinate national status is also clear.

2.11 From hierarchical citizenship to transnational citizenship?

The international political developments examined in this article add up to the construction of a new global order of domination, in which the legal principle of equality of nation-states and of citizens is in stark contradiction to a reality of hierarchy and exclusion. Does this mean that

Table 2   International hierarchies of citizenship

Types	Characteristics
Differentiation of citizenship rights	Tier 1: Citizens of the USA Tier 2: Citizens of other highly developed countries Tier 3: Citizens of transitional and newly industrializing countries Tier 4: Citizens of less developed countries Tier 5: People of failed states, stateless people, and non-citizens
Right to migrate	Stratified on the basis of place of origin and human capital (education and qualifications), following the above tiers
Naturalness of violence and chaos in less developed regions	Discourses which legitimate imposition of Northern models of governance on the South
Transnational racism	Discourses which legitimate strict immigration rules, as well as differential treatment of immigrant populations to create differentiated national and global labor forces

hierarchical citizenship is inevitable under conditions of globalization? That would be a pessimistic conclusion, which would imply that democracy – in the sense of conditions that allow active citizens to participate in law-making and government – has no future. I do not think that it is the case. Globalization cannot be reversed, but there could be more democratic and inclusive forms of global governance. This is not just a theoretical possibility. Recent debates over such issues as military intervention, international law, human rights, trade policy, the environment, and culture show that the hierarchical nation-state system is neither monolithic nor free from countervailing forces. Dissenting voices can be found at the transnational, the national, and the subnational levels. There is no space to describe or analyze these here, but it is important to remember the historical strength of democratizing tendencies in modern societies. The rise of democratic tendencies from the seventeenth century onwards was not the result of inexorable structural processes, but rather of human agency in the form of social and political movements (Habermas, 1996). Such movements exist in this latest phase of modernity too. They include environmental, anti-racist, pro-development, and anti-war movements, as well as political parties. They campaign for citizenship rights for excluded groups within nation-states, and for more democracy at the international level.

Moving from hierarchical to transnational citizenship would have three main elements. First, since the nation-state remains the most important focus of power, it is necessary to introduce more inclusive and effective forms of citizen participation at this level. Groups that suffer from exclusion need special measures to allow genuine participation in the mainstream activities of society. Depending on the circumstances, such measures might include special representation (like the reserved seats for Maori in the New Zealand parliament), social and educational programs, anti-discrimination rules, or equal opportunity laws. Measures are also needed to allow greater participation for all citizens. The complexity of decision-making processes, the dominance of mass media in opinion formation, and the distance of national legislatures from local concerns all make it hard for citizens to do more than vote for one party or another every few years. Devolution of decisions to local and regional levels, information provision using new technologies, democratization of administrative bodies (such as health, housing, or education authorities), and even electronic voting procedures could help revive democracy.

Second, many crucial decisions are now made by international bodies, so democracy needs to be established at this level as well. Decision-making in the IMF, the WTO, and the World Bank is dominated by financial and commercial interest groups within the rich countries. The governing councils of these bodies consist mainly of the finance and trade ministers of the North. Southern governments have little say, and the farmers, workers, and poor people of the world are not represented at all (Stiglitz, 2002: ch. 9). The result is policies that ignore the needs and interests of the great majority of people. Broadening participation to include not only Southern governments but also directly elected representatives of the world's people would be an enormous step toward transnational democracy.

Third, if global institutions had a democratic mandate and represented broader interests than they do today, there would be greater legitimacy for international intervention in situations of oppression or conflict. The military interventions of the period since 1992 have mainly been about securing Northern interests, by containing refugee flows, controlling strategically important areas, securing vital commodities (especially oil), and combating threats of terrorism. Human rights and democracy have often been mere legitimations. The belated and ineffective actions in Somalia and Rwanda, and the failure to help rebuild society in Afghanistan and Iraq are indicative of the true interests behind intervention. With greater democracy and transparency in international decision-making, there might be more willingness to act to prevent massacres and genocide, to curtail racial, ethnic, or religious repression, and to depose despots who oppress their own people. These ideas may seem utopian in view of current trends. But it is important to realize that the hierarchical global order is neither natural nor inevitable, but rather the product of human action. It can therefore also be changed by human action. As always in history, democratization is not likely to come from those who hold power, but through the activities of political and social movements. Such movements are emerging, and it is important that they have clear objectives. The anti-globalization slogan has proved unproductive, since globalization is a process that cannot be rolled back, but the struggle for a more humane, inclusive, and participatory form of globalization could offer a perspective for change.

Notes

1. An earlier version of this paper has been published in Spanish in *Anales de la Cátedra Francisco Suárez*, 37 (University of Granada, 2003: 9–33) and in *International Politics*, (Basingstoke: Palgrave, 42 (2), 2005: 203–224). I thank Rainer Bauböck for comments and suggestions on an earlier draft.
2. This section is based on Chapter 1 of Castles and Davidson, 2000. Detailed information and references are provided in that text, and will not be repeated here.
3. There is a growing literature on this theme. For overviews see Aleinikoff and Klusmeyer, 2000, 2001; Koopmans and Statham, 2000.
4. This trend is so far confined to Western countries. The new immigration countries of Asia, like Japan, Malaysia, Taiwan, and South Korea, still reject any form of long-term integration for immigrants (Castles, 2003).
5. Again, the extensive literature on this topic cannot be summarized here. See, for instance, Bauböck, 1996; Gutmann, 1994; Kymlicka, 1995; Young, 1989.

References

Aleinikoff, T. A., and Klusmeyer, D. (eds), *From Migrant to Citizens: Membership in a Changing World* (Washington, DC: Carnegie Endowment for International Peace, 2000).

Aleinikoff, T. A., and Klusmeyer, D. (eds), *Citizenship Today: Global Perspectives and Practices* (Washington, DC: Carnegie Endowment for International Peace, 2001).

Bauböck, R., 'Social and Cultural Integration in a Civil Society', in Bauböck, R., Heller, A., and Zolberg, A. R. (eds), *The Challenge of Diversity: Integration and Pluralism in Societies of Immigration* (Aldershot: Avebury, 1996).

Bauman, Z., *Globalization: The Human Consequences* (Cambridge: Polity, 1998).

Beauftragte der Bundesregierung für Ausländerfragen, *Bericht über die Lage der Auslander in der Bundesrepublik Deutschland* (Berlin and Bonn: Beauftragte der Bundesregierung für Ausländerfragen, 2002).

Brecht, B., *Flüchtlingsgespräche* (Frankfurt am Main: Suhrkamp, 1961).

Castells, M., *The Rise of the Network Society* (Oxford: Blackwells, 1996).

Castles, S., 'Migrant Settlement, Transnational Communities and State Strategies in the Asia Pacific Region', in Iredale, R., Hawksley, C., and Castles, S. (eds), *Migration in the Asia Pacific: Population, Settlement and Citizenship Issues* (Cheltenham and Northampton, MA: Edward Elgar, 2003).

Castles, S., 'Why Migration Policies Fail', *Ethnic and Racial Studies*, 27:2 (2004): 205–27.

Castles, S., and Davidson, A., *Citizenship and Migration: Globalisation and the Politics of Belonging* (Basingstoke: Palgrave Macmillan, 2000).

Castles, S., and Miller, M. J., *The Age of Migration: International Population Movements in the Modern World* (Basingstoke: Palgrave Macmillan, 2003).

Chimni, B. S., 'The Geo-Politics of Refugee Studies: A View from the South', *Journal of Refugee Studies*, 11:4 (1998): 350–74.

Cohen, R., *Global Diasporas: An Introduction* (London: UCL Press, 1997).

Duffield, M., *Global Governance and the New Wars: The Merging of Development and Security* (London and New York: Zed Books, 2001).

Fukuyama, F., *The End of History and the Last Man* (London: Penguin, 1992).

Gallagher, T., 'My Neighbour My Enemy: The Manipulation of Ethnic Identity and the Origins and Conduct of War in Yugoslavia', in Turton, D. (ed.), *War and Ethnicity: Global Connections and Local Violence* (New York: Rochester University Press, 1997).

Geddes, A., *The Politics of Migration and Immigration in Europe* (London: Sage, 2003).

Giddens, A., *The Third Way: the Renewal of Social Democracy* (Cambridge: Polity, 1998).

Global Commission, *Our Global Neighbourhood: Report of the Commission on Global Governance* (Oxford: Oxford University Press, 1995).

Gutmann, A. (ed.), *Multiculturalism: Examining the Politics of Recognition* (Princeton, NJ: Princeton University Press, 1994).

Habermas, J., *Die Einbeziehung des Anderen: Studien zur politischen Theorie* (Frankfurt am Main: Suhrkamp, 1996).

Hardt, M., and Negri, A., *Empire* (Cambridge, MA: Harvard University Press, 2000).

Held, D., McGrew, A., Goldblatt, D., and Perraton, J., *Global Transformations: Politics, Economics and Culture* (Cambridge: Polity, 1999).

Huntington, S., 'The Clash of Civilizations', *Foreign Affairs*, 72:3 (1993): 22–49.

Kaldor, M., *New and Old Wars: Organized Violence in a Global Era*, 2nd edn (Cambridge: Polity, 2001).

Kaplan, R., *The Ends of the Earth: A Journey at the Dawn of the 21st Century* (New York: Random House, 1996a).

Kaplan, R., 'Was Democracy Just a Moment?', *Atlantic Monthly* (Boston, MA: Atlantic Monthly, 1996b), pp. 55–80.

Koopmans, R., and Statham, P., (eds), *Challenging Immigration and Ethnic Relations Politics* (Oxford: Oxford University Press, 2000).

Kymlicka, W., *Multicultural Citizenship: A Liberal Theory of Minority Rights* (Oxford: Clarendon, 1995).

Marshall, T. H., *Class, Citizenship and Social Development: Essays by T. H. Marshall* (New York: Anchor Books, 1964).

Martiniello, M., 'Citizenship of the European Union: A Critical View', in Bauböck, R. (ed.), *From Aliens to Citizens* (Aldershot: Avebury, 1994).

Mead, L., *Beyond Entitlement: The Social Obligations of Citizenship* (New York: Free Press, 1986).

Portes, A., Guarnizo, L. E., and Landolt, P., 'The Study of Transnationalism: Pitfalls and Promise of an Emergent Research Field', *Ethnic and Racial Studies*, 22:2 (1999): 217–37.

Rawls, J., 'Justice as Fairness: Political Not metaphysical', *Philosophy and Public Affairs*, 14:3 (1985): 223–51.

Renan, E., *Qu'est-ce qu'une nation? et autres essais politiques* (Paris: Presses Pocket, 1992).

Roberts, A., 'More Refugees, Less Asylum: A Regime in Transformation', *Journal of Refugee Studies*, 11:4 (1998): 375–95.

Schnapper, D., *La Communauté des Citoyens. Essai sur l'idée moderne de nation* (Paris: Gallimard, 1994).

Stiglitz, J. E., *Globalization and its Discontents* (London: Penguin, 2002).

Turton, D., 'War and Ethnicity: Global Connections and Local Violence in North East Africa and Former Yugoslavia', *Oxford Development Studies*, 25:1 (1997): 77–94.

United Nations Population Division, *International Migration Report 2002* (New York: United Nations, 2002).

Van Hear, N., *New Diasporas: The Mass Exodus, Dispersal and Regrouping of Migrant Communities* (London: UCL Press, 1998).

Vertovec, S., 'Conceiving and Researching Transnationalism', *Ethnic and Racial Studies*, 22:2 (London: Routledge, 1999): 445–62.

Wieviorka, M., 'Introduction', in Wieviorka, M., Bataille, P., Couper, K., Martuccelli, D., and Peralva, A. (eds), *Racisme et Xénophobie en Europe: une Comparaison Internationale* (Paris: La Découverte, 1994).

Young, I. M., 'Polity and Group Difference: A Critique of the Ideal of Universal Citizenship', *Ethics*, 99 (1989): 250–74.

Yuval-Davis, N., Anthias, F., (eds), *Woman-Nation-State* (London: Macmillan, 1989).

Zolberg, A. R., Suhrke, A., and Aguayo, S., *Escape from Violence* (Oxford and New York: Oxford University Press, 1989).

3
Cultures of Equality, Traditions of Belonging

Anja Rudiger

3.1 Introduction

At the turn of the millennium, the European Union (EU) made a promise of equality to its diverse citizenry. By inscribing the principle of equality in the Charter of Fundamental Rights – and subsequently in the Constitutional Treaty – and by adopting concrete legislation in the form of the Race and Employment Equality Directives under Article 13 of the European Community (EC) Treaty,[1] a future of harmonized equality laws, policies, and practices across Europe has come within reach. The broad scope of the Race Equality Directive in particular has raised expectations for progressing racial justice in Europe. For the first time in EU history, all member states are required to adopt specific legal provisions that protect racial and ethnic minorities from direct and indirect discrimination in most walks of life.

However, this equality framework emerged out of a specific political constellation rather than a shared understanding of equality. Towards the end of the 1990s, a rise in racial violence and electoral successes for far-right parties had galvanized anti-racist struggles to the point where EU leaders were propelled into action. However, since the events of 11 September 2001, this context has undergone a radical transformation. Europe is witnessing a retreat from the fragile multicultural terrain of the late twentieth century. The idea of a homogeneous collective identity, embodied in the resurrected imagery of the nation-state, has returned to assuage anxieties over economic and military insecurity. The EU equal treatment framework, with its pluralist equality promise covering differences on the grounds of race, gender, sexuality, religion, disability, and age, looks set to weaken under pressures to strengthen national identity and cohesion. Racial and religious differences in particular – often

41

perceived as external rather than internal – are subject to renewed scrutiny by legislators and policy makers. Even before the first steps towards creating inclusive cultures of equality in Europe are taken, exclusionary traditions of national belonging are re-emerging, blocking pathways to democratization.

These contradictory developments reflect an underlying paradox that engulfs policy-making at the junction of equality, cohesion, and migration. While the emerging EU equality framework signals the recognition of the need for a joint, integrated, and inclusive approach to equal treatment across Europe, each member state accords special rights to its citizens on the basis of classifying and differentiating them from noncitizens and populations elsewhere. The universal principle of equality clashes with the particular rights conferred by nation-states on the basis of national identification and belonging. In the era of globalization, Europe remains the home to nation-states whose invented political boundaries create communities separated from others and rendered sovereign even in the face of European integration. The imagined nation uses criteria such as nationality, race, and religion to unite and divide populations for the purpose of maintaining a cohesive and stable entity. It is no coincidence that the EU Equal Treatment Directives include an explicit exemption for nationality discrimination, as a marker of the most obvious distinction nation-states make between insiders and outsiders. While such distinctions are constitutive elements of any concrete community, particularly the value-based delineation of the nation, the principle of equality aims to level these in a universal, integrative sweep. This core tension raises the question of whether Europe's newly minted legal equal treatment framework – now one of the most advanced in the world – will in fact be translated into practical measures at the national level. How can EU Member States adopt a rights-based approach to anti-discrimination and develop a culture of equality that negotiates their exclusionary traditions of belonging?

3.2   Cultures of equality in Europe

In legislative terms, the incentive for member states to develop comprehensive anti-discrimination provisions – as provided by the EU Directives – has been unprecedented and may yet lead to significant legal changes in national approaches to equality. Prior to this EU initiative, the majority of member states did not have specific anti-discrimination laws in place, let alone a rights-based equality framework. Joint EU action in this field has enabled, on average, a more progressive and comprehensive approach than national policies would have allowed. Nevertheless, the transposition of the Directives into national law has been a slow and cumbersome process, which – well over a year after the transposition deadlines – is far from completed. Many states did not meet the Race Equality Directive's implementation deadline of June 2003, causing the European Commission to initiate legal infringement procedures against six countries the following year.[2] Other states have interpreted the provisions in such a way that closer scrutiny by the Commission may find that the Directive's requirements have not been fully met.

While this chapter will apply theoretical considerations to identify barriers at the national level, empirical investigations into the specific legal and policy issues that impede full compliance by individual member states have already yielded useful results (European Monitoring Centre, 2002; European Commission, 2004b). In the following, a prism of conceptual perspectives, reflecting concrete policy concerns, aims to elucidate the role of national cultures and traditions in stifling progress on advancing equality in Europe.

Although EU equality provisions remain tied to a rather narrow, compliance-driven anti-discrimination approach (European Commission, 2004a; Hepple, 2004), the Directives' introduction of the principle of equal treatment, particularly on the grounds of race and ethnicity, calls for more interventionist legal and policy instruments than most states were previously willing to provide. Even in the absence of a clear shift from a negative anti-discrimination approach to a positive promotion of equality, EU standards now require proactive policies that go beyond the provisions available in most member states. In many countries it has long been assumed that generic equality promises entailed in constitutional principles are sufficient in regulating how people live together. The reluctance of most member states to acknowledge, in principle as well as for practical policy-making purposes, the profound differences inscribed in the profile of their populations, has obscured the need for concrete legal and policy instruments to ensure equal treatment. Insofar as certain collective experiences mark some groups as different, even a minimal equal treatment approach requires an awareness of such difference to rectify the disadvantages that may accompany it. To advance equality in a more substantive sense, an understanding of people's different choices, needs, and perspectives is required as a basis for responsive policy-making.

It is not, then, a commitment to equality but an understanding of difference that poses the key challenge to implementing equality frameworks at the national level. Most member states have yet to develop an equality culture that combines equal treatment with respect for difference. Even after two decades of rhetorical exploration of the multicultural terrain, the paradigm for much policy-making across Europe rests in classic liberalism's conflation of equality with sameness. As a constitutive element of liberal democracies, the principle of granting the same rights to each citizen and treating them in the same way has historically assumed a powerful progressive – and often subversive – force. It has guided struggles for extending equal rights to an ever wider, more inclusive spectrum of people, and for exercising these rights in practice. But over the course of this contentious history, the political limits of a liberal concept of equality have become increasingly obvious and elicited a proliferation of discursive concessions to diversity. Equality as sameness entails an emancipatory teleology only insofar as it is guided by the prospect, however distant, of human homogeneity. Where empirical differences cannot be fully leveled, they also fail to register as relevant for the purposes of equal treatment. Such differences are perceived as remnants of private particularities within the subsuming public order of the modern state. In practice, these supposedly pre-modern identities, based for example on religion, language, or race, are excluded from a public sphere that is anything but neutral, and disadvantaged by institutions unable to act as impartial arbiters.

Of related ideological provenance, the principle of equal treatment set out by the EU Directives could be interpreted by member states as a call for uniform procedures and practices guided by a pre-existing standard of human needs. For example, such procedures could give everyone the option not to work on Sundays, taking account of religious needs. Everyone would receive the same treatment. The fact that such an option would be meaningless to people whose religious services take place on Fridays or Saturdays would be irrelevant, as the baseline of equal treatment has already been established. However, such an understanding of equal treatment could potentially contravene the Directives' prohibition of indirect discrimination, which signals an understanding that people should be treated equally with regard to their differences as well as their similarities. Thus the right to observe religious practices might involve treating people differently to enable an equal outcome. Depending on what a particular right entails in a specific context, appropriate measures to enable the equal exercise of that right can be negotiated in processes of democratic engagement, rather than imposed by traditions or abstract standards. The Directives provide sufficient latitude for such discursive openings, as emphasized in their explicit call for dialogue with civil society. This could help facilitate a reflection on how cultures have universalized their understanding of 'sameness' and created a dominant, context-blind standard of equality that in fact perpetuates unequal treatment.

Policy-making in EU Member States would benefit significantly from the recognition of how the same treatment can affect people differently. Because people tend to differ from the abstract standards that policy makers use as guidance, a more realistic understanding of equality would enhance the responsiveness of public policies to the many different strengths, needs, and aspirations people have. While setting the baseline by which such differences are measured (e.g., practices other than Sunday prayer are considered different) is itself an indication of an established dominant position, the recognition of difference is the first step towards identifying hierarchies that might impede equal treatment. Policies can only be effective and fair if they detect and address power differentials between the groups of people they intend to serve.

The impact of the EU's new equal treatment framework, especially with regard to race equality, depends to a large extent on member states' understanding of the interplay between equality and difference. In the first instance, European countries will have to learn their 'lesson of otherness' (Balibar, 2003). They need to acknowledge the realities of contemporary societies, which are characterized by social, cultural, and ethnic diversity, segmented by structural hierarchies of power, and manifested in people's widely differing perspectives and needs. Most countries have not yet come to terms with this diversity, and herein lays a key barrier to implementing EU equal treatment provisions in a meaningful manner. A considerable culture change is required throughout Europe's nation-states, a change that would go beyond revisions of legal frameworks and institutional tools and take root in wider social relations.

3.2.1 The lessons of diversity

Within the constellation of Europe's market democracies, three paradigmatic responses to the challenge of race equality can be identified, all broadly anchored in liberal tradition but based on different assumptions and resulting in a disparate array of policies and instruments. In general terms, Anglo-American pragmatism, also expressed in widely varying forms in Sweden, the Netherlands, and Belgium, has moved the furthest from a liberal individualist to a multicultural pluralist understanding of equality and difference. The above countries have all enacted special anti-discrimination legislation and established independent public equality bodies whose mandate is defined by law. In its most pragmatic expression, embodied by the United Kingdom, this model is predominantly procedural, based on a management approach to social relations, with few substantive values to guide it. It is thus subject to frequent revisions based on the policy needs of the day. Influences from the United States are obvious, even though the US race equality framework emerged in a different historical context, driven by the civil rights struggle of historically marginalized groups. As a result, the US approach acknowledges diversity as inherent to society, rather than caused by external developments such as immigration. Although the UK race relations framework was developed in response to immigration, its emphasis on managing group relations links it to the American experience. The focus has been on how society can achieve the fair treatment of different groups, not on how newcomers blend into society. This means that Anglo-American race equality frameworks have been designed to address the rights of distinct groups and their mode of interaction, not merely the rights of individuals. The challenge of negotiating difference and equality has been recognized as integral to the policy goal of cohesion in a pluralist society. In the United Kingdom, the social management model aimed at regulating relations between different ethnic groups, solidified by the Race Relations Act of 1976, became the basis of an institutionalized equality regime that encompassed – prior to the implementation of the Directives – the grounds of race, gender, and disability. Pragmatism gave rise to a regulatory framework informed by the experience of policy-relevant racial and ethnic differences within the national population. It raised expectations of equal treatment derived from the actual process of managing diversity rather than a substantive assumption of sameness.

For the more substantive, value-based approaches to equality, found both in the republican and the ethno-cultural traditions usually associated with France and Germany, diversity has posed a greater challenge. Both rely on constitutional guarantees to secure citizens' rights, rather than policy-driven race relations machinery or specific measures against discrimination. Variations in the historical development and empirical manifestation of diversity in EU Member States cannot explain such distinct national approaches to race equality. A country such as France, with an immensely diverse population and a long colonial history, has developed along a different ideological path than, say, the United Kingdom, by not acknowledging diversity as the real-life corollary to its constitutional equality promise. Its route has been based on a strict separation between public and private spheres, combined with the propagation of a national civic faith (Favell, 2001: 85) shaping the public identity of individual citizens, irrespective of their collective racial, ethnic, or religious backgrounds. This imposition of pre-existing public values onto the seemingly blank canvas presented by isolated individuals runs counter to a pluralist understanding of a democracy constructed by processes of social interaction.

3.2.2 Pluralism

The distinction between individualist and group-centered approaches is one of the main determinants of equality cultures. Without the recognition of collective identities, the constitutive nature of difference and its significance for public policy is rendered invisible. Continental policy makers tend to disregard the collective needs of people who share certain experiences and encounter similar barriers, by overlooking that such experiences affect groups of people and not just isolated individuals. In France, for example, the public emergence of group interests based on race or ethnicity would be perceived as a breakdown of national unity. The state does not officially recognize minorities as groups with distinct needs and experiences which public action would have to take into account. There are no policy-relevant differences which distinguish individuals – provided they are French citizens.

This reluctance to identify people as groups for the purpose of policy-making can diminish the impact of policies if they fail to correspond to patterns of shared needs, and exclude those whose needs remain unrecognized. Accountable and effective policy-making requires monitoring tools to assess group needs and performance, as well as measures to address such needs through targeted or mainstream initiatives, so that those collective experiences that signal disadvantages can be mitigated by equal treatment provisions.

It is not entirely clear whether the EU Equal Treatment Directives adopt and encourage such a pluralist perspective. On the face of it, the Directives' principle of equal treatment aims to provide protection from discrimination for people as individuals, regardless of their background. There does not appear to be similar protection available for people by virtue of their membership of disadvantaged or minority groups. For example, there is no link between combating racial discrimination and protecting minority rights. More generally, within the wider EU legal and policy context, minority rights appear limited to EU accession requirements, thus reflecting the reluctance of the old member states to acknowledge the existence of distinct collective identities within their territories that have not been formed by a unifying national discourse.

While falling short of advocating group rights, the EU Directives do, however, recognize that individuals may belong to groups (defined as grounds of protection, such as racial or ethnic origin, sexuality, religion, age, and disability) that have collective experiences and protection needs. This is exemplified in the concept of indirect discrimination, which stipulates that certain provisions, criteria, or practices can affect people of a racial or ethnic origin differently than others. An even stronger recognition of the potentially disadvantaged position that individuals have as members of minority groups can be found in Preamble 17 and Article 5 of the Race Equality Directive, which point to the possibility of compensatory measures for those groups. This nod to positive action constitutes a crucial step towards addressing inequalities as an expression of power differentials between groups of people, not simply as a failure to treat individuals the same.

3.2.3 Institutional change

If an awareness of the experiences and needs of different groups in society is a precondition for policy-making in general, as well as for remedial action against particular disadvantages, it does not in itself entail an analysis of the forces behind inequalities or of measures to counter them. A group perspective does suggest, however, that discrimination suffered on, say, racial grounds (by virtue of belonging to a certain racial group) is unlikely to be merely the result of inappropriate behavior by individuals. Instead, such behavior is indicative of systematic patterns of discrimination permeating relations between social groups. Inequality is a structural relationship within society, not an occurrence triggered by individual actions or attitudes. Individualist approaches, on the contrary, tend to focus on issues related to behavior or performance, such as prejudice on the one hand, and human capital deficits on the other. While both can certainly act as contributory factors, they also serve to obscure structural inequalities. Moreover, well-meaning and often useful policy responses such as improving educational qualifications and the employability of disadvantaged individuals implicitly suggest that certain differences found in minority groups form obstacles to equality, rather than unequal treatment received from mainstream society. The emphasis on individual agency and adaptation to existing standards often turns a blind eye to the institutions that shape public life, social interaction, and individual behavior.

Anti-discrimination frameworks based on individualist perspectives concentrate on prohibiting direct discrimination and providing complaints mechanisms for discriminatory acts suffered by, and perpetrated by, individuals. Such a narrow, retrospective approach continues to be preferred by policy makers in many EU countries. While it offers a necessary minimum level of protection from discrimination, it is insufficient as a centerpiece around which a national culture of equality could develop.

In Britain, the unequivocal identification of institutional racism by the 1999 Macpherson Report has compelled policy makers to move beyond a reactive, complaints-driven approach in order to revise legal and institutional frameworks to address structural inequalities. While the effective implementation of systematic measures against deeply entrenched institutional discrimination is a long-term and ongoing process, the United Kingdom now commands an array of procedural and substantive measures to advance race equality. These range from penalizing discrimination (legal prohibition enforced in tribunals and courts), creating opportunities (equal opportunities policies), managing diversity, and promoting cohesion (in the form of ethnic monitoring, impact assessments, and consultation procedures) to positively influencing outcomes (positive action). Such measures are supported institutionally by an independent public body with a range of promotional, investigative, and enforcement powers (the Commission for Racial Equality, established in 1976).

While the Race Equality Directive requires member states to establish similar specialized bodies as an institutional support for equal treatment provisions, it is arguable whether it also endorses proactive measures to promote equality within institutions. The objective of institutional change, to which Anglo-American equality frameworks respond in some degree, demands proactive, positive measures that compel public and private institutions to intervene in a preventive and reform-oriented way. Many commentators, however, have argued that the positive action clause in the Directives, which is phrased as an exception rather than as an explicit means to achieve equal treatment, offers an insufficient basis for such an approach, and that the Directives remain focused on individual litigation against specific acts of discrimination once they have occurred (European Commission, 2004a; Hepple, 2004: 12). This would not encourage interventions against institutional cultures characterized by a 'collective failure of an organization to provide an appropriate and professional service to people because of their color, culture, or ethnic origin' (Macpherson, 1999: 6–34). Moreover, the independence of the required equal treatment bodies remains questionable, as some member states' implementation efforts have pursued a literal take on the Directive's requirement of independent operation rather than independent status and basis in law. Therefore, while the EU framework indicates a path towards challenging structural inequalities through institutional change, promoted and enforced by independent equality machinery, this is by no means prescriptive. Much more explicit provisions would be needed to require member states to move beyond a reactive, complaints-driven approach.

If a focus on institutional mechanisms is necessary to highlight the structural nature of inequality, this does not imply an underestimation of the agency of civil society movements, whose pressures revealed institutional failures in the first place. A structural approach does not denigrate collective agency; on the contrary, it is the focus on human capital development that marginalizes the role of civil society as well as public and private sector leadership, as the onus for change remains on those individuals who are considered different. A structural change approach, on the other hand, is based on the understanding that equality requires everyone's participation in a society's resources, institutions, and democratic processes. To enable that, institutions must become more open and flexible, as well as adapt to and manage the consequences of social change. Despite the timidity of the EU equal treatment framework, it is possible to channel the impetus for change that emanates from the Directives into institutional reform, for the purpose of, and sustained by, the public engagement of diverse social groups.

3.2.4 Equality of outcome

A pluralist, structural concept of equality, which stresses proactive, preventive, and positive action over prohibition and penalization, is focused on results. The goal is equality of outcome in a context of diversity, or substantive equality, rather than equality of opportunity, or formal equality. Outcome-oriented approaches have become rare in an age when equal opportunities policies are regarded as the high-water mark of organizational change processes, and differences appear to manifest themselves in variable results. However, such views essentialize difference as much as they formalize equality. The dynamic relationship of equality and difference, and the balance of these two components, can best be assessed in a review of 'outcomes'. Whereas equality of opportunity is based on a standardized and inflexible determination of 'opportunity' (assuming that everyone can make use of opportunities in the same way), equality of outcome requires differences to be taken into account at every stage, from devising opportunities to supporting participation and achieving proportionate results.

Equality of outcome has been most persistently, though not always successfully, pursued under the US equality framework. Affirmative action programs – such as 'set asides' for minority businesses, contract compliance mechanisms, and recruitment quotas – are designed to influence socio-economic outcomes for a range of minority groups, including non-citizens. In Britain, the Race Relations Amendment Act of 2000 introduced a statutory duty for public bodies to take proactive measures to promote race equality. Although these remain below the threshold of enforceable quotas for the participation and representation of disadvantaged groups, they indicate a certain willingness to achieve equal outcomes at least in the public sector. This implies that equality considerations must be taken into account in everything a public body does, and at every level of its operation.

While the EU equal treatment Directives signal a shift towards supporting a substantive equality culture, notably through displaying some affinity for positive action, the concept of formal equality remains dominant (Bell, 2003: 9). However, additional tentative steps towards equality of outcome can be detected in the Constitutional Treaty, which introduces the requirement to combat discrimination in defining and implementing policies and activities of the Union (Article III-118), which resembles an obligation to equality-proofing. This has been welcomed as a 'constitutional mandate for the mainstreaming approach [which] is a distinct novelty and not a common element within national constitutions' (Bell, 2003: 19).

3.2.5   Equality and human rights

While the preceding discussion has focused on race equality, the EU's approach to equality opts for a broader, horizontal thrust, with Article 13 of the EC Treaty encompassing a range of grounds on which protection from discrimination is required. Much has been made of this move towards an integrated equality agenda, both in terms of its potentially unifying impetus, but even more so because of the remaining distinctions between each ground (and also the limitation to a list of six specified grounds, excluding countless others). Protection extended on the grounds of race and ethnicity is currently the widest, followed by gender and then religion, sexuality, disability, and age. This suggests a combination of a single equality approach with some separate provisions for specific groups, in an essentially threefold regulatory approach embodied by three equal treatment Directives (including one on gender equality). The different level of provisions has in fact been dismissed as the opposite of a horizontal approach, marking instead a hierarchy of equality (European Commission, 2004a: 5, 13). However, another perspective suggests that the distinctions between equality grounds merely reflect 'the need for precise responses to different forms of discrimination'

(Bell, 2003: 19). Hence the legal commentary to some extent mirrors policy makers' concerns with determining the point at which difference ceases to be an expression of diversity and instead becomes an indicator of division or inequality.

The dilemma of diversity arises not only with regard to variations in protection provisions, but also in relation to the groups of people targeted by such provisions. The wider reach of equality legislation to cover an increasingly broad spectrum of the population could signal an emerging appreciation of a more complex concept of equality based on the needs of a diverse range of social groups. However, it could also indicate the opposite: an individualistic anti-discrimination approach which considers the majority of people in need of protection from some form of discrimination, with an ever-widening list of grounds rendering traditionally disadvantaged groups such as ethnic minorities less relevant for policy-making purposes. In the latter scenario, the United Kingdom's pluralistic race relations approach would yield to a focus on anti-discrimination as a concern for a wide range of people, rather than for distinct groups. Drawing on continental European traditions – which include race equality, if it is addressed at all, as part of basic anti-discrimination or human rights guarantees – such an approach could significantly enhance the profile of an equality agenda in mainstream policy-making. But it would also mean that equal rights for individual citizens would take precedence over recognizing the situation of diverse and disadvantaged groups in society. In the United Kingdom, this could mean a shift from a group-based equality approach to a focus on individual rights. It might squander the strengths of a community perspective that identifies some groups as more, or differently, affected by disadvantage than others. The emphasis would change from managing diversity to protecting human rights.

Developments at the EU level indicate that the equality agenda might already be on the verge of being superseded by a new focus on human rights.[3] Despite their prominent role in the liberal tradition, which underpins modern constitutional guarantees, human rights have rarely served as a basis for policy-making, particularly at the EU level, where legislation was driven by market integration and where competencies for human rights issues remain limited. In this context, the adoption of the Charter of Fundamental Rights raised expectations for rights-based EU policy-making, and plans for developing corresponding institutional machinery in the form of a human rights agency suggest broader EU ambitions in this area. Charting the relationship between human rights and equality has thus become an imminent task for policy makers. As part of the implementation process of the equal treatment Directives, expectations for the role of human rights include, for example, that these provide a common ground for negotiating conflicting claims made by distinct groups on the basis of different equality grounds.

The high-level policy shift towards human rights has not, however, been accompanied by an influential civil society movement with the capacity to forge links between different equality grounds and develop a joint, rights-based agenda that could help shape the emerging EU policy and institutional framework. In light of the important role played by non-governmental networks in advancing the development of the equal treatment Directives, this absence suggests certain difficulties in marshalling a human rights discourse – with its traditional focus on civil and political rights for individuals – for the struggles of disadvantaged groups, especially once these have already voiced their claims to substantive equality on the basis of particular group characteristics. In modern liberal democracies, the issue of universal rights for people as individuals tends to evoke a broad based but silent consensus. If advancing human rights, and particularly the right to equality, is to be a matter that engages a broad spectrum of society, the rights-based discourse has to enable an understanding of society that goes beyond a mere conglomerate of individual claimants to an abstract set of entitlements.

While grounded in claims for rights, struggles by disadvantaged groups in Europe have over the past few decades emphasized the needs of particular groups in relation to economic, social, and cultural participation. The traditional human rights discourse has a history of marginalizing many of those vulnerable groups, as well as disregarding the significance of economic, social, and cultural rights. Gradually, however, it has been shaped by those struggles and embraced a successively wider range of disadvantaged groups as well as new types of rights. Nevertheless, in many EU countries it is the prospect of equality within a context of diversity, rather than the human rights tradition, that drives the engagement of disadvantaged groups. At the same time, approaches to equality have undergone a similar transformation, expanding from anti-discrimination or formal equality to more positive and proactive measures, thereby extending equal opportunities to equal outcomes, with an emphasis on effecting social and institutional change.

If we have now entered an era in which equality and human rights are increasingly merged, there is a risk that the more minimalist aspects of both could become predominant. This could result in a civil rights and anti-discrimination agenda for individual citizens, thus neglecting group rights and needs, as well as wider economic concerns and positive measures for achieving change. On the other hand, human rights and equality, indivisible as they are, could also enhance each other, by including economic, social, and cultural rights, as well as civil and political rights specifically for marginalized groups, including non-citizens. This could lead to a proactive equality agenda with a focus on socio-economic outcomes and political participation based on substantive rights, rather than a managerial approach to social relations.

While the EU equal treatment Directives do not provide an unequivocal lead for such action at the national level, they give momentum to a possible new articulation of rights and equality at the EU level. Legal commentators have pointed out that EU equal treatment and human rights provisions have distinct roots, with the former – in its initial form relating to gender – originally aimed at preventing discrimination from distorting market competition (European Commission, 2004a: 15). If equality objectives have now been integrated into the EU framework in a less instrumental and more horizontal manner, the previously separate agendas of rights and equality could be linked in new ways, without equality being submerged into the human rights discourse. This could potentially enhance the rights-based thrust of anti-discrimination provisions on the one hand, and situate equality and difference at the core of human rights on the other.

3.3   Traditions of belonging

Equality and human rights have a common adversary, the nation-state's classification of people according to their designated status of national belonging. Belonging introduces a dynamic of inclusion and exclusion which marks some people as more equal than others and limits the universal aspiration of human rights claims. Translated into policy-making, this dynamic is embodied in the principle of citizenship. Understood as citizens' rights, this principle designates people as equal members of a democratic society and can help challenge entrenched practices of privilege and preference. However, citizenship clashes with equality where belonging to a polity is lacking or denied. In the early phase of liberal democracy, this affected groups such as women and people without property. In contemporary society, the main line of demarcation is that of nationality. Most European states equate citizenship with nationality, although traditions of regulating access to nationality vary considerably and thus shape member states' varied approaches to equality and diversity. Insofar as national traditions perpetuate a distinction between those who belong and those who do not, universal claims of rights become particularized in the drive towards national cohesion. The delimited principles of the modern polity are both undermined and sustained by the boundaries of the nation. Citizenship as national belonging entails an exclusionary dynamic that functions as a formal barrier to equality. Since equality requires inclusion into society as well as absence of discrimination, the struggle for equality enters a terrain dominated by national traditions of belonging.

3.3.1 Contradictions of citizenship

In most EU Member States the dynamic of belonging has turned equal rights and equal treatment into a privilege of the majority group in society, and thus constitutes a mechanism of discrimination that complements and contradicts legal anti-discrimination provisions. Parekh notes how this sense of belonging has turned into a possessiveness that supersedes the principle of equality: 'Although in many multicultural societies the majority community is willing to grant its citizens equal rights, it feels possessive about the country for democratic, historical and other reasons and insists that the definition of national identity should reflect its privileged status' (Parekh, 1997: 233). Following the imperatives of nation-building, the desire to keep outsiders out of the property of the imagined nation is part of a collective process of identification that is expected to build and maintain social cohesion. Among EU Member States, this process takes on various forms which employ different exclusionary measures, such as racialization in the ethnocultural tradition and abstraction from empirical needs and differences in the republican model. As a result, rights asserted as universal become dependent on particular access privileges conferred upon insiders, those in possession of citizenship. As a tool to formalize national identification, citizenship becomes a mechanism to regulate inclusion and exclusion, thus constructing a hierarchy of people based on criteria determined by the specific ideological model prevailing in a particular nation-state. These criteria of exclusion, which block an understanding of equality based on diversity, tend to be resistant to policy fluctuations in the face of economic needs and political expediency. For example, faced with a growing demand for migrant labor, Germany's ethnocultural model recently revised its naturalization rules, facilitating easier access to citizenship while supporting the ideological perpetuation of a *Leitkultur*.[4]

Within an equality discourse, citizenship thus fulfils multiple and contradictory functions. It provides a basis for claiming equal rights and inclusion, as well as a mechanism of discrimination and exclusion.

Access to citizenship is combined with the promise of equal rights (and obligations) as members of a community constructed by an ideology of belonging, which is expected to generate national cohesion, stability, and unity. This is the basis for linking citizenship, a civic principle, with nationality, a territorial and ethno-cultural principle. However, it is this connection that undermines the possibility of equality, as the particular national character of citizenship is maintained by exclusion and marginalization along racial, ethnic, and cultural lines. The split personality of the rational, modern nation-state sustained by a feeling of belonging espoused by its citizens as nationals has 'an inbuilt tendency to create differences and to racialise minorities' (Castles and Davidson, 2000: 82). The ambiguous identities emerging from this contradictory process, which are neither equal nor different, neither included nor excluded, generate social tensions rather than cohesion. Citizenship as national belonging thus undermines its progressive promise of rights and bends back on itself in an exclusionary dynamic that interprets social tensions as a need for further restricting access. Hence, a deeply racialized citizenship culture, which prevents black citizens from exercising their rights, is unable to instill a widespread sense of belonging and instead tightens regulations of access, for example through migration controls. The failure of cohesion is seen as a function of access to citizenship for outsiders, not as a lack of equality in the exercise of citizens' rights.

This dynamic can be observed even in those states where the link between nationality and citizenship is comparatively weak. In the United Kingdom, for example, most people from black and minority groups are British citizens and entitled to full civic rights, even if they hold Commonwealth nationality. This means the struggle for race equality can build on citizens' rights that have been reinforced within a specific legal and institutional equality regime. This has enabled race equality issues to be placed squarely within mainstream policy-making, as part of general targets of social inclusion and equal opportunities for all, which do not question belonging to and participation in society. Moreover, as discrimination on the basis of nationality is prohibited by the Race Relations Act, newer migrants are, in theory, also able to benefit from equal opportunities policies. However, since the 2001 disturbances in some Northern cities, concerns about social cohesion have led to a search for a closer link between citizenship and nationality, which could provide citizens with a sense of national belonging by distinguishing them from non-citizens. This process has been accompanied by increasingly restrictive asylum policies, which exclude asylum seekers from certain social and economic rights and benefits, and thus create a more visible distinction between insiders and outsiders. This approach to social cohesion risks achieving only further fragmentation by effectively exacerbating the differences between new and established communities.

3.3.2 Migration and security

The tensions between national belonging, citizenship, and equality manifest themselves openly in contemporary migration policies and their mechanisms of exclusion and inclusion. National sovereignty has become increasingly defined as a function of control over inward migration, with a view to ensuring the security and stability of a national community increasingly fearful of infiltration from outside. Asylum seekers and refugees in particular, as the only migrants with an internationally recognized, albeit minimal, legal right to admission in other countries, have become targets of exclusionary measures, reflecting a resentment of perceived constraints on sovereignty amidst resurgent fears about national security.

In the age of globalization, the nation-state, far from being superseded by an amorphous, multilevel empire, has succeeded in reintroducing national security as the 'homeland's' primary concern, thereby reasserting the inside–outside dynamic of national identification and belonging. The modern idea of the nation-state as the only source and site of a cohesive polity has acquired new force since 11 September 2001. The security discourse renationalizes the political space (which is manifested in the prominent role of migration issues) at the same time that globalization denationalizes economic developments (see Sassen, quoted in Dauvergne, 2004). Feeding on social fragmentation and fueling fears of instability, the issue of security invokes the mistrust of difference and the desire for assimilation, which in turn inform policies of exclusion and practices of discrimination. The detrimental effects of the security discourse on cohesion is confirmed, for example, by the links that migrants maintain with their countries of origin, which have been shown to be strongest in countries with particularly exclusionary citizenship regimes. The protective reaction is forever undermining that which it seeks to create.

3.3.3 Can rights be separated from belonging?

The question is, then, whether the right to equality, especially as a means to social, economic, and political inclusion, can be advanced at all in the context of the nation-state's mechanisms of exclusion. The intricate link between the state and the nation, and thus between rights and belonging, effectively restricts equality to those who already identify with and belong to a predefined community whose composition is controlled by conformity. The process of national identification is dependent on the simultaneous presence and absence of minorities, by negating difference through homogenization and producing it as an excluded residue.

Current developments appear to suggest that this link between citizenship and nationality has already been undermined by the processes of globalization, European integration, permanent migration, and growing diversity. The relevance of national citizenship seems to be waning as fewer people identify themselves as belonging to a single, national community and as sites of socio-economic as well as civic and political participation multiply. The new rights-based legal framework of the EU, supported by consolidated institutions, illustrates that rights can be claimed outside national contexts. European citizenship, while still tied to member state nationality, introduces a small but noticeable displacement within the hegemonic articulation of citizenship and nationality. It could open national confines and provide new spaces for both difference and equality to flourish, where belonging could be chosen and rights could be claimed at different levels (Costa, 2004). The equal treatment Directives have been seen as an indicator of such a development, with several commentators placing them in the context of an EU citizenship that offers, despite its minimal conception, progressively evolving rights through the EU's increasingly welcoming embrace of rights-based social and economic policies (European Commission, 2004a; Bell, 2003).

Are we then at a junction where post-national cultures of equality could emerge, replacing the exclusionary dynamics of belonging with multi-tiered models of rights and justice? At the European level, civil society groups are campaigning for rights based on residence instead of nationality, and the new EU Directive on long-term residents, granting equal treatment in key socio-economic areas, could be an initial step in that direction.[5] Although residence is, by definition, tied to a defined territory, it also implies territorial mobility and could lead to variable and multiple forms of belonging. These in turn could be linked to a post-national citizenship, with rights differentiated according to the type of bonds developed (Castles and Davidson, 2000; Soysal, 1994). As flexible, overlapping constructions, such forms of belonging could be deterritorialized and assume a political meaning in tune with a decontextualized, universalistic understanding of rights. Post-national belonging combined with claims to relevant rights in multiple sites would undermine ideologies of national cohesion based on the exclusiveness of citizens' rights – ideologies that form the main obstacle to equality (Kastoryano, 2002).

In practice, however, the emergence of economic, social, and political spaces beyond the nation-state has not replaced national citizenship as the primary tool to access full and equal rights. In fact, multiple attachments still work against those unable to claim full rights in a national context. The exercise of rights remains dependent on state institutions, which are also the prime site of regulating opportunities and outcomes for their citizens, and as such the relevant point of reference for equality claims (Kastoryano, 2002; Dauvergne, 2004) An increase in transnational forms of belonging denotes, in fact, that more and more people are unable to access rights at all, especially if their status is undocumented. At best, they are granted economic and social benefits, such as in Germany where foreigners have long been allocated a non-civic, social type of citizenship, similar to the third-country national denizenship developed at the EU level. Neither equality nor inclusion can follow from such a hierarchy of citizens' rights.

Anticipation of a meaningful post-national citizenship is premature. Not only has migration failed to undermine the nation-state as the site of institutional power, but post-national and multicultural claims have been outmaneuvered by liberalized naturalization regimes on the one hand, and communitarian policies on integration and cohesion on the other. While Germany, for example, restated the importance of nationality for equality and inclusion by liberalizing its naturalization laws, the United Kingdom has aimed to do the same by introducing a value-based citizenship regime that develops closer links to nationality (Hansen, 2003).

If post-nationalism does not in practice offer a route for uncoupling rights from belonging, it is their relationship, the interplay between cultures of equality and belonging, that invites closer scrutiny. Since approaches to equality and traditions of belonging vary among EU Member States, so does the dynamic between them and their impact on social cohesion.

At the policy level, pragmatic solutions that minimize exclusionary tendencies can be identified. For example, where discrimination on grounds of nationality is prohibited, rights are protected regardless of national belonging. Although the EU Directives explicitly exclude nationality as a ground for protection, member states are free to introduce provisions that relax this link between equal treatment and nationality, in order to provide equal opportunities for all their residents. This would shift the prime location of policy-making from the areas of migration and security to the socio-economic field, the site of mainstream social inclusion strategies. Social cohesion would be seen as a function of equality of opportunity or, from a more ambitious perspective, equality of outcome, and therefore approached as nothing more – and nothing less – than a public policy challenge. In this policy scenario, the relationship between equality and belonging would effectively be reversed, with belonging becoming an outcome of equal rights and opportunities, not a precondition for their exercise.

3.4   Longing for equality

Despite constructive policy options, the fundamental tension characterizing contemporary democracies, the relationship between rights-based cultures of equality and national traditions of belonging, is not about to disappear into an ideology-free zone. Moreover, we have come to a juncture where this relationship is not in a balance, but in the process of being hegemonized by ideologies of belonging which threaten to dominate the discourse of equality. To complete the example from Britain, security policies have begun to displace legal provisions, as in the detention without trial of foreign nationals (accompanied by a derogation from the European Convention on Human Rights), rather than building on a comparatively strong equality framework and promoting it among European partners.

If such developments illustrate an emerging hegemonic constellation across Europe, they are also subject to challenges. The equal treatment Directives can be seen as playing an important role in such a challenge, as can policies aimed at strengthening European citizenship and the rights of third-country nationals in the EU. As part of the perpetual reinvention of Europe, a rights-based EU citizenship that gradually seeks detachment from member states' nationality could help generate a new space for the exercise of rights. However, it appears that such Europe-building is already subject to the same tensions that prevail at the national level. Not content with a basis in rights, a more substantial source of collective identification with Europe is sought to propel unification. It is found, *inter alia*, in Christianity, in geographic borders to the South and East, in restrictions on immigration, and in assertions of 'European culture' and 'European values'. A tradition of belonging is invented to supplement the granting of rights and to place the exercise of rights within the boundaries of a community. The construction of a Fortress Europe symbolizes the price paid for belonging to such a community.

If citizenship is always grounded in a symbolic sense of belonging as much as in the actual exercise of rights, as the striving for a European identity seems to suggest, EU citizenship may not turn out to be very different from national citizenship. In fact, it may be less conducive to realizing people's claims to equality, as it lacks an obvious site for civil participation[6] – a persistent problem for an EU that has limited its claims to democratic legitimacy.

The development of democratic cultures of equality has been a history of excluded groups' struggles for rights and against discrimination in the exercise of those rights. These struggles have democratized modern societies and thus shaped national identity, as well as the meaning and scope of rights. Today, a well-developed culture of civil, political, and social participation not only signals the exercise of citizenship but continues to be a precondition for the practical implementation of equal treatment provisions. Collective engagement and participation can break down barriers between groups, barriers that marginalize some and privilege others, and encourage a cross-fertilization of cultures and identities. This can help overcome power differentials and generate a sense of belonging that is based on equality, not opposed to it. Active relationships between majority and minority groups, for example, tend to transform everyone involved. It is the absence of such relationships that leads to fear and exclusion of that which is difference. Social cohesion is built on recognizing and negotiating different needs and perspectives, at a collective as well as individual level, not a prescribed national identity that demands assimilation. Democracy requires a participatory culture of contesting differences in order to thrive.

In today's Europe, such a culture has not yet taken root. While European states display a variety of approaches to equality, they are motivated by an emphasis on social cohesion as derived solely from a strong sense of belonging, be it civic or ethno-cultural. The complex relation of equality and difference is denounced as a potentially disruptive force. But it is the disruptive impulse that drives democratization by exposing the exclusionary dynamic on which cohesive communities invariably rely. Far from undermining cohesion, it ensures that strong communities are compatible with democratic openness by rendering exclusion visible, contestable, and temporary. The emotional need for boundaries, manifested in belonging, and the rational claim to equality based on sameness, are both sources of exclusion and enemies of difference. A challenge to equality as sameness must be accompanied by a questioning of the complacent safety of belonging. In their current hegemonic articulation, equality and belonging both serve to exclude difference and foreclose the contests that render democratic interaction open and accountable. As in past struggles, this relationship can be challenged and displaced in processes of democratic engagement. Such a challenge does not call for an end to the desire to belong, but offers an ethical starting point for democratizing this desire. Thus, 'a democratic ethos, at its best, introduces an active tension between cultural drives to identity and the persistent ethical need to contest the dogmatization of hegemonic, relational identities' (Connolly, 1995: 93). Democracy takes on the form of continuous displacement, inviting identification on the basis of its ability to render processes of exclusion temporary and contestable. Shared responsibility is generated in continual contests over shifting and permeable boundaries, which affect everyone equally. A sense of belonging arises from the collective struggle for something that may well be unattainable in the context of any particular community: universal rights and equality. The longing for equality has displaced the desire to belong.

Notes

1. Council Directive 2000/43/EC of 29 June 2000, Implementing the principle of equal treatment between persons irrespective of racial or ethnic origin, Official Journal I. 180/22; Council Directive 2000/78/EC of 27 November 2000, Establishing a General Framework for Equal Treatment in Employment and Occupation, Official Journal L 303/16.
2. Cf. news release issued by the Commission in Brussels on 19 July 2004: 'Commission goes to the European Court of Justice to enforce EU anti-discrimination law' (IP/04/947).
3. See, for example, plans to turn the European Monitoring Centre on Racism and Xenophobia into an EU human rights agency; Communication from the Commission, COM(2004) 693 final (25 October 2004), *The Fundamental Rights Agency: Public* Consultation Document (Brussels: Commission of the European Communities).
4. Meaning 'mainstream or guiding culture' in German.
5. Council Directive 2003/109/EC of 25 November 2003, concerning the status of third-country nationals who are long-term residents, Official Journal L 16/44; for the scope of equal treatment provisions, see Article 11.
6. For an elaborated concept of citizenship as comprised of rights, belonging, and participation, cf. Bellamy 2004.

References

Balibar, E., 'Europe: Vanishing Mediator', *Constellations: An International Journal of Critical and Democratic Theory*, 10:3 (2003): 312–38.
Bell, M., 'Equality and the European Constitution', *Industrial Law Journal*, 33:3 (2003): 242–60.
Bellamy, R., 'Introduction: The Making of Modern Citizenship', in Bellamy R., Castiglione, D., and Santoro, E. (eds), *Lineages of European Citizenship: Rights, Belonging and Participation in Eleven Nation-States* (Basingstoke and New York: Palgrave Macmillan, 2004).

Castles, S., and Davidson, A., *Citizenship and Migration: Globalization and the Politics of Belonging* (Basingstoke: Palgrave Macmillan, 2000).

Connolly, W. E., *The Ethos of Pluralization* (Minneapolis, MN and London: University of Minnesota Press, 1995).

Costa, P., 'From National to European Citizenship: A Historical Comparison', in Bellamy R., Castiglione, D., and Santoro, E. (eds), *Lineages of European Citizenship. Rights, Belonging and Participation in Eleven Nation-States* (Basingstoke and New York: Palgrave Macmillan, 2004), pp. 207–26.

Dauvergne, C., 'Sovereignty, Migration and the Rule of Law in Global Times', *Modern Law Review*, 67:4 (2004): 588–615.

European Commission, *Critical Review of Academic Literature Relating to the EU Directives to Combat Discrimination* (Brussels: European Communities, 2004a).

European Commission, *Expert Reports on the Implementation of EU Anti-Discrimination Laws Regarding Race and Religion* (Brussels: European Communities, 2004b).

European Monitoring Centre on Racism and Xenophobia (EUMC), *Anti-Discrimination in EU Member States: A comparison of national anti-discrimination legislation on the grounds of racial or ethnic origin, religion or belief with the Council Directives* (Vienna: EUMC, 2002).

Favell, A., *Philosophies of Integration: Immigration and the Idea of Citizenship in France and Britain* (Basingstoke and New York: Palgrave Macmillan, 2001).

Hansen, R., 'Citizenship and Integration in Europe', in Joppke C., and Morawska E. (eds), *Toward Assimilation and Citizenship: Immigrations in Liberal Nation-States* (Basingstoke and New York: Palgrave Macmillan, 2003).

Hepple, B., 'Race and Law in Fortress Europe', *Modern Law Review*, 67:1 (2004): 1–15.

Kastoryano, R., 'Citizenship and Belonging', in Hedetoft U., and Hjort M., *The Postnational Self: Belonging and Identity* (Minneapolis, MN: University of Minnesota Press, 2002).

Macpherson, Sir William Of Cluny, *The Stephen Lawrence Inquiry: Report of an Inquiry*, Presented to Parliament by the Secretary of State for the Home Department by Command of Her Majesty (1999).

Parekh, B., 'Equality in a Multi-Cultural Society', in Franklin J. (ed.), *Equality* (London: IPPR, 1997), pp. 123–55.

Soysal, Y. N., *Limits of Citizenship: Migrants and Postnational Membership in Europe* (Chicago, IL and London: University of Chicago Press, 1994).

4

Does Anti-Discrimination Require Recognition?

Estelle Ferrarese

4.1 Introduction

Less and less distinction is being made between anti-discrimination and recognition. Both are identified as a result of demands expressed by the same groups, or the fractures they can create in the principle of equality before the law, and yet they correspond to diverging logics. The meaning of anti-discrimination is broadening progressively, based on an ever-expanding conception of equality. It extends from a will to overcome discrimination written into the law, to a concern for giving people who have been victims of discrimination the possibility of making effective use of formal equality, to the demand for the compensation of a de facto inequality, in other words attacking intentional discrimination, then indirect discrimination, before becoming affirmative action. However, it does not incorporate recognition, whose target is nonetheless the same: discrimination. There is, indeed, no demand for recognition if there has been no initial discrimination, no original denial of equality.

The notion of recognition, an old Hegelian concept, suddenly reappeared in political theory and the social sciences, at the beginning of the 1990s, first of all in the writings of Charles Taylor, reformulating George H. Mead's theory of the Self. It has quickly become the master concept for reflection upon a disparate array of multinational societies, social movements, and global flows of people, discourses and signs supposed to give culture and difference a new salience. Following Mead's *Mind, Self and Society from the Standpoint of a Social Behaviorist*, Charles Taylor (1989), Jürgen Habermas (1992, 1999, 2003), Axel Honneth (1995, 2000, 2003, 2005), Hans Joas (1991), Nancy Fraser (1995, 1998, 2000), James Tully (1995, 2000), and Paul Ricoeur (1989) all theorize the stabilization of identity as a consequence of reciprocal recognition, hence the human need to attain the recognition of others. The Self can only develop in a process that begins in interaction; the appearance of a Self always implies the experience of another person. Individuality is therefore constituted in the conditions of intersubjective recognition, and understanding of Self is mediated through intersubjectivity. The above authors share the same dialogical conception of identity and Mead's insight of 'significant others'. This line of argument has led to the reformulation of the problems of inequality, and the fate of members of minority groups in terms of misrecognition.

Nevertheless, the meaning of recognition is above all grasped when it is lacking, the modalities of which are: discrimination, humiliation, disrespect, disparagement, invisibility, and their effects, the formation of a ruptured or distorted Self, making the individual incapable of living and acting as an autonomous being. The theme of recognition thus provides the missing link between the experience of subordination and the mutilation of the subject. While it is a more difficult undertaking to characterize granted, successful or accomplished recognition, the politics of recognition can nonetheless lead to collective rights being granted to minority groups in order to accommodate cultural differences, such as defended, for example, by Charles Taylor, or Will Kymlicka. They can also bring about measures to amend or prevent institutionalized models of values which deny certain members of the political community 'the status of full partners in interactions – whether by burdening them with excessive ascribed "difference" from others or by failing to acknowledge their distinctiveness' (Fraser, 1998: 36). Examples include a reform of divorce that rejects the idea of fault, thus reasserting the status of women, or a regulation of prostitution. Finally, insofar as a politics of recognition relates to the idea of *harm* being suffered, it can lead to quotas or economic subsidies, the restoration of rights and compensatory payments. Coming after debates and praxis bringing anti-discrimination into play – as well as in its ultimate form, affirmative action – recognition therefore constitutes a reaction, and a correction to the latter, since it is directed against the same target.

To highlight the orientation that recognition imposes on the fight against discrimination, and to discuss its validity in normative terms, I will first of all seek to more precisely define the respective conceptual and practical properties of anti-discrimination and recognition, following which I will aim to demonstrate the specific contribution of the paradigm of recognition in thinking about discrimination, and therefore anti-discrimination. I will then outline the risks inherent to recognition when it turns into policy, when the institutions are no longer simply the framework or the background of recognition, but one of the partners in the interaction.

4.2   Crossed logics

In the case of anti-discrimination as in that of recognition, the central issue is that of difference, forever the source and frequently the finality of the demands expressed. It is the source of demands insofar as the members of a group are subject to differentiated treatment on an institutionalized or at least generalized level, and that the resulting handicap is what must be overcome. It is a finality insofar as it is by carrying out a new distinction that the first one is supposed to be overcome, compensated or put right. However, in the case of anti-discrimination, the difference tends to be treated above all as a *problem* facing multicultural societies; a politics of recognition introduces the possibility (not used by all the authors[1]) of difference being considered as a *value*, something to be celebrated. Indeed, the concrete object of the need for recognition not only expresses the demand that behavior toward me be just, that is to say that I be treated with proper respect for my dignity and universal value, it also expresses my need to be recognized as the *particular* individual I am (Habermas, 1992: 149–204).

Moreover, the two logics have radically different relationships with time, even if both can express the will to redress past injustices. One, including when it takes the form of affirmative action, is supposed to disappear as equality comes closer to being achieved. Even if the empirical evidence in countries where the practice of affirmative action has been around for a long time, such as in India or the United States[2] shows that it has tended to endure, even to spread and become institutionalized. The reasons for this are threefold: the persistence of inequality which the anti-discriminatory measures are supposed to attenuate; pressure from the beneficiaries of affirmative action who argue their privileges as entitlements; and the electoral strategies that aim to constitute and reproduce stable and homogeneous electoral constituencies. In spite of this, affirmative action is still *conceived of* as a temporary measure. On the contrary, recognition is thought of as the condition of persistence of a group, a lifestyle, a choice, a difference, in other words, on the condition of persistence of a uniqueness. In Taylor's account for instance, state intervention, which is required to protect the networks of interlocution in which the constitution of the Self through intersubjectivity occurs, is conceived in terms of giving distinct societies the opportunity to survive.

Above all, more than the finality, which is potentially the same, what differs from one concept to the other is the intention with which one works toward it. In the case of anti-discrimination, the action is motivated in reference to an abstract principle of justice; in the case of recognition, it implies a reflexive detour taking into account the other's dignity/good/autonomy.

The ultimate justification for anti-discrimination is the moral principle of equal treatment, interpreted with varying degrees of complexity, depending on whether it is a question of treating individuals in a strictly equivalent manner or rectifying long-term unequal treatment. At the core of struggles for recognition is the idea that not being recognized means being unable to maintain a practical relation-to-self and being unable to develop a non-mutilated Self. Therefore, the idea of a constitutive and shared vulnerability is inherent to recognition. It founds the necessity of taking into consideration not the common good but the good of the other, insofar as the other is the person I need to be recognized. The theoretical passage through a general, all-seeing point of view traditionally found in theories of justice is thus avoided. This represents a rupture with the monological Kantian approach, in that the moral subject is no longer expected to put his propositions to the test in his inner Self by appealing to the criterion of universalizability. In fact it is the real confrontation of arguments between interlocutors in a position of mutual recognition which enables the activation of this criterion. A close bond is thus created between the concern for another person's well-being and the interest of the common good, to the point that the idea of common good can simply be constructed on that of the other's good, community taking the form of Mead's generalized Other.

The impact of this change of approach is not just limited to the history of thinking. The general normative orientation is affected by this recourse to the idea of recognition: in contrast with the principle of equal treatment, here the idea of equal *dignity*, as the external aspect of self-respect (Margalit, 1996: 52), is the normative principle upon which all others are founded. Let us take the example of autonomy: while autonomy is ensured in the case of anti-discrimination by guaranteeing rights, in the case of recognition the relation is indirect. The existence of rights only provides the necessary conditions for self-respect, and it is from self-respect that autonomy will (eventually) grow (Honneth and Anderson, 2005).

The respective effects sought by anti-discrimination and recognition are not the same either. The logic of anti-discrimination tends toward reducing exclusion; hence the aim is access to existing standards, which are those of the group in a dominant position. The politics of recognition, on the contrary, implies changing the framework for the interpretation and organization of society as a whole. The aim is less to obtain the real application, corrections or even exemptions from well-established principles, but to modify the dominant interpretation of needs – decentering the dominant group's perspective and thus pushing for pluralization within society.[3]

This property can be explained in part through the fact that recognition arises with the idea of struggle. This is the form in which it appears in Hegel's work, and which can be found in all the writings of its current defenders or theorists. Therefore, the terms of its expression alone imply that there is a demand or a claim, signifying that recognition cannot be *bestowed* to members of a group by the state or other groups. Insofar as the premises upon which the idea of recognition is based are those of fundamental intersubjectivity and the existence of two consciences which, to be constituted, need mutual approval, to speak of a denial of recognition, as Honneth has demonstrated, implies adopting the internal perspective of individuals involved in intersubjective relations, as opposed to *the external perspective of an objective observer* which only pays attention to distinctions between groups resulting from socially institutionalized relations of subordination. One cannot, except through misuse of the term 'recognition', decide that harm has been committed and attribute compensation without having received a claim.

The emphasis placed on struggle opposes recognition and the logic of tolerance, which in comparison becomes insulting and patronizing benevolence. By placing the motive of power, combined with the idea of uniqueness (the focal point of the expectations of recognition) and the renouncement of an external and neutral point of reference at the heart of its reasoning, it makes it possible to interpret the issue of recognition as a means to redistribute power and transform the framework of dominant representations and interpretations in a society.

4.3   How recognition affects anti-discrimination

The contribution or change of orientation which recognition imposes on anti-discrimination can perhaps be approached first by default; for example, through what one can learn form the policies of territorial affirmative action implemented in France (urban planning policies for priority development or education zones; facilitated admission to elite schools for students from certain districts; local preference in employment, etc.) which make it possible to reach members of different discriminated groups without naming them. Such groups cannot benefit from a specific legal discourse given that 'all citizens are equal before the law, without distinction of origin, race or religion' (first Article of the French Constitution). These therefore constitute (anti-discriminatory) policies without recognition. In other words, tending to define inequality in vague terms of unfortunate social factors to be righted, they do away with the idea of there being *harm* suffered and therefore inflicted. Furthermore, they do not recognize the formation or the existence of one or several group(s) that are both objects and products of discrimination. Consequently they fail to recognize these groups and their members as interlocutors or as authors of a request or a claim.

This exercise of confrontation, whose terms I will re-examine point by point, reveals that while recognition goes beyond anti-discrimination, notably because it is also an ethic, in addition, it casts a new light on discrimination, and hence, on what is entailed by anti-discrimination.

In thinking on the subject of discrimination, the paradigm of recognition, particularly in the way it is conceived of by Nancy Fraser, first and foremost offers a normative criterion to identify and reflect upon involuntary or indirect discrimination. This is based on the analysis of *effects* and on opposing discrimination not with equality, but with the possibility of participation as a peer in all spheres of social interaction, independently of the intentions of actors or texts. As soon as this parity is not satisfied, harm exists. As it happens, the form taken by anti-discrimination, whether codified in the law or institutionalized through government policies, the codes of administrations or professional practices, sometimes results in the State constantly signalling to groups that it tolerates them, in the sense of 'puts up with them'.

Such is the case with the French PACS law allowing civil union between same-sex people, which seems to counter discrimination against homosexuals, but in reality reproduces a normal versus deviant model. While the deviance is tolerated, it is still defined in reference and opposition to a norm in that homosexuals are offered an option of inferior status to that of heterosexual marriage. To really overcome discrimination, there is a choice between two courses of action if one places oneself in the perspective of recognition: 'One way would be to grant the same recognition to homosexual partnerships that heterosexual partnerships currently enjoy by legalizing same-sex marriage. Another would be to deinstitutionalize heterosexual marriage, decoupling entitlements such as health insurance from marital status and assigning them on some other basis, such as citizenship and/or territorial residency' (Fraser, 2000: 114).

The problematic of recognition therefore proposes reformulating discrimination from the idea of harm: because of misrecognition which constitutes some categories of social actors as normative and others as deficient, even when in a tolerant form, it is impossible for them to act and to live as autonomous beings. It consequently brings to light the fact that when this idea is not taken into consideration, the blame for the shortcoming is disdainfully attributed to the oppressed party. Furthermore, the problematic of recognition doubly accounts for the degrading power of the ascribed characteristic upon which discrimination is based.

On the one hand, because the individuation of persons occurs through socialization, their identity can only be protected when they have free access to contexts of communication and mutual recognition in which people can acquire and consolidate their identity, articulate their understanding of themselves, and develop their own life plan. In Kymlicka's words, 'it is only through having access to a societal culture that people have access to a range of meaningful options' (Kymlicka, 1995: 83). The problematic of recognition, while it doesn't necessarily bring about a reformulation of the experience of injustice in the language of collective identities (a possibility which is refused equally by Habermas, Honneth, and Fraser, for different reasons and according to different modalities), in any case establishes the individual's need to be integrated into a network of intersubjective relations guaranteeing him a non-distorted image of himself, by making it a minimal condition for achieving freedom (Honneth, 2000: 328–38).

On the other hand, and based on this same reasoning related to the construction of identity, recognition highlights the insufficiency and even the harmfulness of anti-discrimination policies given that they recommend and assert neutrality in relation to certain groups. In doing so, they do not take into account that groups and identities can be constructed through the ascription of properties not chosen by the 'members' themselves, but imposed through policies of repression and coercion. Injurious taxonomies develop a force of their own. As Judith Butler describes, 'by being called a name, one is also, paradoxically, given a certain possibility for social existence' (Butler, 1997: 2). An ascribed identity can shape social reality so much that members of groups cannot avoid identifying with it. If the normative discourse now addresses these groups and their needs with a conception of tolerance that serves the protection of members of the group, then it only reproduces the offences and the heartfelt experiences they generate: 'It reiterates the existence of an identity whose present past is one of insistently unredeemable injury' (Brown, 1995: 73).

At the same time, recourse to the concept of recognition affords a definite importance to the idea of participation and thus allows the introduction of the problematic of citizenship into anti-discrimination. This is particularly clear in the work of Nancy Fraser, for whom recognition is construed in terms of *participation* and where the goal of recognition is to establish the members of a discriminated group as full members of society, capable of participating on a par with other members in all spheres of interaction. Hence, it is a condition for full membership. But this reasoning can be broadened to the whole problematic of recognition insofar as it conditions autonomy on intersubjective consideration.

A homology between the integrity of identity arising from socialization in relationships of reciprocal recognition and the integrity of legal persons can be established through the idea of public autonomy, this collective and deliberative process of society's self-government or self-determination. Because people are able to acquire and consolidate their identities and develop their life projects if, according to Taylor, Habermas, and Kymlicka, they have access to contexts of communication and mutual recognition, this access also guarantees their development as legal persons. My aim here is not to defend the subordination of moral and public autonomy to the vivacity of collective identities, induced by the assumed equivalence between the recognition of my group and the recognition of myself, which underlies the politics of identity as formulated by Taylor for example. Rather it is a question of revealing that individuals' capacity for action is threatened when they are not in a position to fuel the conviction that their aspirations are worth pursuing, as a consequence of institutionalized patterns of cultural value in whose construction they have not participated equally and which disparage their distinctive characteristics or the distinctive characteristics assigned to them. It then can be argued that being unable to assert their claims and aspirations, they are denied the status of fully fledged partners in deliberative interaction, or of being legitimate co-legislators, a hypothesis which is easily verified by the connection between a deteriorated relationship with oneself and disaffection with politics.

4.4   The force of recognition

If we are constituted by the other's recognition, the latter is, then, capable of *creating* what he names. That is why, when the other's address takes the form of a discourse of hatred, the subject is constituted by the very act of being assigned a subordinate position. The imposed identity is constantly limiting our room for maneuver. The force of what Althusser calls *interpellation* (Althusser, 1977: 127–86) continues to take its toll, indifferent to any protest on our part. Thus, the key concept of recognition, a constitutive and shared vulnerability, while reformulating the implications and scope of anti-discrimination, also makes recognition a problematic issue when it becomes policy.

Recognition is thus a performative act; the act of recognition creates the status, the definition of the Self it recognizes, and it creates it precisely by seeming only to cognize the existence of what it is it constructs, that is to say, by seeming only to ascertain. And this creation is the act of the party granting recognition. Two characteristics are therefore inherent to the act of recognition: the exercise of a power and the pinning of the recognized party to a singularity.

As for the first feature, here is always the exercise of a power even when he who recognizes, recognizes exactly and unreservedly the claim (to uniqueness) being addressed to him. The other *can* refuse to grant recognition and thereby refuse to grant equality. The fact that power is being exercised is thus verified whether one adopts a substantial definition of an object of recognition, or one limits oneself to the narrowest conception of recognition, according to which all that is recognized is the person's status as a subject capable of replying, judging, and criticizing (Habermas, 1992).

The second point draws heavily on the theory developed by Foucault, who studies, in *Discipline and Punish* (1977), the modality of power through which each person receives the status of his own individuality and is bound to the features, measurements, gaps, and 'marks' which characterize this status. Foucault focuses here on the institution of techniques such as (medical. psychological) examination, however, what I refer to as the pinning of self to one's own singularity describes recognition equally well.

This pinning and the exercise of a power are both particularly evident if one considers the case of the recognition of culture in multicultural societies. Not only does recognition tend to treat cultures as coherent and strictly distinct totalities, but the reifying effects of recognition are particularly strong when the performative act is accomplished by the State.

Legal discourse and public policies constitute differences by treating them as pre-existing social facts which the State is merely reacting to. A particularly striking example of this is to be found in the European Charter for Regional or Minority Languages.[4] By obliging the signatory states to implement a series of measures to acknowledge and preserve the specificity of their linguistic minorities, it not only affects, it also sometimes creates identities and groups, for example, Frisian or

Danish-speaking minorities in Germany, which had probably never been considered in such terms before.[5]

Furthermore, political movements for the recognition of certain groups only confirm their own subordinate political status by accepting the constitution of personal or social statuses by the State. Ultimately, the politics of recognition result in individuals' very calls for justice being formulated as calls for the recognition of identifiable groups. The themes of recognition thus converge with the logic of the State of administration of a territory and of a population, by rendering the latter legible and therefore governable. Not surprisingly, as demonstrated by Žižek, this type of justice for victimized minorities requires a vast array of experts and social workers, a 'complex policing apparatus', intended to identify the group in question, to punish those who have infringed its rights, for example to give legal definition to sexual harassment or racial insult suffered, and to devise the preferential treatment capable of compensating the harm caused to the group in question.

The act of recognition states reality, both on a collective and individual level, for example by introducing a constraint to identitary coherence and legibility. On the one hand, this means that the interplay between recognition and identity fuels modes of action where the aim is to do away with or control the contingency and unpredictability of interaction. On the other hand, it means that the pinning of individuals and groups to a singularity negates the complexity of individuals' existences, the multiplicity of their identifications, and the cross-dual dynamic of their different affiliations.

Not only do these policies pin the subject to a unique identity and impute individuals' intentions and actions to this identity, *thereby denying their ability to rewrite the meaning of their own actions*, they also wall them into meanings which they may have sought to escape from, for example by constructing, deconstructing, and reconstructing self-definitions for strategic purposes or by slipping into determined roles which they knew would gain them recognition.

This can be illustrated through the example of 'Cultural Defense' and its effects in the United States. This term refers to a series of legal cases in which defense lawyers presented, and the court accepted cultural evidence as an excuse for the otherwise criminal conduct of defendants. One of the most famous cases concerned the rape of a young Laotian-American woman by a Laotian immigrant, who explained that among his tribe this behavior is accepted as a customary way to choose a bride. His argument was allowed. Apart from the issue of the rape, the problem here is that the court disregarded the woman's US citizenship, and pinned her to her Laotian origin, whereas she had chosen to abandon it (Benhabib, 2002; Coleman, 1996). Moreover, in the discourse Cultural Defense applies to the defendant (and in this case to the victim also), it deduces intention from *culture*.

The same feature can also be easily observed in the successive occurrences of the French debate on the veil through 1990s and 2000s. On either side of the divide between the positions and arguments on the question, one finds the same depiction of individuals riveted to a culture, admittedly a culture that may be in a process of negotiation, but in any case a clearly identifiable and all-encompassing culture. Among the different motives attributed to the young girls concerned by the issue, the notions of ploy, role playing, or strategic action, for example, were mentioned the least, if at all. Not to say that this is definitely the correct interpretation of their motives, but it is striking to note all the same that the explanations put forward, ranging from manipulation by religious or paternal authorities to moral coercion and even the courageous empowerment of young people with restricted room for maneuver, all revived the idea of a 'natural' entity – culture – to which a person 'belongs'. The way in which the concerned individuals' intentions were interpreted rarely gave them a status greater than that of 'cultural puppets'.[6]

Finally, leaving little room for dissidence and cultural experimentation, the interplay of recognition and identity is also congruent with the logic particular to a group elite. The institutional confirmation of the existence of groups consolidates, or even constructs, the position of privileging some of their members – the recognition of cultural forms of practices also implying the recognition of representatives for legal or political finalities. Moreover, policies of multicultural accommodation tie the distribution of rights and resources to the maintenance of existing cultural forms or practices, and recognize powerful subgroups within a culture as its 'authentic' representatives according to this logic (thereby reinforcing their status).

The paradigm of recognition is therefore a double-edged sword: on the one hand, it acknowledges the fact that reality is limited for certain parties because of a denial of recognition insofar as individuation takes places through socialization; it therefore explains the deep effects of discrimination, which are not restricted to simply not having an equal share of what others receive (in terms of rights, redistribution, opportunities, etc.), but affect what we *are*. On the other hand, incautious recourse to the idea of recognition as a means of fighting against discrimination is ultimately tantamount to endowing cultures with naturalness and innocence in a way that has not been possible for nation-states for a long time, effacing the equally constructed and 'imagined' character of the unit 'culture'. It obscures the fact that cultural coherence is simply a product of the State which has ordered its society in that way, of certain elites seeking to impose themselves, of the employee of a NGO, of the defender of the cause of a minority, or of a theorist of recognition acting as an observer. The well-known criticisms of the anthropological conception of culture, such as those expressed by James Clifford, who insists on the 'complex historical processes of appropriation, compromise, subversion masking, invention and revival' (Clifford, 1988: 338), are paid little attention among current theorists of multicultural societies. Many discussions of justice and injustice in cultural relations continue to be framed in terms of an encounter among the members of distinct, coherent totalities called 'cultures'. The performative act stating the existence of a group remains unquestioned. This blindness, which is already problematic from a theoretical point of view, comes coupled with the most perverse practical effects when the thus formulated recognition becomes policy, requested from, and granted by the state.

I therefore believe that it is necessary both to question the validity of transposing recognition, a moral category, into policy and legal discourse, and to ask if it would not be preferable, from a normative point of view, to consider recognition as being limited to having either a negative use, or a positive use restricted to the public sphere and intersubjective relations.

Notes

1. See Maeve Cooke's five interpretations of demand for recognition: (1) Recognition of the (potential equality of) individual (and groups) distinctiveness, understood as originality. (2) Recognition of individuals' (and groups') equal capacity to form and define their specific identities and lives. (3) Recognition of the specificity of individual (and group) needs. (4) Recognition of the (potential of equality of the) distinctiveness of individual (and group) achievement. (5) Recognition of the (potential of equality of the) specific conceptions of the good around which individuals (and groups) orient their self-understandings and lives (Cooke, 1997: 266).
2. Cf., for example, Parekh, 2000.
3. However, it remains true that expressing a claim to recognition amounts to recognizing the sovereignty of the state this claim is addressed to: the logic of a struggle for recognition therefore differs radically from a logic of revolution or of territorial partition.

4. Council of Europe, *European Chart for Regional or Minority Languages* (Strasbourg: Council of Europe, 1992).
5. For a study balancing the discourse of linguistic human rights with the examination of resource allocation, see Grin, 2003.
6. This expression is borrowed from Seyla Benhabib (2002: 89).

References

Althusser, L., 'Ideology and Ideological State Apparatuses', in *Lenin and Philosophy and Other Essays* (London: New Left Books, 1977), pp. 127–86.

Anderson, B., *Imagined Communities. Reflections on the Origin and Spread of Nationalism* (London: Verso, 1991).

Barry, B., *Culture and Equality: An Egalitarian Critique of Multiculturalism* (Cambridge, MA: Harvard University Press, 2001).

Benhabib, S. (ed.), *Democracy and Difference: Contesting the Boundaries of the Political* (Princeton, NJ: Princeton University Press, 1996).

Benhabib, S., *The Claims of Culture, Equality and Diversity in the Global Era* (Princeton, NJ: Princeton University Press, 2002).

Brown, W., *States of Injury: Power and Freedom in Late Modernity* (Princeton, NJ and Oxford: Princeton University Press, 1995).

Butler, J., *Excitable Speech: A Politics of the Performative* (New York: Routledge, 1997).

Clifford, J., *The Predicament of Culture: Twentieth-Century Ethnography, Literature and Art* (Cambridge, MA: Harvard University Press, 1988).

Coleman, D. L., 'Individualizing Justice through Multiculturalism: The Liberals' Dilemma', *Columbia Law Review*, 5 (1996): 1093–167.

Cooke, M., 'Authenticity and Autonomy: Taylor, Habermas and the Politics of Recognition', *Political Theory*, 25:2 (1997): 258–88.

Council of Europe, *European Chart for Regional or Minority Languages* (Strasbourg: Council of Europe, 1992).

Emcke, C., 'Between Choice and Coercion: Identities, Injuries, and Different Forms of Recognition', *Constellations*, 7:4 (2000): 483–95.

Fabre, C., Fassin, E., *Libertés, égalité, sexualités* (Paris: Belfond, 2003).

Forst, R., *Toleranz im Konflikt. Geschichte, Gehalt und Gegenwart eines umstrittenen Begriffs* (Frankfurt am Main: Suhrkamp, 2003).

Foucault, M., *Discipline and Punish: The Birth of the Prison*, trans. A. Sheridan (London: Allen Lane, 1977).

Fraser, N., 'From Redistribution to Recognition? Dilemmas of Justice in a "Postsocialist" Age', *New Left Review*, 212 (1995): 68–93.

Fraser, N., 'Social Justice in the Age of Identity Politics: Redistribution, Recognition and Participation', *The Tanner Lectures on Human Values*, vol. 19 (Salt Lake City: Grethe B. Peterson, 1998), pp. 1–67.

Fraser, N., 'Rethinking Recognition', *New Left Revue*, 3 (May-June 2000), pp. 107–20.

Fraser, N. 'Distorted Beyond all Recognition: A Rejoinder to Axel Honneth', in Honneth, A., and Fraser, N., *Redistribution or Recognition? A Political-Philosophical Exchange* (London: Verso, 2003).

Grin. F., *Language Policy Evaluation and the European Charter for Regional or Minority Languages* (Basingstoke and New York: Palgrave Macmillan, 2003).

Habermas, J., 'Individualization through Socialization. On George H. Mead's Theory of Subjectivity', in *Postmetaphysical Thinking: Philosophical Essays* (Cambridge, MA: MIT press, 1992), pp. 149–204.

Habermas, J., 'Struggles for Recognition in Constitutional States', in *The Inclusion of the Other* (London: Polity Press: 1999), pp. 203–39.

Habermas, J., 'Intolerance and Discrimination', *International Journal of Constitutional Law*, 1:1 (2003): 2–12.

Honneth, A., *The Struggle for Recognition: The Moral Grammar of Social Conflicts* (London: Polity Press: 1995).

Honneth, A., *Dans Andere der Gerechtigkeit: Aufsätze zur praktischen Philosophie* (Frankfurt am Main: Suhrkamp, 2000).

Honneth, A., 'Redistribution as Recognition: A Response to Nancy Fraser', in Honneth, A., and Fraser, N., *Redistribution or Recognition? A Political-Philosophical Exchange* (London: Verso, 2003a).

Honneth, A., 'The Pointe of Recognition: A Rejoinder to the Rejoinder', in Honneth, A., and Fraser, N., *Redistribution or Recognition? A Political-Philosophical Exchange* (London: Verso, 2003b).

Honneth, A., and Anderson, J., *Autonomy, Vulnerability, Recognition, and Justice*, unpublished manuscript, 2005.

Joas, H., *Communicative Action: Essays on Jürgen Habermas' "Essays on the Communicative Action* (Cambridge: Polity Press, 1991).

Kymlicka, W., *Multicultural Citizenship: A Liberal Theory of Minority Rights* (Oxford: Clarendon Press, 1995).

Margalit, A., *The Decent Society* (Cambridge, MA: Harvard University Press, 1996).

Markell, P., *Bound by Recognition* (Princeton, NJ: Princeton University Press, 2003).

Mead, G. H., *Mind, Self and Society from the Standpoint of a Social Behaviorist* (Chicago, IL: Chicago University Press, 1934).

Parikh, S., *The Politics of Preference, Democratic Institutions and Affirmative Action in the United States and India* (Ann Arbor, MI: The University of Michigan Press, 2000).

Rawls, J., *A Theory of Justice* (Cambridge, MA: Harvard University Press, 1971).

Ricoeur, P., *Parcours de la reconnaissance. Trois études.* (Paris: Stock, 2004).

Taylor, C., *Sources of the Self* (Cambridge: Cambridge University Press, 1989).

Taylor, C., 'The Politics of Recognition', in Gutmann, A. (ed.), *Multiculturalism*, (Princeton, NJ: Princeton University Press, 1994).

Tully, J., *Strange Multiplicity* (Cambridge: Cambridge University Press, 1995).

Tully, J., 'Struggles over Recognition and Distribution', *Constellations*, 7:4 (2000).

Waldron, J., 'Minority Cultures and the Cosmopolitan Alternative', in Kymlicka, W. (ed.), *The Rights of Minority Cultures* (Oxford: Oxford University Press, 1995).

Williams, M., 'The Uneasy Alliance of Group Representation and Deliberation Democracy', in Kymlicka, W., and Norman W. (eds), *Citizenship in Diverse Societies* (Oxford: Oxford University Press, 2000).

Young, I. M., *Justice and the Politics of Difference* (Princeton, NJ: Princeton University Press, 1990).

5

Social Citizenship, Ethnic Minorities, and the Welfare State

John Rex

5.1 Introduction

In opening this topic, I find it useful to discuss two related statements on policy, which have played their part in the political development of the United Kingdom. The first is that contained in T. H. Marshall's *Citizenship and Social Class* (1951) on the nature of social citizenship. The second is that of the British Home Secretary, Roy Jenkins, in 1966 relating to the integration of immigrants (see Rex and Tomlinson, 1979).[1] Starting from this base, I will go on to show how the context and the content of the debate about citizenship have changed over 50 years in Europe and America and the way in which the question of the integration of immigrants has been reformulated in relation to them.

5.2 The general problem of citizenship and the welfare state

5.2.1 Marshall's concept of citizenship

What Marshall was addressing in his book was the question of whether British politics would continue to be based upon a process of class struggle. In this profoundly anti-Marxist perspective the primacy of class loyalty over any other in the British working class would be overcome by the identification of all individuals with citizenship. Citizenship was first a matter of equal legal recognition by the courts; second, a matter of enfranchisement; and third, the acquisition of social rights. The process of the acquisition of social rights, although begun earlier, attained a new momentum in the creation of the welfare state. Drawing on the ideas of Beveridge in his *Full Employment in a Free Society* (1944) and in his report to the government on Social Insurance and Allied

Services (1942), Marshall suggested that social citizenship would come to involve a guaranteed minimum income in times of ill health, unemployment, and old age, the fixing of wages by free collective bargaining, and the guarantee of minimum standards of housing, health, and education for all. It did not suggest universal equality of outcome for all, nor did it simply call for equal opportunity. Rather it envisaged a guaranteed minimum for all, together with recognition of the right of individuals to obtain more for themselves over and above this minimum.

The attainment of social citizenship in this sense could be contrasted with the idea of social exclusion. This is a question to which we shall have to return.

5.2.2 Cultural diversity and citizenship

The concept of multiculturalism is now widely discussed and is often celebrated as an important ideal separate from that of citizenship. A good example of this kind of celebration is to be found in the work of Parekh (2000). What is striking about this work is that it does not relate the discussion of multiculturalism to questions of political conflicts and their resolution on other grounds. This is clearly brought out in Barry's (2001) powerful critique of Parekh and other theorists of multiculturalism such as Kymlicka (1995) and Charles Taylor (1994). Significantly too, Parekh makes no reference to the work of T. H. Marshall or to the formulation of the concept of 'integration' by the British Home Secretary in 1966.

The Jenkins statement suggests that integration of minorities should not be conceived as a 'flattening process of uniformity' but as the recognition of 'cultural diversity, coupled with equal opportunity in an atmosphere of mutual tolerance'. What is perhaps most significant here is that, unlike other theories of multiculturalism, the notion of the recognition of cultural diversity is coupled with that of the necessity of equal opportunity. Though this notion is actually rather less radical than that of Marshall's social citizenship, its inclusion in Marshall's theory does nonetheless real the question of cultural diversity with that of shared citizenship.

I have suggested repeatedly that the Jenkins formula implies the existence of two institutional domains. On the one hand, there is that of the public political sphere which includes the institutions of the welfare state but also, of course, legal and political equality; on the other, there is the set of institutions which structures the life of separate ethnic minority communities. These include speaking their own language in private, practicing their own religions, and maintaining their own family practices. In my book *Ethnic Minorities in the Modern Nation State* (Rex, 1996b), I have discussed some of the difficulties which are involved in this notion of two institutional domains. They include (1) the difficult question of the role of the educational system which straddles the two domains; (2) the attempt by human rights activists to extend the ideas of the public into the separate communal domain and, vice versa, the attempts by some ethnic communities to extend their own values into the public domain; and (3) the possibility of a limited intermediate domain as instanced by the arts and cuisine.

Apart from these difficulties there is the fact that insistence on separateness may mean exclusion from the rights of the public institutional sphere. Just as there is a special problem relating to the inclusion of ethnic minorities in the public domain, so there is a special problem of their exclusion. In their case, exclusion takes the form of racial and ethnic discrimination.[2]

5.2.3 Gellner and the theory of the modernizing nation-state

Along with Marshall, Gellner (1983) has developed a highly influential theory of citizenship in the modernizing nation-state. Like Marshall, Gellner rejects the idea that class is or should be a main focus of identification in modern conditions. The modernizing nation-state, as represented above all by the French state after the Revolution, replaces the notion of class loyalty with the notion of a common citizenship fostered by a universal education system. Equally, in this nation-state there is, in principle, no room for any ethnic ties. Thus, in contrast with Anthony Smith, who has written extensively about the continuing importance of ethnicity and, indeed, the ethnic origins of nations (Smith, 1981 and 1986), Gellner has little place for ethnicity. Citizenship for him is the only important structuring principle in the modern nation-state.

5.2.4 Social citizenship, class struggle, and social policy

My own reaction to Marshall's (1951) thesis about social citizenship was to agree that it gave a useful account of the kind of society which was coming into being after the 1939–45 World War in Europe. It seemed to me, however, that this was only possible if there was a balance of power between the major classes (Rex, 1961). It occurred, in fact, when the bourgeoisie and proletariat recognized that neither could achieve a victory and that they had to accept some kind of consensus or middle way. Also involved was a limited acceptance of the market mechanism as a way of distributing goods, while allowing for governmental intervention to guarantee a social minimum for all.

The notion that the precedence of social citizenship over class loyalty was dependent upon an historic class compromise implied that, if the balance of class forces was disturbed, that compromise would not be maintained and there would be a reversion to class struggle. These questions were at the heart of British politics from the end of the 1960s through the 1980s. First, the Labour Party agreed that the assertion of trade union power through strikes and similar actions was no longer necessary, and that a new system of industrial relations could now operate. This led to the publication of the White Paper entitled *In Place of Strife* (Department of Employment and Productivity, 1969). As Barbara Castle, the Minister concerned, put it, this was not intended to replace collective bargaining with state intervention. Rather, it was a way of getting unions to face up to their responsibilities, 'to ensure that workers do not down tools before they have used the procedure for examining disputes which their own unions have negotiated' (Tribune Archive, 1969). This recognized that there were differences of interest, but suggested that they could be resolved in negotiation rather than through disruptive industrial action. Given such a system of industrial relations, the creation of a social citizenship which would replace class struggle was possible.

Similar ideas were being pursued by political sociologists in the Scandinavian countries. Thus, in Sweden, Korpi argued that the class struggle could be pursued by peaceful and democratic means (Korpi, 1978) and that working class mobilization had a part to play in the welfare state (Korpi, 1983). Esping-Anderson, on the other hand, saw the welfare state as taking different forms in different times and places (Esping-Anderson, 1990). His is a complex argument about the different ways in which the market mechanism and the 'commodification of labor' might be modified. There are thus three types of welfare capitalism. The first is one in which income is seen as related to need rather than being a reward for performance, and is given after a means test. The second one is that which was developed in Bismarck's Germany, in which there was compulsory social insurance and benefits were given at different levels according to contributions. The third, which is represented by the Beveridge Report, is that which offers 'a basic equal benefit to all irrespective of prior earnings, contributions or performance'.[3]

Whatever the form of the welfare state, however, it seemed to be challenged in Britain with the revolution in social policy brought about by the Prime Minister, Margaret Thatcher, between 1979 and 1992. Crucially, she broke the power of the trade unions and no longer needed the consensus looked for in *In Place of Strife* (Marshall, 1951). Oddly, she did claim that she would 'defend the welfare state', but, in saying this, she limited the notion simply to social insurance against unemployment, ill health, and old age rather than involving all the wider issues which Marshall had had in mind. Her successor, John Major, in some ways went even further, saying that he believed in a classless society, meaning by this one in which there would be equality of opportunity for all individuals without any kind of class mobilization.

5.2.5 The consequences of the breakdown of welfare capitalism

In the previous section I have assumed that the welfare state was the result of class mobilization, class struggle, and class compromise. A rather more cynical view is taken by Crowley (1994). For him, welfare payments were offered to the working classes because they were a necessary cost for the preservation of capitalism. The problem which he then poses is what will happen when these payments can no longer be met. It is in these circumstances, he believes, that nationalism and xenophobia will be appealed to rather than a sense of social citizenship.

A rather different perspective is taken by Delanty (1996). When I argued that there was likely to be tension between the sense of national identity of the European nations and the threat posed by new immigrant identities, he argued that this was a secondary factor. For him, the real problem was precisely that posed by Crowley, namely the breakdown of social citizenship deriving from a secure system of social welfare.

Finally, in this section I should like to draw attention to an important recent article by Schierup (2000). In this article, Schierup draws attention to the fact that, whereas Marshall envisaged a society in which nearly all people could enjoy social citizenship and relatively few were excluded, in the present situation in most advanced capitalist countries there is a large proportion of the population living in relative poverty and relative deprivation. The concept of social citizenship would seem to need redrawing in these circumstances, as would any conception of the welfare state based upon the assumptions which Beveridge was able to make.

5.2.6 The rights and duties of citizenship

For Marshall, the notion of citizenship was based upon the idea of social rights. Quite obviously, the guarantee of such rights is the performance by others, especially by the state, of social duties. It is a striking fact, however, that there has also been another theme in many policy discussions which has emphasized duties to the exclusion of rights. In my earliest research in Birmingham, I recorded the claim by the City Council's so-called Liaison Officer for Coloured People that immigrants had now got their rights and must now be compelled to perform their duties (Rex and Moore, 1967). A similar conception of citizenship guided Conservatives during the period of the Thatcher government. *Inter alia, Education in citizenship* was seen as a way of combating crime and hooliganism. The work of Bernard Crick (1998) who was called upon to advise the government on education in citizenship, left open the question of whether rights or duties should be emphasized. By the beginning of the twenty-first century, however, all the emphasis was laid upon duties. In other versions, the notion of *Education for citizenship* was applied particularly to ethnic minorities. This had been true in much French discussion of the matter. According to a proposal for joint research put to the Centre for Research in Ethnic Relations by French colleagues, the main object of citizenship education was seen as being the education of immigrant minorities in the displacement of the traditional non-secular cultures of immigrants, rather than an education of white children in challenge of their colonialist and racist assumptions. This view was reinforced in Britain after 2001 by two factors. One was the fear of immigrants after the attacks on the World Trade Center in New York and the Pentagon in Washington, DC. The other was the fear felt in government circles after racial disturbances between Asian and white communities in Northern British cities. The major policy response was to suggest the introduction of identity cards and tests of language which would apply especially to Asians who, it was thought, needed to be integrated. Another research proposal put to the Centre was a comparative one designed to study the integration of Turkish citizens in London. The fact that many of these Turks were in fact Kurdish asylum seekers struggling to become citizens seemed to have escaped the authors of this research proposal.[4]

All in all, what this discussion shows is that the notion of citizenship in the Marshallian sense is far from universally shared. There is a conservative alternative which strongly affects government policy and the funding of social research. This is true both of discussions of citizenship in general but even more true when what is being discussed is the citizenship of immigrants and minorities. It is to the place of these minorities that we must now turn.

5.3 Minorities and citizenship

The question of the citizenship of minorities and the manner of their integration into national societies breaks down into two. On the one hand, there is the degree to which territorially concentrated groups share in a common citizenship or claim a separate one. On the other hand, there is the question of the immigrants who are dispersed in the general population. This latter question has to be discussed both in relation to economic migrants and in relation to political migrants, refugees, and asylum seekers.

5.3.1 National minorities within nations

The problems involved in the citizenship of territorial groups may be illustrated by considering the cases of Catalonia and Scotland on the one hand,[5] and the Basque country and Ireland on the other. In the case of Catalonia and Scotland, the claim that is made for special rights is not made on behalf of all those who are linguistically or ethnically Catalonian or Scots, but rather for all those living in Catalonia or Scotland. Only a minority of Catalonians or Scots seeks independence. The majority seeks devolved rights within a national state whose citizenship they would retain. From the point of view of the Spanish or British state, this is a problem which must be solved by the devolution of some governmental powers.

A different set of problems arises in the cases of the Basques in Spain and Irish Republicans in Northern Ireland. In these cases, Basque and Irish nationalists do not seek citizenship rights within the Spanish and British states. Rather, they claim a right to secede from a citizenship which has been imposed on them, an ethnic affiliation to a nation which transcends national boundaries, and, in the case of the Northern Irish Republicans, in another state. In both of these cases, those concerned have resorted to armed struggle or terrorism rather than pursuing their aims through the ballot box. The state has used its military and police powers against them, while at the same time promoting a so-called peace process, which would bring relations with the minority nationalists within the framework of a national state with some devolution to regional assemblies. Clearly, these situations are unstable, but the discourse of national governments of Spain and Britain seeks to treat them as though they were comparable with the cases of Catalonia and Scotland.

The Catalonian/Scottish and Basque/Irish cases are used here as examples. They are reproduced in most other European countries in some degree, and have to be dealt with either by devolution or through armed struggle and consequent peace processes. Problems are, however, more acute where previous central states have broken up, and ethnically based civil wars occur, as in the former Yugoslavia.

5.3.2 The integration of immigrant minorities

Western European countries during the nineteenth century were countries of emigration. Millions of their citizens migrated to North America or as settlers in colonial territories. After 1945, however, Europe began to import immigrants on a large scale until the halt in immigration for new immigrants in the late sixties and early seventies. Thereafter, it faced the problem of dealing with increasing numbers of refugees.[6]

5.3.2.1   Economic immigration

The major population movement involving migrants in search of work in the nineteenth century was from Europe to the United States. In the world after 1945, however, the largest movement was of economic migrants into Europe. From a situation in which European countries were sending societies, the United Kingdom, France, Germany, Austria, Switzerland, and the Benelux and Scandinavian countries were targeted by economic migrants, and, in the period between 1945 and 1970, this was the major movement of economic migrants. The former imperial countries actively encouraged migration from their former colonies in the fifties and sixties, when there were large numbers of job vacancies in jobs which native born citizens of the European countries were unlikely to fill. In Germany, which had no former colonies to which it could turn, resort was to Turkey and the southern European countries. By the late sixties in the United Kingdom, and by the early seventies in other countries, such immigration was feared and, apart from family completion and small numbers of highly skilled immigrants, immigration came to a stop. In the eighties and most of the nineties, there were actually more people leaving the United Kingdom than there were economic immigrants coming in. This situation, however, changed at the end of the nineties. It was recognized amongst policy makers, both in the separate countries and at the European level, that there would be a need for considerably increased immigration during the first 20 years of the new millennium. This was partly to cope with a demographic deficit produced by the small family size of European families, and partly to fill jobs, particularly those requiring high skill. There was, however, a new and influential organization of right-wing politicians and academics called 'Migrationwatch UK' in Britain which warned of the dangers to European identity of any further increase in the proportion of residents born overseas.[7]

There were different ways of counting these immigrants. Some countries simply counted those born abroad, and some those of foreign nationality, while in the United Kingdom an attempt was made to classify the population according to their own perception of the ethnic group to which they belonged. But, whatever the method of counting, there was now a problem in the societies of West Europe of how these immigrants were to be integrated. The Swedish political scientist Tomas

Hammar (1990) drew attention to the fact that the population of Europe included some who were 'denizens' rather than citizens. He had in mind here especially the German guestworkers, who were not accorded the rights of citizens. There was, however, a problem even in those of the former imperial metropolitan countries like Britain and France, that the majority of their immigrants were legally and politically citizens. In these cases, there was a question of whether they were in some sense excluded even though they were formally citizens.

In France, policy was informed by the idea of assimilation. Immigrants from the French overseas territories were entitled to equal legal treatment and could vote. They also had many social rights. There was, however, in practice a considerable amount of discrimination against these immigrants and they were also the target of racial abuse and attack, even though this was hard to document in a country which rejected the very idea of counting these immigrants separately.

The crucial German idea was that Germany was not an immigration country and this idea was reproduced in Austria. They could, if they won the support of German churches or trade unions, enjoy social rights. Even these rights, however, were paternally dispensed and, without a political voice of their own, the immigrants were wholly dependent on such paternalism. A new report to the German Parliament in 2001 called for the recognition that Germany was now, indeed, an immigration country and for a consideration of the policy implications of this change. Such a change, however, was weakly defended by the Social Democratic Party in the subsequent election, and very dependent upon the government's Green partners in any practical situation. The alternative to French assimilationist policy and the guestworker policy of the German-speaking countries was some form of multiculturalism, and this, it was generally thought, was exemplified by policy in the United Kingdom, the Netherlands, and Sweden.

'Multicultural', however, is a very loosely used term. It may often be used interchangeably with the terms 'multiethnic' and 'multiracial', and mean no more than recognizing that the population includes many who are visibly different in their physical appearance and their culture. This may not involve according these minorities significant rights, and may indeed be coupled with the notion that some cultures are superior to others.[8] In this context, what I have called the Jenkins formula, which combines the recognition of cultural diversity with equal opportunity and mutual tolerance,[9] represents a stronger and more political form of multiculturalism which, as I have suggested, is not defended in Parekh's influential work any more than it is in popular discussion.

Because the term 'multiculturalism' is loosely used, it has been rejected as an ideal by a number of important European sociologists.[10] Wieviorka in France has suggested that the very term ethnicity is used only to refer to inferiors (Wieviorka, 1994). Jan Rath in the Netherlands suggests that in the much-vaunted Dutch form of multiculturalism, ethnic minorities are recognized, but actually marked for unequal treatment (Rath, 1991).

Two other significant interventions in this debate are those of Radtke in Germany, and Schierup and Alund in Sweden. Radtke places great emphasis upon what he calls the Social Democratic welfare state. In this welfare state, the conflicting interest of different classes has led to a series of compromises. Turkish immigrants who are exploited or oppressed by their marital partners, employers, or landlords should have their interests defended within this system. The mistake of multicultural policy as represented by the Multicultural Bureau in Frankfurt seems to him to be misguided in setting up a separate organization for immigrants (Radtke, 1994). Radtke, however, does not consider the possibilities raised by the Jenkins formula of recognizing cultural diversity without denying the minorities' rights to protection within the institutions of the welfare state.

Schierup and Alund (1990) are suspicious of Swedish multiculturalism, which they see as directing attention away from other forms of struggle. Multicultural consultation too often suggests that minorities can best be dealt with through representatives chosen for them by the government. Rank and file members of the minority communities, particularly among the young, may form alliances across ethnic boundaries not merely with other minority groups, but with disadvantaged and disaffected Swedes.

All of these criticisms of actual forms of multiculturalism by serious social scientists should be accepted. What they do, however, is to make even more necessary the insistence upon the strong political form of multiculturalism implicit in the Jenkins formula, rather than the abandonment of the very ideal. True citizenship can be multicultural.

5.3.2.2   The culture of minority groups

Many of the critics of multiculturalism imagine that to speak of minority cultures at all is to be guilty of what is called essentialism. Essentialism is the doctrine which sees minority cultures as fixed traditionally and unchanging. It is important therefore to emphasize in the discussion of the cultures of minority groups that they are subject to change. What I have suggested in my writing (Rex, 1996a, 1996b) is that minority cultures must be thought of as involving not simply a body of ideas, but all the forms of mobilization and all the goals and aspirations of minority groups. The changing culture of these groups, I argue, has three points of reference, namely the changing structure of homeland society, the struggle for survival and equality in the land of first settlement and the aim of possible migration to another society. Crucially, in the land of first settlement, which is what we are discussing when we talk of integration of immigrant minorities in Europe, they have an interest in obtaining equality of treatment and in fighting racist exclusion. For this reason, they tend to be very supportive of the idea of social citizenship in the welfare state. The fact that lands of possibly onward migration are another point of reference draws our attention to the fact that immigrant minorities are part of transnational communities. This is an important aspect of globalization, which we will discuss in a later section.

5.4   Refugees and political migrants

In the previous section, we looked first at the concept of citizenship in general terms and then at its applicability to sub-national territorially concentrated groups on the one hand, and economic migrants on the other. We must now turn, however, to the group whose rights to citizenship result from their status as asylum seekers and refugees, or who might be called more generally political migrants.

5.4.1   The numbers of refugees

According to the United Nations Convention of 1951, a refugee is a person who has a genuinely held fear of persecution because of race, religion, nationality, membership in a particular social group, or political opinion, and who cannot return safely to his or her country of origin. According to the *Guardian* of 18 August 2000, there were in the world some 25 million 'internally displaced persons, many of them victims of civil wars now asking the UN refugee Agency for help'. Not all of these would qualify as refugees in terms of the 1951 Convention, but they might nonetheless seek asylum. In 2000, the 38 industrialized countries received 550,000 new applications for asylum, and in 2001, 595,700. The United Kingdom received the largest number of asylum seekers (92,000), followed by Germany (88,300) and the United States (83,200). The leading country of origin for asylum seekers was Afghanistan, accounting for 10 percent of all applications, followed by Iraq (9 percent), Turkey (6 percent), Former Yugoslavia (5 percent), China (4 percent), Republic of Iran (4 percent), Russian Federation (3 percent), Sri Lanka (3 percent), India (3 percent), and Somalia (3 percent).

5.4.2 The treatment of asylum applicants in the country of application

These figures refer to applicants for asylum making their application at the borders of, or in, the country in which they claim refugee status. While they await decisions on their cases, there are a number of ways in which they are excluded from any of the rights of citizenship. They may be kept in camps or detention centers in which their rights are not unlike those of prisoners. They may be allocated to local Councils who are expected to house them and provide education for them and their children. So far as housing is concerned, they are likely to be allocated houses not wanted by the host population. Some children were allowed to attend ordinary schools, but where the asylum seekers lived in segregated circumstances they might be offered schools of their own apart from native children. They are not permitted to work, but, in any case, the houses in which they lived were vacant mainly because there was no work in the vicinity. Finally, they received minimal financial assistance, and, for a while at least, were given vouchers instead of money. These vouchers were not accepted in all shops so that the asylum seekers were partially excluded from the role of consumer at the same that that they were denied the rights of citizens.

The fortunate minority would be given refugee status and go on to attain the full rights of citizenship. Some, however, would be given only 'temporary protection' on the understanding that they might at any time be returned to their own countries if circumstances change. In other cases, although the applicant was denied refugee status, the circumstances in his or her home country would be so dangerous that the applicant was given 'exceptional leave to remain'.

5.4.3 The treatment of asylum seekers before their migration

The number of applicants for asylum in the country where they sought it was made smaller by the fact that a number of measures had been adopted to prevent their presenting themselves in the country itself. The receiving society would declare some countries safe, and thereby prevent anyone from such a country applying for asylum. In some cases, 'safe havens' were established in which, although there was great danger in their home societies, there would be limited regions under the protection of the armed forces of the society of application and its allies. Applicants might be required to present themselves at the embassies of the society of application to obtain visas in the first place. Those who came through a third country *en route* to application might be returned to that country, and carriers would be subject to heavy fines for carrying them. Many potential applicants therefore entered the country of application illegally, and were aided in doing this by traffickers who provided their services for payment which might be paid after the illegal migrant had settled and obtained employment. There was also the possibility that traffickers would place immigrant women as prostitutes or in ill-paid and even slave domestic employment.

5.4.4   The exclusion of asylum seekers from citizenship

In all of the suffering and deprivation which asylum seekers endured they would, of course, not be without allies. At all points there would be NGOs offering advice and assistance, including that provided by specialist lawyers.

What all this amounts to is that those awaiting asylum decisions and those who were able to stay openly or clandestinely could hardly be said to be citizens. They were the most excluded section of the population, lacking the rights of the poorest economic migrants. On the other hand, they would themselves be accused of really being economic migrants posing as asylum seekers. For example, the term 'bogus asylum seekers' was frequently heard in anti-immigrant discourse in the media.

5.4.5   The numbers of asylum seekers, refugees, and illegals in European cities

It is very hard to obtain any kind of reliable statistics of the numbers either of asylum seekers or various types of illegals. There is, however, a great deal of anecdotal evidence, and there is hardly a town in some major European countries in which there are not such clandestine communities of illegal political migrants.

5.4.6   Policy toward asylum seekers

The fact that different European Union (EU) countries have different policies, and that several different countries are involved in any asylum case, has led to demands that there should be some coordination of policy at the European level. Unfortunately, what is often suggested is harmonization at the level of the lowest common denominator of the harshest policy toward immigrants. Some politicians moreover have used the present crisis to call for the scrapping of the 1951 Convention. The matter was taken up at the meetings of the EU under the Finnish presidency at Tampere (1999) and under the Belgian presidency at Laeken (2001). A Directive on Minimum Standards on Reception of Asylum Seekers in Member States was reconsidered at the end of April 2002 (EU Directive, 2002). This, however, was subject, as had been previous drafts of the Directive, to criticisms by a number of NGOs, particularly the European Council for Refugees and Exiles (ECRE) and Caritas. A paper signed by Martina Liebsch of Freiburg, then Vice-President of ECRE and a member of Caritas, entitled 'Migration and Integration in Europe – The Role of Citizenship Education' was submitted to a conference in Kirscheen, Germany, by ECRE on Demands on a New Refugee Policy in Europe in July 2001. This sets out very well some of the major criticisms of present asylum procedures, which many liberal minded critics of refugee policy accept (Liebsch, 2001).

5.5 The rise of far-right parties and their effect on immigration policy

As early as the late 1980s, anti-immigrant political parties were beginning to have electoral success. This was true of the National Front led by Le Pen in France, of far-right parties in Germany, and the Vlaams Blok in Belgium. By the turn of the century, however, it seemed that such parties were achieving more and more success in a number of countries. The emergence of Jörg Haider's Peoples Party as one which had to be included in any government coalition provided a shock to the whole of Europe and the EU sought to break off relations with the new Austrian government. This exclusion of Austria, however, was not sustained and right-wing anti-immigrant parties gained more success in several countries. Le Pen's party in France emerged as the largest party in 2002 and a right-wing party with extreme anti-immigrant proposals because a part of the government in Demark. Finally, in the Netherlands, thought to be the stronghold of social democracy and multiculturalism, the strange new figure of Pim Fortuyn, anti-immigrant and anti-Muslim, emerged as the leader of the most electorally successful party.

The new parties of the right did not actually take power, but the mainstream parties modified their own policies on immigration and refugees in order to win back the vote. In Austria, where Haider's party eventually collapsed in the election of 2002, the success of the conservative parties was due to the fact that they had modified their policies to make them more hostile to immigrants and refugees. In the United Kingdom, there were riots involving the far right and British Asians with the far right gaining some seats in local elections. The Labour government made a curious interpretation of Blair's formula 'tough on crime, tough on the causes of crime' in speaking of being tough on anti-immigrant racism, but understanding of the causes of White racism. Multiculturalism was now seen as implying segregation and policy was directed toward not merely integration but rapid assimilation of Asians. Such policies involving a fear of Asians and of Islam were even more single-mindedly pursued after the attacks on the World Trade Center in New York and the Pentagon in Washington, DC.

At a European level, the idea of Fortress Europe gained ground. There was to be free movement of capital and labor at least in the Schengen countries, but, at the borders, immigrants from the South and the East were to be kept out as much as possible. The fact that there were many such potential immigrants and refugees because of civil wars going on in the Balkans and Africa meant that these migrants would be treated as part of a temporary emergency, which, it was thought, would end with their return to their countries. The other side of this coin was that the immigrant and refugee populations began to mobilize resistance. Various forms of fundamentalism or Islamicism gained ground amongst Muslims, and other immigrant groups began to organize for resistance. This was as true in Belgium as it was in the Northern British cities.

Against this background, the notion of a shared social citizenship amongst natives, immigrants, and refugees could hardly be discussed as a main point of policy.

5.6   Citizenship in a global world

In Western Europe there were strong nation-states which were having difficulty in coming to terms with the international institutions and policy of the European Union, but social scientists increasingly pointed to the fact that neither of these was as important as the new globalism. While Hammar was troubled by the coexistence of citizens and denizens, Bauböck in Austria calmly discussed the relative costs and benefits of citizenship and denizenship for Turkish immigrants (Bauböck, 1991), and he later explored the possibilities of a citizenship which was transnational (Bauböck, 1994). Meanwhile, Soysal suggested, in a highly influential book (Soysal, 1994), that national citizenship was now no longer important in the light of a new consciousness of *human* rights and the growth of institutions which could enforce these rights.

These writings would seem to suggest that the concerns of this chapter are no longer relevant. This, however, is not so. There may indeed be emergent global institutions, but the day-to-day struggle for rights by natives, and by ethnic and immigrant minorities, goes on. The task of social scientists must be to document them in their full complexity.

Notes

1. For convenience, I shall refer to this statement as 'the Jenkins formula' in what follows.
2. I do not wish to raise at this point the problem of the use of the term 'race'. I fully understand the objections which are made to the use of the very term 'race', but this does not mean that there may not be forms of exclusion based upon racist beliefs. It is in this sense that I refer to exclusion on racial and ethnic grounds.
3. This is slightly misleading in that in the first place benefits as of right followed from contributions which had been paid, though there was also a supplementary system of social assistance which covered others regardless of contributions.
4. It was a permanent problem in the shaping of research plans that many social scientists adopted research strategies which were concerned with imposing duties of citizenship on immigrants and minorities. Jacqueline Costa-Lascoux, a French academic principally concerned with legal questions, put the proposal to the Centre for a comparative study of citizenship in Britain and France. Steven Vertovec suggested the study of the education in citizenship of Turkish students as part of an Anglo-German study sponsored by the Volkswagen Foundation.
5. We may leave out here cases like that of Wales in Great Britain or some of the relatively autonomous regions in Spain which may be seen simply as having less powers than the devolved governments of Catalonia and Scotland.
6. Calculation of the numbers of immigrants settling is a difficult matter and the different countries have different methods of counting them. A good source giving an indication of what happens country by country is Migrant Information Source, Website: http://www.migrationinformation.org.
7. This organization was chaired by Sir Andrew Green, former UK ambassador to Saudi Arabia, and had its honorary consultant Professor David Coleman, Professor of Demography, who had been a long-term supporter of the Conservative Party and who had maintained his opposition to immigration, especially of Muslim immigrants, throughout the seventies and eighties.
8. See, for instance, the writings of the working-class Conservative headmaster and publicist, Ray Honeyford, who both advocated an inegalitarian version of multiculturalism and accused the State bureaucracy of seeking to impose it (Honeyford, 1998).
9. The word 'tolerance' unfortunately seems to some to imply a paternalistic attitude to those who lack power. Probably 'mutual respect' would be a better term.
10. This was the topic of a conference organized by the Centre for Research in Ethnic Relations at Warwick University, whose findings were reported in a book edited by myself and Beatrice Drury (Rex and Drury, 1994). Wieviorka, Rath, Radtke, Schierup, and Alund were among the most important contributors to the discussion which followed.

References

Barry, B., *Culture and Equality: An Egalitarian Critique of Multiculturalism* (Cambridge: Polity Press, 2001).

Bauböck, R., *Immigration and the Boundaries of Citizenship* (Coventry: Centre for Research in Ethnic Relations, Monograph No. 4, 1991).

Bauböck, R., *Transnational Citizenship* (Aldershot: Edward Elgar, 1994).

Beveridge, W., *Social Insurance and Allied Services* (London: HMSO, Cmnd 6404, 1942).

Beveridge, W., *Full Employment in a Free Society* (London: Allen & Unwin, 1944).

Crick, B., *The Crick Report: Final Report of the Advisory Group on Citizenship* (London: Qualifications and Curriculum Authority, 1998).

Crowley, J., 'Social Complexity and Strong Democracy', in *Innovation, the European Journal of Social Sciences*, 7:3 (1994).

Delanty, G., 'Beyond the Nation State: National Identity and Citizenship in a Multicultural Society – a Response to Rex', *Sociological Research Online*, 1:3 (1996): http://www.socresonline.org.uk?1/3/1.html

Department of Employment and Productivity, *In Place of Strife: A policy for Industrial Relations* (London: HMSO, Cmnd 3888, 1969).

Esping-Andersen, G., *The Three Worlds of Welfare Capitalism* (Cambridge: Polity Press, 1990).

EU Directive on *Minimum Standards on Reception of Asylum Seekers in Members States*, 29 April 2002.

Gellner, E., *Nations and Nationalism* (Oxford: Blackwells, 1983).

Hammar, T., *Democracy and the Nation State: Aliens, Denizens and Citizens in a World of International Migration* (Aldershot: Avebury, 1990).

Honeyford, R., *The Commission for Racial Equality: British Bureaucracy in a Multiethnic Society* (New Brunswick, NJ and London: Transaction Books, 1998).

Korpi, W., *The Working Class in Welfare Capitalism* (London: Routledge & Kegan Paul, 1978).

Korpi, W., *The Democratic Class Struggle* (London: Routledge & Kegan Paul, 1983).

Kymlicka, W., *Multicultural Citizenship* (London: Oxford University Press, 1995).

Liebsch, M., 'Migration and Integration in Europe – The Role of Citizenship Education', Paper presented in Kirscheen, Germany on behalf of the European Council for Refugees and Exiles to a round table at a conference on Demands on a New Refugee Policy in Europe, organized by the Bundeszentrale fur Politische Bildung in the framework of the political network for citizenship and democracy in Europe (2001).

Marshall, T. H., *Citizenship and Social Class* (Cambridge: Cambridge University Press, 1951).

Parekh, B., *Rethinking Multiculturalism: Cultural Diversity and Political Theory* (Cambridge, MA: Harvard University Press, 2000).

Radtke, F.-O., 'The Formation of Ethnic Minorities: The Transformation of Social into Ethnic Conflicts in the So-Called Multicultural Society, The German Case', in Rex, J., and Dreary, B. (eds), *Ethnic Mobilisation in a Multicultural Europe* (Aldershot: Gower, 1994).

Rath, J., *Minosering: De social Constructe van Ethnische Minderheden* (University of Utrecht: PhD Thesis, 1991).

Rex, J., *Key Problems of Sociological Theory* (London: Routledge & Kegan Paul, 1961).

Rex, J., 'National Identity in the Democratic Multicultural State', *Sociological Research Online*, 1:2 (1996a): http://www.socresonline.org.uk/1/2/1.html

Rex, J., *Ethnic Minorities in the Modern Nation State* (Basingstoke: Macmillan, 1996b).

Rex, J., 'The Basic Elements of a Systematic Theory of Ethnic Relations', *Sociological Research Online*, 6:1 (2001): http://www.socresonline.org.uk/6/1/rex.html

Rex, J., 'The Fundamentals of the Theory of Ethnicity', in Malesevic, S., and Haugaard, M. (eds), *Making Sense of Collectivity: Ethnicity, Nationalism and Globalisation* (London: Pluto Press, 2002).

Rex, J., and Dreary, B. (eds), *Ethnic Mobilisation in a Multicultural Europe* (Aldershot: Gower, 1994).

Rex, J., and Moore, R., *Race, Community and Conflict: A Study of Sparbrook* (London, New York: Oxford University Press, 1967).

Rex, J., and Tomlinson, S., *Colonial Immigrants in a British City* (London: Routledge & Kegan Paul, 1979).

Schierup, C.-U., 'Multi-Poverty Europe, Reflections on Migration, Citizenship and Social Exclusion in the European Union', in Gundara, J. and Jacobs, S. (eds), *Intercultural Europe, Diversity and Social Policy* (Aldershot: Ashgate, 2000).

Schierup, C.-U., and Alund, A., *Paradoxes of Multiculturalism* (Aldershot: Avebury, 1990).

Smith, A., *The Ethnic Revival in the Modern World* (Cambridge: Cambridge University Press, 1981).

Smith, A., *The Ethnic Origins of Nationalism* (Oxford: Blackwells, 1986).

Soysal, Y., *Limits of Citizenship: Migrants and Post-National Membership in Europe* (Chicago, IL: Chicago University Press, 1994).

Taylor, C., 'Multiculturalism and the Politics of Recognition', in Guttman, A., (ed.), *Multiculturalism: Examining the Politics of Recognition* (Princeton, NJ: Princeton University Press, 1994).

Tribune Archive (24 January 1969): http://www.tribune.atfreeweb.com/archive/240169/htm

Wieviorka, M., 'Ethnicity in Action', in Rex, J. and Dreary, B. (eds), *Ethnic Mobilisation in a Multicultural Europe* (Aldershot: Gower, 1994).

Part II

The EU Fight against Discrimination

6
Social Exclusion, Diversity, and the EU's Anti-Discrimination Agenda

Carl-Ulrik Schierup

6.1 A hegemonic concept: diversity and the vicissitudes of 'social exclusion'

The notion of *social exclusion* originates from the French political scene. Here, even since the mid-1970s, it has been an important political concept for the definition of the moral-political rationale behind the *République* and French citizenship. In France, it has a particular meaning attached to social Catholicism as well as to Durkheimian sociology. It is, as discussed by Silver (1994), concerned with moral integration and social solidarity. *Exclusion* is understood 'as the breakdown of the structural, cultural and moral ties which bind the individual to society' (Levitas, 1998). In the French context, moreover, the notion of *exclusion* has traditionally been, and still is, a contested one, exposed to competing Catholic and Socialist/social democratic understandings (Chamberlayne, 1997).

A similar situation arose when, 15 years after the term's first adoption as a key concept in French social policy, the discourse of *social exclusion* came to penetrate the wider political scene in the European Union (EU) and was elevated to a hegemonic notion, guiding political strategy as well as scientific enquiry.[1] Its powerful status can be seen as emerging from the fact of its inclusiveness as a concept, providing a common language of 'solidarity' for a wide spectrum of political directions in the Union.

The language of 'exclusion-inclusion' came, like its beginnings in France, to merge the concerns of two main broad political traditions. One was a Christian democratic concept of citizenship associated with the conservative-corporatist type of welfare regime, traditionally prevailing in Central and Southern Europe. The other approached a social democratic orientation conforming to an egalitarian interpretation of citizenship and social justice, similar to the well-known theory of T. H. Marshall (1992 (1950)). This is a tradition dominant in Scandinavia and, partially, in pre-Thatcherist Britain (e.g., Mann, 1987), but influential among much of the traditional social democratic left across the EU. While the former, the 'conservative' Christian democratic tradition, stresses moral integration and social order, the latter, the social democratic, has traditionally been deeply concerned with poverty and broad issues of social participation with a focus on 'equality'. The strategic advantage of the concept of 'social exclusion' was thus that it could draw from the two main, traditionally dominant welfare regimes and traditions of social policy of the Union, even though they would attach substantially variable meanings to the concept.

This potentially hegemonic concept of social exclusion and its antonym of *social inclusion*, merging conservative concerns centered on *social order* with socialist concerns centered on *social equality*, is succinctly articulated by Ralph Dahrendorf (1985), who, by the mid-1980s, stood forth as a pioneer for the adoption of social exclusion as a basic European policy concept.

Dahrendorf formulates the question of social exclusion in terms of the moral-political premises of citizenship on which the twentieth-century welfare states were constituted. He presents a range of new forms of marginalization and poverty, developing in the economically advanced welfare states from the mid-1970s, as an ongoing process expressed in the exclusion from established rights, encoded in national charters on social citizenship (Dahrendorf, 1985, 1987; Schmitter-Heisler, 1992). The new odd miscellany of socially marginalized and poor categories of the population – among them an incongruously high proportion of immigrants and ethnic minorities – make up a deviant, restless, but disorganized new 'underclass', excluded from the social compact of the welfare state. Dahrendorf persisted that citizenship was thus becoming an exclusive rather than inclusive status (see also Lister, 1990: 24), and this to a degree that would threaten the social stability (that is, 'cohesion') which had for decades marked the post-Second World War Western European welfare states.

This close connection with a broad democratic conception of citizenship summarizes quite well the essence of the notion of social exclusion as it went into general European discourse and policies on poverty and social exclusion at the beginning of the 1990s. Social inclusion was understood to be preconditioned by civil, political, and, in particular, social rights of citizenship, sanctioned by the overall political compact of the welfare state. This also implicated the reality of a *substantial citizenship*,[2] contingent on the existence or establishment of overall institutional and social conditions, which would indeed facilitate the exercise of these rights for individuals and social groups, and thus their actual participation as full and equal members of society. Social exclusion was, conversely, seen as signifying an exclusion from citizenship in the broad sense of the blocking of actual opportunities for individuals to exercise full and fundamental social, political, or civil rights in a liberal democratic welfare society.

This original usage of the conception of social exclusion in the context of EU policy was originally almost completely void of references to issues of racism and the discrimination of ethnic minorities. This changed radically during the 1990s, however, particularly after the Amsterdam treaty emerged as a proliferating EU reform agenda for combating racism and discrimination. We have seen a new manifest antiracist orientation being turned into mandatory directives and large-scale transnational development programs, which impose compelling demands for combating the discrimination and social exclusion of ethnic minorities on the member states. This has certainly endowed the whole issue of social exclusion and inclusion with an essential focus on *diversity*. However, we have also seen a strong effort made to estrange the meaning of social exclusion/inclusion from its original association with a broad notion of substantial citizenship, and a subsequent narrowing of the connotation to that of exclusion from or inclusion into *paid work or self-employment*.

We see this as a general tendency conditioned by current trends to dismantle the social rights of citizenship with the aim of removing barriers to the establishment of 'the market' as the dominant form of regulation of economy and society. The overall movement is, in essence, from one type of European political coalition and discourse to another; that is, from a conservative/social democratic coalition attempting to merge differential political concerns with 'social order' and 'equality' – which was also so vividly exposed in Dahrendorf's discourse on social order – toward a neo-communitarian/neo-liberal coalition concerned with reconciling 'social cohesion' with 'efficiency'. The central question of race, class, and democracy raised by this chapter is whether the theory that a sustainable policy targeted at equal opportunities can actually succeed without the precondition of some form of a broad social compact on citizenship and social welfare, in terms of normative political consensus and strong institutions beyond and complementary to the market.

6.2   The poverty program: social exclusion as the denial of rights of citizenship

Dahrendorf analyzed the problem of social exclusion in terms of a major contraction of the welfare state, which has created a 'crucial boundary ... between the majority class and those who are being defined out of the edifice of citizenship' (Dahrendorf, 1985: 98). There is, as he sees it, a social cleft, which threatens to fundamentally undermine the legitimacy of the central political institutions of the liberal democratic state. The essence of the term 'social exclusion' is, as used here, its denotation of *the denial of citizenship*: that is, citizenship largely understood in the sense theorized by the British sociologist T. H. Marshall (1992) in his influential work *Citizenship and Social Class*. Consequently, the precondition for combating social exclusion and social unrest would be to uphold an ideal of citizenship as universal entitlement. This would implicate a distinctly redistributive welfare policy, unconditionally guaranteeing every citizen a certain socially acceptable standard of living; a solid foundation to build on.

This was, sheltered by the President of the Commission, Jacques Delors's stress on forging a powerful *social dimension* of the Community, also to become the dominant connotation of *social exclusion*, when – from the beginning of the 1990s – the term became one of key importance in the political vocabulary of the EU. A focus on tackling a broad range of social disadvantages, connected with poverty and inequality, was strongly articulated in the *Background Report* to the European Poverty Programme in 1991. Here the poor are defined as 'persons whose resources (material, cultural and social) are so limited as to exclude them from the minimum acceptable way of life in the Member State in which they live' (European Commission, 1991).[3] This echoes T. H. Marshall's (1992) conception of social inclusiveness in *Citizenship and Social Class* where he describes social citizenship as that 'whole range (of rights of citizenship) from the right to a modicum of economic welfare and security to the right to share to the full in the social heritage and to live the life of a civilized being according to the standards prevailing in the society'. Del Castillo (1994: 616) observes that the general orientation here is on social exclusion as it relates directly to the contemporary challenge to one of the cornerstones of justice, and addresses 'the system of "social contract" associated with democracies since the Second World War, namely, the equality of opportunity which should be guaranteed by law'.

In the subsequent work of the Commission, 'social exclusion' was widely adopted as a theoretically based concept for identifying, analyzing, and forming policy in respect to groups exposed to conditions of enduring and multiple deprivation. Marshall's concept of social citizenship was explicitly adopted as the basis for the work of the *Observatory on National Policies to Combat Social Exclusion*, which was founded by the Commission of the European Communities in 1990 (Room, 1992). Seeking what they describe as a precise and theoretical conception of the notion of *exclusion*, the Observatory defines social exclusion 'first and foremost in relation to the social rights of citizens'. Social exclusion can, accordingly, 'be analyzed in terms of the denial – or non-realization – of social rights' (Room, 1992: 13–15). On the basis of this definition, the Commission went on to produce evidence of a significant degree of widespread and growing poverty throughout Europe, which, at the same time, was seen as being variable in extent and form.[4] The Observatory includes other types of rights of citizenship in its analyses, such as Marshall's civil and political dimensions, insofar as they appear important in concrete cases for analyzing exclusion from or realization of social rights (Room, 1992: 16 ff.). It investigates the various social rights (to employment, housing, health care, child care, and so on) individuals have in the individual member states. It makes use of studies of multiple, persistent, and cumulative disadvantage (in terms of education, training, employment, housing, and financial resources), and it addresses the question 'whether those who suffer such disadvantages have substantially lower chances than the rest of the population of gaining access to the major social institutions' (Room, 1992: 16 ff.).

6.3 Combating racialized exclusion: the 'post-Amsterdam' social agenda

The work of the Observatory suffered, from the beginning, from what critics have identified as one of the soft spots so often present among protagonists of the citizenship paradigm derived from T. H. Marshall. That is, an apparent blindness to matters of ethnic diversity and the social position of immigrants (see, for example, Turner, 1990). A number of important national surveys, studies, and academic discussions on social exclusion and poverty from the 1980s and early 1990s contain, with notable exceptions,[5] quite inadequate material, or lack data altogether, concerning the situation of immigrants and ethnic minorities;[6] and they too often lack a discussion as to this apparent scarcity.

This state was, in the course of the 1990s, gradually redressed as the Commission sponsored important comparative studies concerned with discrimination and racism and with the situation of immigrants in irregular labor markets.[7] It was, however, only the Amsterdam accord in 1997 that gave the Commission genuine leeway for developing social policy initiatives, including policies on combating racism and discrimination (see, for example, Kostakopoulou, 1999). Here, in the context of the new post-Amsterdam policy agenda in general, we see an increasing confluence of social policy with labor market and employment policies taking place. This is, among others, currently being implemented through large-scale community programs supposedly pushing in the direction of integrated EU practices and institutional frameworks formulated top-down. But they are envisaged to be implemented in the form of processes of transnational integration from below. This is supposed to take place through the trans-border dissemination of 'best practices' produced by *development partnerships* focused on regions, branches, or local communities in different member states.

Although the process may, in several ways, appear spurious and contradictory (Kostakopoulou, 1999), the EU is now in the position to, and has actually started to, take concrete and determined action in terms of policies of inclusion addressing racism and discrimination as central issues. This policy agenda, emphasizing 'fundamental social rights and civil society' is, among others, being implemented through the 'Community Action Programme to combat discrimination' (2001–06).[8] A particularly noteworthy milestone was The Council Directive, which was adopted in June 2000, *Implementing the Principle of Equal Treatment between Persons Irrespective of Racial or Ethnic Origin* (European Commission, 2000). The directive aims to put into action Article 13 of the EC Treaty regarding the struggle against racism and xenophobia. Here, the Council strongly expresses the need to promote 'a socially inclusive labor market' for the EU to be able to achieve the objectives of the EC Treaty, 'in particular the attainment of a high level of employment and of social protection'.

Currently, the new large-scale and transnational *Equal Programme 2000–06*,[9] managed by the European Social Fund, ties together these two parallel developments in policy formation mentioned above – the new social policy *cum* employment agenda and the *anti-discrimination agenda* – within the overall framework of an integrated transnational development strategy. The program echoes the 'Third Way' (as theorized by Giddens, 1998) and stakeholder capitalism with an emphasis on the *social inclusion* of disadvantaged groups through employment (see the discussion by Levitas, 1998). This is supposed to take place through the collaboration of the 'different worlds of public administration, non-governmental organizations, social partners and the business sector' within the framework of mostly local development partnerships, which are supposed to pool 'their different types of expertise and experience'. The program has become a privileged testing ground for trying out new ways of dealing with problems of discrimination targeted on a range of disadvantaged groups in the name of 'diversity', but with a marked emphasis on the inclusion of refugees, immigrants, and ethnic minorities and on combating racism and xenophobia in the labor market. It stresses, in particular, the need to analyze and to combat structurally and institutionally embedded discrimination. It also emphasizes the urgency of intercultural training and the training of social workers or mediators of immigrant origin as well as the need to take positive action in order to improve the opportunities of migrants and ethnic minorities.

The implementation of the program is in accordance with the general decentralizing principle of subsidiarity of the Union, which has gradually been developed within the context of its practices belonging to the Employment and Social Policy agenda (Geddes, 2001, in passim). In this context, so-called development partnerships, including partners in 'civil society' together with businesses and the public sector, which cooperate on specific local or regional objectives, are privileged instruments. Development partnerships are expected to build on and to produce 'empowerment from below', which is in line with a general stress on regionalism, localism, and 'civil society' in a range of contemporary programs for enhancing social participation and equal opportunities across the Union. While each member state develops its own particular priorities within the general framework and orientation of the Equal Programme, the implementation of each single (regional, local, or branch-oriented) development partnership must include close cooperation with similar development partnerships in other EU Member States for the purpose of joint development and dissemination of 'good practices' in the form of inventive strategies for employment inclusion. The development, communication, and exchange of transformative practices strive to mainstream and progress the integration of practices vertically, horizontally, and through the boundaries of member states across the Union.

Equal and other large-scale EU programs for combating racialized exclusion are still in progress and will be studied and evaluated in due time. But there is a good deal of experience to share already from other programs and local partnerships for social inclusion from different parts of Europe, albeit they were not so ambitiously targeted on the specific aim of combating ethnic/racial (and other forms of) discrimination.

A number of analytic country reports were collected in the edited volume, *Local Partnerships and Social Exclusion in the European Union* (Geddes and Benington, 2001), which provides a critical appraisal of partnerships as new forms of local governance. The experience reviewed is not unanimous. Some report a potentially genuine increase in a broad influence for social movements on a new and more attentive social policy agenda, like in the case of Portugal (Rodrigues and Stoer, 2001), while the Finnish report (Kautto and Heikkilä, 2001) gives the impression of an overall state-bureaucratic grip on the whole process.[10] The British report (Geddes, 2001), in turn, observes that the form of 'partnership' belonging to the 'new social agenda' looks like a sales offer for people to buy shares in the overall neo-liberal project, but wholly on terms set by business, the much propagated 'corporate responsibility' which cannot, however, make up for any overall social solidarity.

Obviously, experience appears to vary greatly, not only from locality to locality, but systematically between member states, according to their still highly different path-dependent economic policies, welfare and labor market regimes, systems of governance, and the factual constitution of civil society. But it is necessary to discuss the changing norms of social citizenship and social welfare on which the new social policy agenda and the anti-racist programs are, in general, contingent. This has to do with the currently strengthened role at the European level in setting the rules of the game for policy formation on social and employment issues, together with an increasing emphasis on transnational mainstreaming of best practices, to which – among others – the new programs targeted at combating racialized exclusion give evidence. Seen in this perspective, there is a particular need for a critical scrutiny of important changes in the wider European discourse and agenda on social exclusion/inclusion, within the framework of which the new programs are conceived and implemented.

6.4   Changing configurations of 'exclusion/inclusion': from 'social order' and 'equality' to 'social cohesion' and 'efficiency'

At the beginning of the 1990s a belief in the Community's role as a successor to the national welfare state, guarding a forceful 'social dimension', was still alive among major representatives of its institutions (e.g., Delors, 1992). But after the Maastricht Treaty in 1992 and the abortive negotiations for reaching an overall accord concerning 'the social dimension' which preceded it, alternative traditions in European social policy and politics of citizenship have gained in influence concerning the major issue of what 'a European Creed' should actually be. This has decidedly modified the scope of the social dimension as well as the critical analytical range of the notion of 'social exclusion'.

The stress has been increasingly placed on labor market integration as a precondition for 'social cohesion', with the wider implications of poverty and inequality moving into the background (see Levitas, 1998). While the initial focus had been on efforts to reconcile the conservative primacy on 'social order' with socialist worries concerning 'equality', the core concern became reconciling 'social cohesion' with 'economic efficiency'. The economic discussion is phrased in terms of efficiency, deregulation, and the demand for economic growth, while a parallel social concern counterpoises 'solidarity, integration, and cohesion' with 'unemployment, poverty, and social exclusion'. But in spite of a language of solidarity, the emphasis is one-sidedly on exclusion from paid work, or on the issue of 'unemployment'. The cure is, universally, inclusion through paid work. Here,

> 'Solidarity' is a device reducing the costs of social provision, not for redistribution. The forms of solidarity invoked are manifold: between those who have jobs and those who do not; between generations; between regions; between 'those who earn their income from work and those who earn their income from investments'; and between men and women 'making it easier to reconcile family life and working life'. (Levitas, 1998: 25, quoting the European Commission, 1994b)

This is not about any unequivocal enthusiasm with the market, which is seen to be in need of regulation or 'management' through collective solidarity mechanisms. The type of 'solidarity' in question here is not synonymous with that of a redistributive welfare state, argues Levitas (1998) in her analysis of central EU documents on social exclusion/inclusion.[11] Welfare state expenditures are deemed too costly to uphold. Instead, solidarity is called upon as a form of restraint for the purpose of reducing the costs of social provision. What is at stake is no longer the duty of the whole community to face up to universal rights of citizenship, but rather, under the banner of civil society and corporate responsibility, a moral commitment of the individual citizen, corporations, individual counties, and social groups to safeguard 'social cohesion'.

This *social integrationist discourse* (Levitas, 1998), becoming dominant in the Community after Maastricht, could indeed be described as a revamped version of a conservative-corporatist moral 'creed' focused on maintaining social order through social solidarity measures. However, merging with an Anglo-American liberal discourse preoccupied with economic expediency, a retreat of the state from the economy, and with the minimalization of welfare expenditures, the Commission's conception of social exclusion/inclusion has become increasingly similar to the neo-communitarianism of 'The Third Way', which – apart from Tony Blair's Britain – profoundly influences social democratic regimes like, for example, Sweden's or Germany's. This turn away from *redistribution* became 'endemic' in the financial and legal framework of the Union as its member states started to employ austerity measures in order to qualify for the single currency. It is ingrained in the practices of the whole range of projects initiated by the structural funds, designed to integrate marginal groups into the labor market or to promote equal opportunities. They exclusively finance projects targeted directly at the labor market, and their rules are designed so as to reinforce the understanding of social participation as labor market activity (see Levitas, 1998: 25).

6.5   Right to welfare or duty to work?

Reserving 'social exclusion' as a term for describing the 'exclusion from paid work', as is the tendency in the EU social policy agenda since Maastricht, may have the advantage of simplicity and precision. But this shift occurs – as analyzed in detail by, among others, Peo Hansen (2002)[12] – together with a general disassociation from more ambitious visions of the European Union's 'social dimension' and the adoption of practices that withdraw attention from the wider issue of poverty and inequality. It is important to raise, as argued by Levitas (1998), a discussion of the consequences of this choice in terms of an estrangement from the broader focus on 'full membership of the community', as implicated in the broad citizenship maxim and the initial redistributive discourse on social exclusion and inclusion.

6.5.1   Between racialized welfare dependency and the new working immigrant poor

An imminent consequence is that of de-legitimizing non-participation in paid work[13] and by, directly or indirectly, discrediting traditional redistributive measures, doing away with any welfare guarantee. This carries with it an innate propensity for endorsing the stigmatization of immigrants and ethnic minority members out of work, often excluded due to exposure to racism or systematic institutional discrimination.

Putting a one-sided emphasis on work and economic expediency, and branding welfare spending, also limits the political latitude for leading a generous refugee policy. We currently see such tendencies all across the EU, but particularly in the 'old' immigration countries of Northwestern Europe. Here, unemployment and welfare dependency among immigrants and new ethnic minorities is consistently high, widely oversteps rates among national majorities, and is the object of negative and stigmatizing attention in the media and popular discourse (see EUMC, 2001). Hence, as argued by Ruth Lister (1990), where 'poverty' becomes 'social exclusion' and where the bearings of social exclusion become constricted to 'exclusion from paid work', there is an imminent risk that the result may turn out to be the sifting out and stigmatization of one particular subgroup among the poor, the 'welfare clients'. A most adverse, but quite typical result, is that the issue of poverty and social exclusion becomes subsumed by an understanding that locates the cause of misery in a moral deficiency of the excluded themselves (Lister, 1990; see Katz, 1989).

Different varieties of this kind of *moral underclass discourse* (Levitas, 1998) have indeed won extension in political struggles over the causes and meaning of social exclusion among immigrants and racial and ethnic minorities all across Europe (see, for example, the analysis by Schierup, 1993). It is in the United States that this kind of discourse has been most influential, however, and forcefully adopted as a recipe for 'social integration through work'. Converted into actual policy measures and processed, through tough disciplinary strategies of workfare, this has proved to lead to the transformation of poor 'welfare clients' into different categories of 'working poor', permanently trapped in enforced low status, deregulated, and under-remunerated work'[14]. Morally induced work enforcement of this disciplinary character, of which a huge American 'prison-industrial complex' (Parenti, 2000) is the ultimate expression, has deprived poor African Americans of their political power and their civil right to withhold their labor from the new service economy's substandard jobs. The implication is, in effect, a substantial deterioration in terms of exclusion from citizenship; not only social citizenship, but civil and political (Fox Piven and Cloward, 1993; King, 1999).[15]

Seen in this perspective, the ongoing 'war on welfare' (Katz, 1989) in the United States is, as argued by Fox Piven and Cloward, nothing but part of a wider 'war against (organized) labor'. Contingent on *The Breaking of the American Social Compact* (Fox Piven and Cloward, 1997), it forms part of a consistent low-wage strategy of employers. The defeat of organized labor and the struggle of radical race and class conscious

black urban 'ghetto' communities have, together with the moral con-
demnation and institutional embargo on 'welfare', opened the gates for
the formation of today's extended deregulated low-wage sector, mainly
staffed by new immigrants from Asia and Latin America, but increasingly also by poor African Americans.[16] Similar tendencies can be
observed all over the 'old' immigration countries of the EU, with Britain
as the most obvious example of this incremental Americanization of
welfare and work regimes.[17]

Here, what Fox Piven and Cloward have called 'regulating the poor'
(1993), is about regulating the poor, not for their own benefit, 'but for
the benefit of protecting work and family values and the corresponding
modes of economic allocation and political entitlement' (Schram, 2000:
87).[18] There is growing political pressure to devise new authoritarian
forms of workfare and, among employers in particular, to extend the
range of a deregulated low-wage service sector, drawing labor from
racialized internal labor reserves as well as from the global labor market.
As observed by Chris Jones and Tony Novak (1999) in a comparative
study of welfare-to-workfare strategies in the United States and New
Labor's Britain, 'work is promoted as the solution to a range of social
issues and problems', but 'with an apparent total amnesia of the damage
that work has done to many people'. This may well be on its way to
becoming a maxim for social and employment policies all across the EU.

The substantial erosion of the ideological foundations for social
citizenship, which the redefinition of social exclusion/inclusion opens
up, may thus – seen in the perspective of the ongoing deregulation and
recommodification of labor all over Europe – pave the way for a deterioration of the actual quality of employment and conditions of work.
Given their systematic concentration in low pay and de- or non-regulated
sections of the labor market, exacerbated through racializing stigmatization and prevalent hiring practices, this affects, in particular, immigrants
and new ethnic minorities. A one-dimensional emphasis on paid work
in conjunction with the currently growing stigmatization of welfare
recipients may reinforce the pressure on immigrants and ethnic minorities to accept any working conditions, and thus deepen current tendencies toward new types of racialized divisions of labor and welfare in
Europe. To this come important gender considerations. A one-sided
emphasis on paid work and self-employment may exacerbate a predominant blindness to 'unpaid work and its gendered distribution' (Levitas,
1998: 26 ff.), which also carries with it particular predispositions to
racialization (Sassen, 1991). It especially pertains to the conditions in
the expanding sector of so-called ethnic business, where 'invisible' and

'unpaid' female and family work often plays an essential role as cheap labor under irregular or hazardous working conditions.[19]

6.5.2 The complexity of 'advanced marginality'

What Dahrendorf, and others with him, focused on during the early 1980s was, in particular, the social and political repercussions of the mass unemployment and subsequent welfare dependency resulting from crisis and restructuring in North Atlantic economies after the mid-1970s (Schierup, 1985). However, during the 1980s and 1990s, the actual multiplicity of contemporary forms of social exclusion became increasingly evident. The unemployed and welfare dependent among Europe's new ethnic minorities have come to enjoy the company of a number of categories among the new *working poor*, to an increasing degree stigmatized and kept apart as ethnic or racial 'others'.[20] These include everything from the undocumented workers on Southern Europe's large building sites to the 'exotic' women in Amsterdam's iniquitous red-light district, but also the growing numbers trying to muddle through on the basis of authoritarian *workfare* schemes. They include Western Europe's so-called new proletariat (Bel Habib, 2001), small self-employed 'ethnic entrepreneurs' in subcontracted 'sweatshops, the new 'contract workers' substituting a defamed guest worker's system, the black housemaids tending middle class homes in Italy (Andall, 2000), and the *new asylum seekers* forced into clandestine jobs due to deteriorating terms of protection and reception in presumptive 'host countries'.

These and other categories of working poor are all found to varying extents in different member states of the European Union, depending on their particular political configuration and policies on migration and integration, their type of welfare regime, and the structure of their economies and labor markets.

Immigrants and ethnic minorities, especially immigrant and ethnic minority women, are – across the Union – heavily overrepresented in new service jobs marked by odd working times, non-regulated working conditions, and a lack of social security benefits. In Southern Europe, in particular, public attention, as well as that of researchers,[21] is on the contingencies and consequences of undocumented migration and the extensive employment of immigrants in the irregular economy. This is, however, a long since extended practice in countries like Germany, France, and the Netherlands, and a rapidly growing phenomenon in Britain and Scandinavia, where the irregular economy draws labor, partly from among racialized populations squeezed by a deteriorating welfare system (Slavnic, 2002) and partly through a growing undocumented immigration.[22] With their exposed position, these and a range of other categories among the new working poor are excluded from essential dimensions of citizenship.

These new working poor European *others* share with their North American contemporaries what the French sociologist, Loïc Wacquant (1996b), has called *advanced marginality*. This signifies that their lives and their exclusion are formed by conditions that belong to the novel and most advanced political and economic configurations rather than representing the imperfections of a passing order. But in this respect they are no different from the poor currently on welfare.

Other papers (Schierup, 2003a, 2003b, 2003c),[23] have analyzed the complexity of this development, arguing that any analysis focusing on poverty or social exclusion as an issue that pertains to a single social category in isolation – like, for example, the 'welfare dependent' so-called ghetto poor or, alternatively, the new migrant working poor[24] – does not merely simplify the matter. It eschews or distorts the dynamics of different, but mutually interdependent, processes of racialized exclusion, which should be analyzed together in their contingency on wider globalizing 'political economies of exclusion', deregulated labor markets, and refractory welfare regimes on the wane. In this perspective, the matter of social inclusion becomes much wider than simply one of employment or entrepreneurship. It emerges as part and parcel of the more comprehensive issue of citizenship in a situation where, as brought forward by Dahrendorf (1985), Fox Piven and Cloward (1997), and others, the social compacts that carried up the established national welfare states are dwindling or collapsing.

The American example, referred to above, is particularly illustrative of this complexity and interdependency (Schierup, 2003a). Studies like that of Fox Piven and Cloward (1993) or Desmond King (1999), clearly demonstrate that the old Marxist thesis embodied in the theory of the 'reserve army of labor' in capitalism, telling that unemployment is always a relative phenomenon, is still not obsolete. Their analyses demonstrate that the welfare poor are hardly superfluous in any absolute sense. That 'work disappears' (paraphrasing Wilson, 1997) and jobs continue to remain unavailable, as contended in well-known American discourses on the so-called (black) urban underclass or the welfare dependent ghetto poor (Wilson, 1978, 1987, 1993), is indeed the expression of a state in a struggle for rights of citizenship and for the terms on which labor may be sold and bought on the market, rather than the manifestation of any absolute surplus of (low skilled) labor.

The character and function of the black, so-called urban ghetto depends largely on the relationship of forces in that struggle. When racialized minority groups hold a strong political position, they may be able to withhold their labor from unfavorable sections of a racially divided, discriminatory labor market. The 'ghetto' may function as a political resource and a stronghold of social and political citizenship, as often started to become the case under the terms of the 'Great Society' in the big cities of the United States during the 1960s (Fox Piven and Cloward, 1993). However, minorities, and African Americans in particular, became weak and dispersed, new political constellations positioned themselves to exploit ever-present potentials of racialization, and exceedingly unfavorable terms of negotiation were set by economic restructuring, spatial relocation, and globalization (in terms of internationalizing the labor market through increasing capital mobility as well as large-scale and continuous immigration of low-wage labor). As a result, the ghetto became an increasingly stigmatized hellhole, with the disciplinary function of deterring anyone attempting to withhold labor from the substandard jobs on the labor market, where employers hold the upper hand.

Thus, subjected to the terms of the particular low-wage strategy backed by the new immigration that came to mark wide sections of the US labor market during the 1980s, the black urban ghetto became an increasingly depressed and haunted labor reserve. Here, the disciplinary function of 'workfare' has become effectively boosted by that of the prison. With the mass incarceration of the poor – hitting poor African Americans to an extremely disproportionate degree[25] – the former ghetto's 'ethnoracial prison' is, as argued and documented by Wacquant (2000, 2002), Christian Parenti (2000), and others,[26] being systematically transformed into the prison's surrogate 'judicial ghetto'. With the privatization of prisons, their introduction into the stock market, and the increasingly commercialized character of forced prison labor, a new post-Fordist mode of the slave economy became de facto reintroduced in the United States less than 150 years after its formal abolishment under the auspices of humanism and mass industrialism. An important difference is, however, that it is now no longer restricted to the Southeast, but is just as present in the North and the West. Institutionalized within the framework of the so-called *prison-industrial complex*,[27] the private prison corporations operate under 'ideal business conditions' (Parenti, 1996: 232). They are guaranteed a labor supply at absurdly low wages, receive direct government subsidies, and have a guaranteed market.

The rising demands and political movements of the Black American ghetto and African Americans' rejection of the new 'slave jobs',[28] belonging to the post-Fordist service economy, have been curbed. In the same fell swoop, American employers have, through workfare and the prison's new slave economy, managed to exploit the gradual conversion of poor African Americans from welfare recipients to labor reserve for further cutting the price of labor, and thus indirectly to impair the bargaining power of wider groups of working poor (African Americans, Asians, Latin Americans, and Caucasians alike); workers, who even before the 1990s' rapid expansion of the wage depressing prison-industrial economy's 'bloody Taylorism'[29] held a weak position in a changing US labor market.

Thus, by the turn of the millennium, the relationship between the 'restructured' black ghetto and the 'new economy's' low-wage pole, run by cheap immigrant labor, had, in a somewhat ironic way, become reversed. State subventioned workfare programs and the prison economy, replacing the 'welfare refuge', have become additional levers for wage-dumping in a dualist post-Fordist economy.

Like in the contemporary United States, the European situation is marked by multiple modes of racialized exclusion and different categories among the excluded cannot be seen in isolation. They are mutually interdependent, embedded in complex ethnic divisions of labor.[30] Extended areas of chronic social disadvantage and welfare dependency are ever-potential 'incubators' for working activities that are 'precarious and underpaid and systematically performed by women, immigrants and disadvantaged minorities' (Mingione, 1996a: 382). The extension of areas of low pay, casual, and precarious jobs, performed by exposed minorities and other groups excluded from substantive rights of citizenship, is, in turn, likely to put pressure on welfare institutions and to support political programs for dismantling the function of social citizenship as a sanctuary and defense of the exposed against market forces.[31]

This kind of development and interdependency is everywhere contingent on labor market deregulation, new flexibility regimes, the growth of an informal economic sector, and the irregular sector of the labor market. Similar processes of economic restructuring and labor market deregulation have racializing effects and shape unequal ethnic divisions of labor all across the European Union. Yet, particular modes of racialized exclusion are forged depending upon the dynamics of the political economy and social struggles in local and national institutional settings, exposed to global pressures. The concrete forms of intersection of different faces of marginality vary, depending on the character of the welfare regime in each single country or groups of countries, and on their policies of migration and incorporation.

6.6   A quest for new-old politics of citizenship

We have focused on how our current dilemmas are highly centered on issues of citizenship and the contemporary 'great exclusion' (paraphrasing Jordan, 1996) in which processes of racialization have become of major concern.

Social citizenship and the welfare state are, like any dimension of citizenship, the result of social struggles and based on particular political, institutional, and structural assumptions and preconditions (Bottomore, 1996). Like any achievement in citizenship, attempts to develop an inclusive multi-ethnic welfare society is vulnerable to radical social and economic change and, in the last instance, contingent on the sustainability of established, or the renewed formation, of powerful political compromises and coalitions (e.g., Carnoy, 1994).

We currently see, under headings like 'social cohesion', 'social inclusion', 'transnational partnerships', the 'mobilization of civil society', 'empowerment from below', and 'combating racism and discrimination through structural and institutional changes', the emerging contours of a *new European social project*; beyond the homogenizing class organizations belonging to industrial Fordism and beyond the centralized national welfare state. New EU policy frameworks, methods, and grand transnational anti-discriminatory development programs are designed and launched top-down. They appeal to the bottom-up mobilization of a large range of movements and networks of 'civil society'. This still, like in the traditional 'social partnership' of the established welfare state, includes the trade unions, but without conceding these their, once, self-evidently privileged position. New policy frameworks endeavor to merge 'civil society' and voluntary associations into 'development partnerships' with local and regional government, business, centers of learning, and science. This overall process is supposed to embrace 'diversity', in terms of gender, ethnic background, and so on, as a central conceptual hub and as a target for practice.

We could see all of these currently emerging anti-racist programs, institutions, and declarations of intent from the European Commission, and their increasingly regular embeddedness within major treaties and transnational framework agreements, as one important new feature of processes of renegotiation of the overall social compacts of citizenship and welfare which, in all their national variation, have dominated the member states of the EU since the Second World War. We may further see this as signifying emerging elements of a more inclusive 'European Creed' and process of identity formation, professing a qualified and differentiated liberal approach through its stress on 'diversity' and the need to combat discrimination – racial and other – in particular local situations and with a professed will to address the conditions of disadvantaged groups in their institutional and structural embeddedness. This is accompanied, moreover, by a multitude of actual day-to-day practices for 'diversity', directed against racial and other forms of discrimination: a truly promising and encouraging development.

The stress on local commitment and civil involvement addresses key problems, which emerged as constraints for the realization of a substantive community of citizens during the heyday of heavily bureaucratized and often inflexible welfare states, ill-equipped for accommodating increasing cultural diversity, complex identities, and differentiating social needs. Yet, seen in a wider perspective, the question and innate dilemma is whether the baby may not in the end risk being thrown out with the bathwater. That is, if the wider sense of the 'social dimension', closely connected with a universalistic liberal-democratic conception of citizenship as an inseparable complex of unconditional rights, will vanish in favor of fragmented, localized, and parochial projects and partnerships targeted at a narrowly conceived inclusion into employment or the engagement in small business. In a possible negative scenario, with no overall social vision or broad democratic representation guiding the process, these 'partnerships' may become the vehicles for transforming the right to welfare into the (unconditional) duty to work; the end of the 'social dimension' rather than its reaffirmation.

Seen in this perspective, the contemporary European dilemma of racialization is centered between an *emerging EU supra-national policy agenda for combating racialized exclusion,* and the current political discourse and *realpolitik,* which may disconnect the important link between the issue of social exclusion/inclusion and the more general question of citizenship and social welfare.

In Western Europe, even the *Gastarbeiter* or the *travailleur emigré* of the post-Second World War often lacked fundamental rights of citizenship in the countries where they worked, but their mode of employment and social trajectory differed from what has become typical for substantial parts of a multifarious *new immigration* of the 1980s and 1990s. Our times' racialized working poor are socially marginal, but essential cogwheels serving the much hailed *flexibility* of the production and labor regimes and the new service economies characteristic of current processes of restructuring. As the broad class-based organizations characteristic of the established European welfare states increasingly lose their integrative power for economy and society, 'multiculturalism' or 'diversity', which have become important idioms for the self-understanding of contemporary North Atlantic societies, emerged from the early 1970s as a coded language obscuring new fragmented divisions of labor and a so-called network economy harboring multiple new forms of racialized exclusion.

But this does not necessarily mean that the particularism of equally fragmented and multifarious social and employment programs, beyond any socially grounded universalism, must or can be the overall answer. We should scrutinize the far-sighted prospects of the European employment and social policy agenda, together with its new strongly voiced anti-racist/anti-discrimination dimension, as vehicles for 'empowerment' in the perspective of today's more general problems of the erosion of frameworks for substantial citizenship. Without, so far, any broader alternative in sight which may effectively confront the challenges of economic globalization and the prevalent 'deregulation' strategies, the issue of citizenship, and in particular that of social citizenship, must in turn be dealt with in its contingency with new economic regimes, structurally bounded ethnic divisions of labor, and the crumbling of the established compacts on social welfare between capital and labor.

Ongoing political struggles revolving around matters of citizenship and social exclusion in increasingly multi-ethnic societies, exposed to continuous immigration, demonstrate the difficulties and choices that any effort to develop a multi-ethnic welfare society is exposed to, confronting the selective forces of economic restructuring and globalization. They single out the contested status of social citizenship at a juncture where the welfare state is exposed to critique and pressure for continued and extensive change concerning its ideological foundations, institutional set-up, and power to legitimately interfere in the regulation of economy, society, and culture. These current struggles evolving around the set-up of a multi-ethnic welfare state in Europe and elsewhere may indeed serve as an illustration and extension of the argument of a number of critical reviews of the allegedly evolutionary air and optimistic modernism of Marshall's theory of citizenship (e.g., Giddens, 1982; Bottomore, 1996). They also draw attention to what has been criticized as another flaw in the Marshallian paradigm: that is the lack of any thorough theory of the *economic foundations and contingencies* of the welfare state (Turner, 1986). Social citizenship and the welfare state are, as it has been argued (Giddens, 1982; Bottomore, 1996), like any dimension of citizenship, the result of social struggles and based on particular political, institutional, and structural assumptions and preconditions. The same is the case with attempts at a 'multicultural' redevelopment of citizenship or any other attempt to forge an inclusive citizenship, accommodating the increasing diversity of contemporary society.

An incipient stratification in ethno-racial terms confronts us with a whole range of differentially excluded population groups, working as well as non-working poor. The 'welfare'/'workfare' dyad is only *one* example of this. But the transformation from 'welfare to workfare' demonstrates the analytical importance for critical social science of guarding a meaning of 'social exclusion' that will be able to capture the transient boundaries between different categories of socially deprived 'Others'. Notwithstanding the wide differences in form and extent of social exclusion across the EU, these, and other categories of racially excluded are becoming an increasingly common political concern. They are among the most conspicuous manifestations of Europe's common 'ethnic dilemma' (Hansen and Schierup, 1998). The common character of this dilemma is not simply based, however, on the emergence and persistence of multiple forms of new racialized poverty, but on certain common contingencies of these racialization and exclusion processes that make them all part and parcel of the wealthy First Europe's *dual crisis* of the *nation* and of the *welfare state* (Schierup, Hansen and Castles, 2004). This calls, in effect, for an apprehensive redevelopment of the politics of citizenship, which is capable of synthesizing both of these dimensions into a concept for an inclusive multi-ethnic welfare society beyond the nation-state. We find it – in spite of changing global and local contingencies – hereby important to retrieve the broader and more original meaning of 'social exclusion'.

Notes

1. Chamberlayne (1997: 3 ff.) provides an illuminating review of the ways in which 'social exclusion' was adopted and debated by social science in different member states. This is indeed a matter, as argued by Chamberlayne (1997: 3 ff.), depending on national traditions and current directions of social science analysis. But given *social exclusion's inherent character of a moral-political term any preference for* analytical premises and definitions will indeed be forced to state its value premises.
2. We refer here to the habitual distinction between formal and substantial citizenship as defined and discussed by, among others, Castles (1994).
3. This is, in effect, an approach to poverty that echoes the so-called relative deprivation theory of poverty, widely publicized through the influential writings of the sociologist Peter Townsend (e.g., Townsend, 1987).

4. See Close (1995: 30 ff.), Strobel (1996), and del Castillo (1994) for examples of seminal discussions concerning the European Commission's perspective on poverty and social exclusion.
5. The most notable exception is that of Britain, which is by far the best researched Western European country in this respect.
6. For example, the important anthology on deprivation and poverty, edited by Ferge and Miller (1987)
7. See the study *Preventing Racism at the Workplace* (Wrench, 1996), based on 16 detailed country reports from across the Community, and *Migrants' Insertion in the Informal Economy* (Reyneri *et al.*, 1999), a detailed TSER report on migration and the informal economy in Southern Europe, including a comparison with parts of Northern Europe.
8. http://europa.eu.int/comm/employment_social/fundamri/prog/index_en.htm
9. http://europa.eu.int/comm/employment_social/equal/index_en.cfm
10. The Swedish interim evaluation for *Equal* (PLS/IPM, 2002) presents a similar (provisional) judgment, concerning the way in which the first round of the national Equal-project has been set up in the country.
11. In particular, two reports from the European Commission in 1994: *European Social Policy* (European Commission, 1994a) and *Growth, Competitiveness, Employment* (European Commission, 1994b).
12. Schierup, C.-U., Hansen, P., and Castles, S., *Migration, Citizenship and the Welfare State. A European* Dilemma (Oxford: Oxford University Press, 2004).
13. For a detailed argument on this point, see Levitas, 1998.
14. See, for example, John Myles's (1996) revealing analysis of the development from welfare to workfare in the United States.
15. Arguments focusing on the impoverishment and deprivation of poor urban African Americans during the past three decades do, of course, not in any way reject the fact that, during the same time, a substantial African-American professional elite has consolidated its position in the United States. But in a situation marked by economic and labor market deregulation and the deterioration of general welfare state policies this has, as argued by Wilson (see 1987, 1993, 1997, 1999), become part of a convoluted social problem of race, class, and deprivation rather than a solution to poverty, social exclusion, and urban segregation. This is an issue that we discuss at length ourselves in another paper (Schierup, 2003a).
16. Black racial pride and class consciousness – embedded in a wider ongoing class struggle concerning the terms on which labor can be bought and sold – have often been conspicuously articulated in submerged conflicts between racial and ethnic minority groups in the 'ghetto'. This is vividly illustrated in Spike Lee's film *Do the Right Thing* (1989) and it formed one of the components of the Los Angeles uprising in 1992.
17. See, in particular, the work by Chris Jones and Tony Novak (1999) on Britain and, for a detailed discussion, Schierup (2003a, 2003b). For a comparison of dimensions of the United States and the British experience, see Sassen (1991) and King (1999).
18. See also the illuminating discussion of US debates on 'welfare' by Roche (1992).

19. See, for example, Ålund (2000), Mitter (1986), Morokvasic (1993), Panayiotopoulos (1996). A particularly penetrating analysis was made by Swasti Mitter (1986), who studied the intersection of class, race, and gender in constituting a heavily exploited female labor force in new 'ethnic' sweatshops produced through restructuring of the English clothing industry during the 1980s (on this, see also Schierup, 2003c).
20. An innovative theoretical perspective on the new working poor, international migration, and ethnic relations was raised by Saskia Sassen (1991, 1998) in a number of important works. Schierup (2003a) discusses strengths and weaknesses of the Sassenian approach.
21. See, for example, the edited volumes on immigration in Southern Europe by Anthias and Lazaridis (1999), King and Lazaridis (2000), and Marin Baldwin-Edwards (1999).
22. For example, the study, Migrants' Insertion in the Informal Economy (Reyneri *et al.*, 1999), which is a detailed TSER report on migration and the informal economy in Southern Europe, including a comparison with parts of Northern Europe.
23. Representing preparatory work included in a more comprehensive analysis of the contemporary European Dilemma (Schierup, Hansen and Castles, 2004).
24. Criticizing and contextualizing the arguments of, respectively, Wilson (1987), Sassen (1991), and Waldinger (1996).
25. The lifelong cumulative probability of doing time in a state or federal prison is, as estimated on the basis of the imprisonment rates of the early 1990s, 4 percent for whites, 16 percent for Latinos, and 29 percent for Blacks (according to Wacquant, 2002: 43, quoting, Bonczar and Beck, 1997: 1).
26. See, in particular, the edited volume by Mauer (2002)
27. In California, for example, subject to the so-called Prison Industry Authority (PIA) (Parenti, 1996: 232).
28. As commonly labeled by ghetto inhabitants (Wacquant, 2002: 54).
29. Term originally coined by Liepitz (1987) for describing the particularly rude character of industrial relations marking the Taylorist production processes 'exported' to low-wage 'newly industrializing countries' after the great leap in Western industrial restructuring processes from the mid-1970s onwards.
30. See, for example, Waldinger (1996), Fox Piven and Cloward (1993), and Carnoy (1994). Contemporary ethnic divisions of labor and the political economy of racialized exclusion in the Unites States and different member states of the EU are analyzed in a comparative perspective by Schierup (2003a, 2003b).
31. A number of important case studies from different countries and local settings in Europe and North America were collected by Mingione (1996b) in the volume Urban Poverty and the Underclass. See also the complex analysis of US politics on work deregulation, welfare, and workfare by Fox Piven and Cloward (1993).

References

Andall, J., Gender, Migration and Domestic Service: The Politics of Black Women in Italy (Aldershot: Ashgate, 2000).
Anthias, F., and Lazaridis, G. (eds), Into the Margins: Migration and Exclusion in Southern Europe (Aldershot, Brookfield, USA, Singapore, Sydney: Ashgate, 1999).

Baldwin-Edwards, M., and Arango, J., (eds), Immigrants and the Informal Economy in Southern Europe (London and Portland, OH: Frank Cass, 1999).

Bel Habib, H., 'Mångfald döljer proletariat', Dagens Nyheter (Stockholm: 21 February, 2001).

Bonczar, T., and Beck, A., Lifetime Likelihood of Going to State of Federal Prison. Bureau of Justice Statistics Special Report (Washington, DC: Bureau of Justice, 1997).

Bottomore, T., 'Citizenship and Social Class, Forty Years On', in Citizenship and Social Class (London: Pluto Press, 1996), pp. 55–96.

Carnoy, M., Faded Dreams: The Politics and Economics of Race in America (New York: Cambridge University Press, 1994).

Del Castillo, Y., 'A Comparative Approach to Social Exclusion: Lessons from France and Belgium', International Labor Review, 5:133 (1994), pp. 613–633.

Castles, S., 'Democracy and Multicultural Citizenship: Australian Debates and Their Relevance for Western Europe', in Bauböck, R. (ed.), From Aliens to Citizens: Redefining the Status of Immigrants in Europe (Aldershot: Avebury, 1994), pp. 3–28.

Close, P., Citizenship, Europe and Change (Basingstoke: Macmillan, 1995).

Chamberlayne, P., 'Social Exclusion: Sociological Traditions and National Contexts', Sostris Working Paper, Social Exclusion in Comparative Perspective, No. 1 (London: University of East London, Centre for Biography in Social Policy, 1997).

Dahrendorf, R., Law and Order (Boulder: Westview Press, 1985).

Dahrendorf, R., The Modern Social Conflict: An Essay on the Politics of Liberty (London: Weidenfeld & Nicolson, 1987).

Delors, J., Le nouveau concert Européen (Paris: Editions Odile Jacob, 1992).

EUMC, Diversity and Equality for Europe: Annual Report, 2001 (Brussels: European Monitoring Centre on Racism and Xenophobia, 2001).

European Commission, Background Report: The European Poverty Programme (Luxembourg: Office for Official Publications of the European Communities, 1991).

European Commission, European Social Policy: A Way Forward for the Union (Brussels: European Commission, 1994a).

European Commission, Growth, Competitiveness, Employment: The Challenges and Ways forward in the 21st Century (Brussels: European Commission, 1994b).

European Commission, Implementing the Principle of Equal Treatment between Persons Irrespective of Racial or Ethnic Origin (Brussels: The European Commission, 2000).

Ferge, Z., and Miller, M. S. (eds), Dynamics of Deprivation (Aldershot: Gower, 1987).

Fox Piven, F., and Cloward, R. A., Regulating the Poor: The Functions of Public Welfare (New York: Vintage Books, 1993).

Fox Piven, F., and Cloward, R. A., The Breaking of the American Social Compact (New York: The New Press, 1997).

Geddes, M., 'Local Partnerships and Social Exclusion in the United Kingdom: A Stake in the Market?', in Geddes, M., and Benington, J. (eds), Local Partnerships and Social Exclusion in the European Union: New Forms of Local Social Governance? (London and New York: Routledge, 2001a), pp. 170–97.

Geddes, M., and Benington, J. (eds), Local Partnerships and Social Exclusion in the European Union: New Forms of Local Social Governance? (London and New York: Routledge, 2001b).

Giddens, A., Profiles and Critiques in Social Theory (Berkeley, CA: University of California Press, 1982).

Giddens, A., The Third Way: The Renewal of Social Democracy (Oxford: Polity Press, 1998).

Hansen, P., Dilemmas of European Integration: Social Policy, Immigration and the Negative Augmentation of European Integration (Budapest: CEUS Working papers, 2002).

Hansen, P., and Schierup, C.-U, Europe's Ethnic Dilemma: Essays on Citizenship and Politics of Identity (Umea: Umea Universitet, MERGE Papers on Transcultural Studies, 1998).

Jones, C., and Novak, T., Poverty, Welfare and the Disciplinary State (London and New York: Routledge, 1999).

Jordan, B., A Theory of Poverty and Social Exclusion (Oxford: Polity Press, 1996).

Katz, M. B., The Undeserving Poor: From the War on Poverty to the War on Welfare (New York: Pantheon Books, 1989).

Kautto, M., and Heikkilä, M., 'Partnerships Against Exclusion in a Nordic Welfare State: A Difficult Mix?', in Geddes, M., and Benington, J. (eds), Local Partnerships and Social Exclusion in the European Union: New Forms of Local Social Governance? (London and New York: Routledge, 2001), pp. 46–70.

King, D., In the Name of Liberalism: Illiberal Social Policy in the United States and Britain (Oxford: Oxford University Press, 1999).

King, R., and Lazaridis, G. (eds), Eldorado or Fortress? Migration in Southern Europe (New York: St. Martin's Press, 2000).

Kostakopoulou, D., 'European Union Citizenship: Exclusion, Inclusion and the Social Dimension', in Anthias, F., and Lazaridis, G. (eds), Into the Margins: Migration and Exclusion in Southern Europe, Perspectives on Europe. Contemporary Interdisciplinary Research (Aldershot, Brookfield, USA, Singapore and Sydney: Ashgate, 1999), pp. 179–204.

Levitas, R., The Inclusive Society? Social Exclusion and New Labor (Basingstoke: Macmillan – now Palgrave Macmillan, 1998).

Liepitz, A., Mirages and Miracles: The Crisis of Global Fordism (Thetford: The Thetford Press, 1987).

Lister, R., The Exclusive Society: Citizenship and the Poor (London: Child Poverty Action Group, 1990).

Mann, M., 'Ruling Class Strategies and Citizenship', Sociology, 21:3 (London: BSA, 1987): 339–54.

Marshall, T. H., 'Citizenship and Social Class', in Marshall, T., and Bottomore T., Citizenship and Social Class (Cambridge: Cambridge University Press, 1992 (1950)).

Mauer, M., and Chesney-Lind, M. (eds), Invisible Punishment: The Collateral Consequences of Mass Imprisonment (New York: The New Press, 2002).

Mingione, E. 'Conclusion', in Mingione, E. (ed.), Urban Poverty and the Underclass: A Reader (Oxford: Blackwells, 1996a), pp. 372–83.

Mingione, E. (ed.), Urban Poverty and the Underclass: A Reader (Oxford: Blackwell, 1996b).

Mitter, S., 'Industrial Restructuring and Manufacturing Homework: Immigrant Women in the UK Clothing Industry', Capital and Class, vol. 27 (London: CSE, 1986), pp. 37–80.

Morokvasic, M., 'Immigrants in Garment Production in Paris and Berlin', in Light, I., and Bhachu, P. (eds), Immigration and Entrepreneurship: Culture, Capital and Ethnic Networks (New Brunswick and London: Transaction, 1993).

Myles, J., 'When markets fail: social welfare in Canada and the United States' in Esping-Anderson, G. (ed), Welfare States in Transition: National Adaptation in Global Economies (London: Sage, 1996), pp. 116–140.

Panayiotopoulos, P. I., 'Challenging Orthodoxies: Cypriot Entrepreneurs in the London Garment Industry', New Community, 22:3 (1996): 437–460.

Parenti, C., 'Pay Now, Pay Later: States Impose Prison Peonage', The Progressive, 60:7 (1996).

Parenti, C., Lockdown America: Police and Prisons in the Age of Crisis (London: Verso, 2000).

PLS/IPM, Interimsrapport. Gemenskapsinitiativet EQUAL i Sverige, Evaluation report (Stockholm: PLS Rambøll Management AB and Institute of Public Management, 2002).

Reyneri, E. et al., Migrants' Insertion in the Informal Economy, Deviant Behaviour and the Impact on Receiving Societies (Contract, No. SOE2-CT95-3005, Brussels: CE/DG XII- Science, Research and Development, 1999).

Roche, M., Rethinking Citizenship: Welfare, Ideology and Change in Modern Society (Oxford: Polity Press, 1992).

Rodrigues, F., and Stoer S. R., 'Partnership and Local Development in Portugal: From "Globalised Localism" to a New Form of Collective Action', in Geddes, M., and Benington J. (eds), Local Partnerships and Social Exclusion in the European Union: New Forms of Local Social Governance? (London and New York: Routledge, 2001), pp. 134–51.

Room, G. et al., Observatory on National Policies to Combat Social Exclusion, Second Annual Report (Brussels: Directorate General for Employment, Social Affairs and Industrial Relations, Commission of the European Communities, 1992).

Sassen, S., The Global City: New York, London, Tokyo (Princeton: Princeton University Press, 1991).

Sassen, S., Globalisation and its Discontents: Essays on the New Mobility of People and Money (New York: The New Press, 1998).

Schierup, C.-U., 'The Immigrants and the Crisis', Acta Sociologica, 28:1 (1985): 21–33.

Schierup, C.-U., På kulturens slagmark: mindretal og størretal taler om Danmark (Esbjerg: Southern Jutland University Press, 1993).

Schierup, C.-U., Political Economies of Exclusion: Transatlantic Convergence or Transatlantic Split? (Norrköping: Working Paper; carl-ulrik.schierup@niwl.se for e-mail requests; homepage: http://www.niwl.se, 2003a).

Schierup, C.-U., Still a European Triptych? Migration, Ethnic Divisions and the Differential Dynamics of Advanced Marginality (Norrköping: Working Paper; carl-ulrik.schierup@niwl.se for e-mail requests; homepage: http://www.niwl.se, 2003b).

Schierup, C.-U., Bloody Sub-Contracting in the Network Society (Norrköping: Working Paper; carl-ulrik.schierup@niwl.se for e-mail requests; homepage: http://www.niwl.se, 2003c).

Schierup, C.-U., Hansen, P., and Castles, S., Migration, Citizenship and the Welfare State: A European Dilemma (Oxford: Oxford University Press, 2004).

Schmitter-Heisler, B., 'Migration to Advanced Industrial Democracies: Socio-Economic and Political Factors in the Making of Minorities in the Federal Republic of Germany (1955-1988)', in Messina, A., et al. (eds), Ethnic and Racial Minorities in Advanced Industrial Democracies (New York: Greenwood Press, 1992).

Schram, S. F., After Welfare: The Culture of Postindustrial Social Policy (New York and London: New York University Press, 2000).

Silver, H., 'Social Exclusion and Social Solidarity: Three Paradigms', International Labor Review, 133:5/6, (1994): 531-78.

Slavnic, Z., 'Informell ekonomi och välfärdssamhället', in Rosing, A., Sundin, E., and Råberg, C. (eds), Marginalisering eller integration. Invandrares företagande i svensk retorik och praktik. En forskningsrapport (Stockholm: NUTEK, 2002).

Strobel, P., 'From Poverty to Exclusion: A Wage Earning Society or a Society of Human Rights?', International Social Science Journal, 148, (1996): 173-89.

Townsend, P., 'Conceptualising Poverty', in Ferge, Z., and Miller, S. M. (eds), Dynamics of Deprivation (Aldershot: Gower, 1987).

Turner, B., Citizenship and Capitalism: the Debate over Reformism (London: Allen and Unwin, 1986).

Turner, B., 'Outline of a Theory of Citizenship', Sociology, 14:2 (1990): 189-217.

Wacquant, L., 'The Rise of Advanced Marginality: Notes on its Nature and Implications', Acta Sociologica, 39:2 (1996): 121-39.

Wacquant, L., 'The New "Peculiar Institution": On the Prison as Surrogate Ghetto', Theoretical Criminology, 4:3 (2000): 377-89.

Wacquant, L., 'From Slavery to Mass Incarceration: Rethinking the "Race Question" in the US', New Left Review, 13 (2002): 41-53.

Waldinger, R., Still the Promised City? African-Americans and New Immigrants in Postindustrial New York (London and Cambridge, MA: Harvard University Press, 1996).

Wilson, W. J., The Declining Significance of Race: Blacks and Changing American Institutions (Chicago, IL and London: The University of Chicago Press, 1978).

Wilson, W. J., The Truly Disadvantaged: The Inner City, the Underclass, and Public Policy (Chicago, IL.: The University of Chicago Press, 1987).

Wilson, W. J. (ed.), The Ghetto Underclass: Social Science Perspectives (Newbury Park, London and New Delhi: Sage, 1993).

Wilson, J. W., When Work Disappears: The World of the New Urban Poor (New York: Vintage Books, 1997).

Wilson, W. J., The Bridge over the Racial Divide (Berkeley, CA and Los Angeles: University of California Press, 1999).

Wrench, J., Preventing Racism at the Workplace: European Foundation for the Improvement of Living and Working Conditions (Dublin: European Foundation for the Improvement of Living and Working Conditions, No. EF/96/23/EN, 1996).

Ålund, A., 'Ethnic Entrepreneurs and Other Migrants in the Tracks of Migration': Self-Employment, Gender and Migration (Paper for the conference in San Feliu de Guixols. A EuroConference EURESCO, 28 October to 2 November 2000).

7

The Europeanization of Anti-Discrimination in Britain and France

Andrew Geddes and Virginie Guiraudon

7.1 Introduction

The politics of immigration in Britain and France now constitute interesting examples of the scope, reach, potential, and limits of European integration. There is something new here and the European Union (EU) could be largely ignored in what were essentially domestic debates about immigration and its effects on the two societies. The EU's reach into these issues could be seen as surprising because immigration issues combine symbolic resonance with high levels of political sensitivity. In the words of Stanley Hoffmann (1966), states may well be loath to expose to the supranational method issues such as immigration and immigrant politics that are closely linked to their identities as states. If they were to play this dangerous game of Russian roulette, as Hoffmann put it, they would do so only if the gun was filled with blanks. European integration would thus be more likely to occur when it sustained and fortified state identities rather than undermining and eroding them.

What, then, are we to make of EU developments? Since the 1980s we see a growing EU role in the areas of immigration and asylum that accelerated after the 1997 Amsterdam Treaty, which also added a new Article 13 to the Treaty of Rome (Geddes, 2000). Article 13 enabled the Council of Ministers to take action to combat discrimination on grounds of sex, ethnic and racial origin, religion and belief, disability, age, and sexual orientation. Article 13 entered into force when the Treaty had been ratified by all member states on 1 May 1999. The purpose of this chapter is to analyze and explain these developments and its effects on Britain and France. The chapter has two main tasks. One is to analyze when, how, and why Article 13 was added to the Treaty of Rome and the role played by Britain and France. The chapter's second task is to explore the scope for 'Europeanization' of immigrant politics and anti-discrimination in Britain and France, as well as thinking about what this might mean in terms of adaptation processes and pressures. It is shown that powerful frames associated with the politics of immigration sustained and underpinned the development of EU competencies in these areas. The first of these was a powerful anti-fascist frame that fuelled much support for EU action in the areas of racism and xenophobia. The second was linked to rather more specific EU aspects of EC law, namely the principle of equal treatment and already existing anti-discrimination law, particularly that relating to gender. It was these two frames that are particularly evident in the debate about inserting Article 13 into the Treaty and the subsequent move to turn this Treaty article into Community law, as happened in June 2000 and November 2000 when anti-discrimination directives were introduced. The third frame was a more specific anti-discrimination frame closely linked to actually existing policy frameworks in Britain and the Netherlands. The ways in which these acquired some purchase at EU level and were then to be broadly reflected in the resultant legislation is an interesting outcome of these debates and tells us quite a lot about the constitution of the EU as a political field and the kinds of political and social capital that are privileged within it. The fourth frame is a relative newcomer to the scene and thus far possesses more resonance at national than EU level. It involves a shift in the debate about the integration of migrant newcomers to emphasize adaptation through, for example, language acquisition combined with the contention that admission policies should be motivated at least to some extent by considerations of the 'integration capacities' of immigrant newcomers (Groenendijk, 2004). How these various frames will then be absorbed within the domestic politics of the two countries is a different question and one that will also be explored.

7.2   Analyzing the impact of EU competencies

There can be two broad areas of focus when analyzing the impact of EU competencies on British and French approaches to integration and anti-discrimination. One is on European integration and the other is on the impact of European integration on domestic politics, or Europeanization. The first – European integration – centers on the processes of negotiation whereby EU Member States agreed to the inclusion of a new Article 13 in the Treaty of Rome covering anti-discrimination, and then agreed in June and November 2000 in two EU Council Directives. In negotiations the analytical focus is on how, why, and when an anti-discrimination framework was included in the Treaty and then enacted, and its relation to existing frameworks in Britain and France. In this area we see closer fit with Britain than with France, so there is a particular emphasis on explaining why France agreed to measures that did not seem to fit very closely with existing approaches. This process of negotiation could be seen as encapsulating the kind of 'two-level games' that Putnam (1988) referred to where preferences at national level (which we could assume to be fairly well embedded in Britain and France) are accommodated at EU level. The EU was proceeding from a low base in this area, which makes some of the more recent developments even more significant because they mark a leveling up of national responses rather than the more usual leveling down and lowest common denominator response. In a decision-making setting where there is a reliance on unanimity then the preferences of the most reluctant states will not determine the outcome, but can have a decisive effect on the range of possible outcomes (Moravscik, 1993). In the area of anti-discrimination we see that despite the reliance on unanimity, there was a legal outcome in terms of the two anti-discrimination directives that far exceeded the provisions in the national laws of most member states. We turn to the explanation for this shortly.

The second broad area of focus is on adaptation by states to measures agreed at EU level, which points toward the burgeoning amount of research focused on so-called Europeanization. In the case of the anti-discrimination directives, transposition is required by law, but the use of a directive as the preferred legal instrument does allow some margins for flexibility when deciding the way in which implementation will occur. Later in this chapter we move on to examine the debate about Europeanization and its application to anti-discrimination legislation in Britain and France. At this stage, suffice to note Sartori's (1970: 1038) caution that 'we cannot measure it until we first know what it is that we are measuring.'

7.3 The development of European competencies

Article 13 of the Amsterdam Treaty gave the EU the power to act in the area of anti-discrimination. The bar was set quite high, though, because EU action would require unanimous agreement in the Council of Ministers. This was an area where intergovernmental forces manifest in the Council were strong and where supranational institutions such as the Commission, the European Parliament, and the European Court of Justice were dependent on the political will of the member states. Yet within three years, two directives had been introduced. On 29 June 2000 a directive was agreed in the Council on the implementation of the principle of equal treatment between persons irrespective of racial or ethnic origin (Council Directive 2000/43/EC 29 June 2000). In November 2000 its sister directive established a general framework for equal treatment in employment and occupation (Council Directive 2000/78/EC 27 November 2000). Transposition into national law was due to be completed by 2003. This does mark a significant shift in anti-discrimination politics because: 'Through the EU legislator, standards have been significantly raised in at least 25 countries, a change that in today's climate it is hard to imagine could (or would willingly) be realized by the respective national parliaments acting alone (Chopin, Cormack and Niessen, 2004: 1). As a side note it is also worth noting that the particular legal instrument chosen has some significance. The EU has the capacity to introduce regulations and directives both of which are legal instruments that bind member states and that must be implemented. A regulation leaves little margin for flexibility as it must be introduced as stipulated. A directive, on the other hand, is a more flexible instrument than a regulation because it allows for flexibility by member states when deciding how to incorporate the measures in national law.

In addition to the introduction of anti-discrimination legislation it is also worth noting that the EU has extended its reach into other areas that affect the rights and conditions of migrants and their families. In September 2003 a directive on family reunification was agreed by the Council of Ministers. This codifies a right to family reunion, sets admission conditions, gives some protection against expulsion, gives admitted family members access to the labor market and equal treatment. As Groenendijk (2004: 118) put it, this is 'an important document [although] the level of protection is rather low and the requirements are high' (Groenendijk, 2004: 118). There is, however, a standstill clause that prevents member states introducing more restrictive national rules. In November 2003 a directive on the status of third-country nationals who are long-term residents was introduced. This secures residence status plus legal and social rights 'comparable but not equal to' EU citizenship (Groenendijk, 2004: 121). This includes free movement rights for third-country nationals (TCNs) after five years residence. Free movement, rights of residence and anti-discrimination would all seem to accord with notions of 'rights-based politics' as advanced by Hollifield (1992) and could raise the prospect of the opening of social and political spaces for migrants at supranational level and linked to the distinct institutional setting at that level centered on the

Commission, European Parliament, European Court of Justice, and Council of Ministers.

The rights-based dimension of EU law and politics has been underdeveloped in areas such as anti-discrimination. Article 14 of the European Convention on Human Rights does state that: 'The enjoyment of the rights and freedoms set forth in this Convention shall be secured without discrimination on any ground such as sex, race, color, language, religion, political or other opinion, national or social origin, association with a national minority, property, birth or other status.' The Treaty of Paris creating the EU's forerunner, the European Coal and Steel Community Treaty contained no specific requirement for the member states or the institutions of the Communities to observe human rights. Pressure grew during the 1970s for acknowledgement of the importance of human rights. In 1977 a Joint Declaration by the Council, Commission, and European Parliament issued a non-binding Joint Declaration affirming 'the prime importance they attach to fundamental rights'. In the Maastricht Treaty Article F.2 required the Union to 'respect fundamental rights, as guaranteed by the European Convention for the Protection of Human Rights and Fundamental Freedoms ... and as they result from the constitutional traditions common to the member states, as general principles of Community law'. But neither the 1977 Joint Declaration nor Article F of the Treaty on the European Union (TEU) gave the European Community (EC) a specific competence to adopt general measures in the sphere of human rights, or to combat discrimination.

The attitudes of the British and French governments to developments in the area of anti-discrimination are interesting. Britain has long been characterized as an 'awkward partner' (George, 1998; Geddes, 2004). This awkwardness has been evident with regards to immigration and immigrant politics. Britain did agree to the June 2000 anti-discrimination directives because this was a relatively costless measure that mapped well with an already existing national framework. In effect, the British framework has been 'uploaded' to EU level. Britain did, however, secure an opt-out from Title IV of the Amsterdam Treaty covering free movement, immigration, asylum, and visas. This gave it the right to opt out of the family reunion directive and the directive covering the rights of long-term residents, which it chose to do. The British government has tended to opt in to the more coercive aspects of the EU framework and opt out of those that are rights-extending (Geddes, 2005). For the French government, it could be anticipated that the anti-discrimination directive would be a real pressure point because, as we will see, this measure brought into European law notions of indirect discrimination, 'race', and ethnicity that had been evident in countries such as the United Kingdom and the Netherlands, where 'ethnic minorities' had long been a policy referent, but not in France. In this first section the task is to explore the reasons why France agreed to anti-discrimination measures that did not appear to fit well with a national approach to immigration and immigrant politics.

To address this issue we use the concept of frames as heuristic devices that individuals use to perceive, organize, and make sense of the social world (Goffman, 1974). There is also a strategic element to the use of frames because individuals and actors (such as national governments, EU institutions, and NGOs) may seek to ensure that their particular framing of an issue resonates and becomes dominant. It may also be the case that there is sufficient ambiguity in a EU-level frame that it is possible for it to make sense in a variety of national contexts because, for example, it relates to a rather vague notion such as 'social cohesion' or because it fits with broader EU economic objectives such as the 'Lisbon process' of single-market consolidation and economic reform (Geddes and Guiraudon, 2004). We identify an anti-fascist frame that was particularly instrumental in securing French support for anti-discrimination legislation. We also see an equal treatment and equality frame with a sounder EU legal basis that served as a template for proposals in this area and that did, to some extent, make sense for the French even though its application to areas of race and ethnicity was potentially problematic. We identify, too, a more specific anti-discrimination frame linked to existing approaches in Britain and the Netherlands. The fourth frame that we identify is the newest and perhaps, too, the one with most relevance for ongoing debates about immigrant integration in the Member States and with regards to the EU role. This is the way in which admission policies are being linked to integration capacities. This has been most evident in the Netherlands, Germany, and Austria, but has been a theme, too, in discussion of immigrant integration in the United Kingdom and France (Groenendijk, 2004).

As a staring point, it is also worth noting the low base from which EU developments in this area proceeded. In 1995 Britain and France were two of only six EU Member States that had specific legislation to combat racism (the others being Austria, Belgium, the Netherlands, and Sweden (ECRI, 1995). The British House of Lords reported in 1999 that

> While some Member States, such as Ireland, the Netherlands and Sweden, have wide-ranging legislation going in some respects beyond that found in the UK, others offer little or no statutory protection against discrimination. There is no uniformity. This means not only

that there is little protection in some parts of the Community for the fundamental rights of, for example, the disabled or members of racial minorities, but also that the principle of free movement is likely to be compromised.

In the early 1990s, following racist and xenophobic attacks, there was growing concern, but how could this be translated into supranational action? Here we need to make connections between the set of issues associated with anti-discrimination and the institutional setting at EU level. In particular, it is important to note that there is at the EU level a clear and well-defined role for expertise. This does not mean that the EU is necessarily a technocracy, but that expertise does play a key role in EU decision-making 'because many EU issues are technical concerns and of low political salience, and this makes them particularly disposed to this decision-making style (Radaelli, 2000: 1). This has tended to privilege networks of expertise, as we will see shortly when the fortunes of two groups active in this area, the Starting Line Group (SLG) and the European Union Migrants Forum (EUMF) are contrasted.

Prior to the Amsterdam Treaty there was no legal basis for EU action in the area of anti-discrimination on grounds of race and ethic origin. Any proposal from the Commission would encounter the demand of 'what's the legal base' from the member states. In the absence of such a base, action was unlikely. The first battle was to secure a Treaty reference. Prior to such a reference, initiatives had tended to falter because of resistance from within the Council. There were, however, cognate frames that could be sued to muster some legal and political resources behind the claim for inclusion of these areas within the EU legal framework. One such cognate framework was in the area of gender equality in which the EU had developed a substantial profile since the inclusion of gender provisions in the Treaty of Rome in 1957. Article 119 of the EC Treaty, member states should 'maintain the application of the principle that men and women should receive equal pay for equal work'. In 1976 the Equal Treatment Directive was adopted to combat sex discrimination in three broad employment-related areas: access to employment and promotion, vocational training, and working conditions, and also provided the basis for an argument that the principle of anti-discrimination should be extended beyond its rather limited focus on nationality and gender. Such arguments were later to provide some justification, as well as a frame for the adoption of anti-discrimination directives (Tyson, 2001). The gender discrimination frame was useful for the French because this was an area in which they had experience and, indeed, had been central to the gender equality provisions of the Rome Treaty, which matched those in French domestic law. There is, however, an important and well-known difference between gender and ethnicity because the French authorities do collect statistics on gender, but do not on ethnic origin. The point is, however, that an equal treatment frame did possess some European resonance. On its own, however, it was unlikely to prove sufficient if the intergovernmental block was to be broken.

We can point to a growing political momentum behind claims for expanded EU competencies in these areas during the 1990s. Of particular importance were attempts to mobilize the first two of the frames that were discussed earlier: anti-fascism and equal treatment. For much of the 1980s and 1990s action against racism and xenophobia was largely declaratory. In 1986 the European Parliament, Council of Ministers, and the Commission issued a 'Joint Declaration against Racism and Xenophobia', partly impelled by the success of Far-Right parties at the 1984 European Parliament elections. A European parliament resolution on racism and xenophobia was passed on 2 December 1993, followed by a further resolution on racism, xenophobia, and anti-Semitism in 1994. In June 1994, the Corfu summit of EU heads of government created the Consultative Commission on Racism and Xenophobia (ECCRX). In May 1996 the final ECCRX report called for an amendment to the Treaty of Rome to take action against discrimination on grounds of race, ethnic origin, or religion. In its 1994 White Paper on Social Policy the Commission called for competence to be extended to include racial discrimination. In 1995 a Commission communication proposed that 1997 be designated as the European year Against Racism. During 1997 a European Monitoring Centre on Racism and Xenophobia (EMCRX) was also established

Anti-discrimination was an issue covered by the 1996 Inter-Governmental Conference (IGC). In the run-up to the 1996 IGC the United Kingdom was the only member state to be openly opposed to the inclusion of a non-discrimination article in the Treaty, despite, or perhaps because of, its own relatively advanced domestic legislation in the field (House of Lords, 1999). On the one hand, the British were awkward in the sense that the Conservative government's White Paper on the IGC argued that 'the problems of discrimination (particularly on such sensitive questions as race and religion) are best dealt with ... through national legislation. Solutions need to be tailored to the particular circumstances and traditions of each Member State' (Foreign and Commonwealth Office, 1996). There was also a suspicion among UK organizations such as the Commission for Racial Equality (CRE) that EU legislation could water down the more advanced – as they saw it – British framework (Favell, 2001). While other member states could agree on the issue, it was more difficult to reach agreement on the specifics. In particular, there was little desire among the member states for the amended Treaty to include any reference to discrimination on grounds other than sex, race, and religion. Finland proposed a 'general prohibition of discrimination, including rejection of racism and xenophobia', and similar suggestions were made by the Foreign Ministers of the Benelux states. In October 1996, Austria and Italy made a joint call for the Union to 'ensure non-discrimination on grounds particularly of race, color, nationality, sex, language, religion, political or other opinion ... disability, or sexual preference'. Following the change of government in Britain in May 1997, a policy change took place. The British opposition was removed in the final stages of negotiation leading up to the agreement of the text of the Amsterdam Treaty in June 1997. Article 13 treated all the grounds of discrimination equally, but it was the political will to combat racial discrimination that was strongest as most member states already had some constitutional or statutory provisions in this area. The French government was viewed as having appreciated the general wording of Article 13, since it complied with the French constitutional concept of equality, but acknowledged during the negotiations that it had difficulty with the expression 'ethnic origin' and would have preferred 'regional origin'(House of Lords, 1999).

To understand the ways in which the debate was framed means looking beyond the often declaratory tone of various resolutions condemning racism and exploring more closely a network of actors that developed in the 1990s around anti-discrimination issues. It is here that we see the relevance of the equal treatment frame based in European law and of the existing anti-discrimination policy frameworks as they had developed in Britain and the Netherlands. Thus while the decision-making process was heavily dependent on the conjunctural context within intergovernmental forums, the tone and content of the proposals, and the ways in which the issues were understood can be linked to a network of actors including NGOs and academic activists with good links to European institutions, particularly the Commission and the Parliament.

The most influential group was the Starting Line Group (SLG) founded in 1991, following racist and xenophobic attacks, as an initiative led by the Dutch NBR (National Office Against Racism), the British CRE and the Churches Commission for Migrants in Europe. This developed into a network of nearly 400 organizations including NGOs, trade unions, churches, experts, and academics (Chopin, 1999: 111). The contrast with the Commission-sponsored EUMF is quite stark. The EUMF was a classic Commission device to co-opt 'civil society', but the main concern of EUMF organizations tended to be with debates and dilemmas in their countries of origin rather than with the rather more technical nature of EU-level developments that could appear somewhat detached from these national contexts. The SLG, in contrast, focused on the mobilization of expertise that can be highly valued by the Commission, which is a relatively small institution that often relies quite heavily on outside expertise in the development of policy (Danese, 1998; Geddes, 2000; Guiraudon, 2001).

NGOs played no role in the negotiation of the directive and were not at the negotiating able, but the kinds of ideas mobilized by the SLG were present and did have some influence on the content of legislation because they had been fed into the Commission policy development process and had attracted allies within the European parliament and with organizations in the member states. The negotiation of the 'race directive' is interesting because, from the Commission proposal in December 1999 to final agreement, a world record was set for legislation in a new area. This is all the more surprising because this was a complex issue as a new inter-sectoral area that encompassed social affairs and employment primarily but linked to other ministries such as interior departments of state. Of importance within negotiations is the role of the Council presidency, which chairs meetings for a six-month period. The Portuguese presidency in the first six months of 2000 was keen to reach a deal, although this would be complex with two proposed directives and an action plan. Presidency plays a key role. The presidency was, however, like all others, keen to point to achievements.

The dynamics of negotiation were heavily dependent on specific conjunctural factors, which also help us understand why a leveling up rather than lowering down of standards occurred. There was a very good reason why the directives were agreed, namely the entry of Jörg Haider's extreme right-wing Freedom Party into the Austrian coalition on 3 February 2000. Martine Aubry, the French Minister for Social Affairs was one of the strongest in calling for the 'quarantining' of the Austrian government. This marked the deployment of a powerful anti-fascist frame, but was in the context of negotiations centered on a rather more specific set of proposals about anti-discrimination legislation. The entry into the Austrian coalition of Haider's party impelled the negotiations, but did not determine the scope and content of the legislation. This we explain is why, at a particular point in time, agreement was reached by focusing on the conjunctural dynamics of intergovernmental negotiation. In order to understand the content of the proposals we need to broaden the discussion and analyze the range of mobilizations that occurred at the EU level around the issue of anti-discrimination and how organized interests within the Starting Line Group influenced the content of legislation in a way that reflected approaches that were quite familiar in Britain, but rather alien in the context of French approaches to immigrant integration.

It would have been difficult for the French government to back away from the Commission's anti-racism proposals while denouncing the Austrian government. In February 2000 a declaration from the French, Belgians, and Italians called for swift adoption of the Commission anti-discrimination proposals 'to promote a diversified, multicultural Europe which espouses equal opportunities for all citizens irrespective of gender, origin, race, religion, opinions, age or disability' (cited in Geddes and Guiraudon, 2004: 347). The negotiations were conducted swiftly, mostly in English, without translation of documents which saved time, and with phone calls to national capitals rather than references back that could take up to three weeks. The French secured a derogation that allowed them to monitor the effects of the legislation without having to collect data on ethnicity. For the British, their bottom line during the negotiations was that the anti-discrimination legislation would not relate to the immigration authorities. As we will see, however, recent decisions of the UK courts have included the immigration authorities within the scope of race relations legislation. The outcome was the directive of 29 June 2000 on the implementation of the principle of equal treatment between persons irrespective of racial or ethnic origin (Council Directive 2000/43/EC 29 June 2000) followed in November 2000 by its sister directive establishing a general framework for equal treatment in employment and occupation (Council Directive 2000/78/EC 27 November 2000).

7.4   The Europeanization of anti-discrimination

What impact have these developments had on anti-discrimination politics in Britain and France? Given that these measures were only introduced relatively recently, it's hard to come to definitive conclusions about impact. What we can do is explore the process of adaptation, some of the issues raised, and their relationship to the various frames discussed earlier.

First, however, it is necessary to consider the concept of Europeanization. Following Buller and Gamble, we understand Europeanization as the situation where distinct modes of European governance affect aspects of domestic politics (Buller and Gamble, 2002). These aspects can include formal and informal rules, beliefs, paradigms, styles, ideologies, and culture (Dyson, 2000; Radaelli, 2000). Europeanization has become a hot research topic and there are some risks associated with its deployment. The first of these is 'concept stretching', whereby terms are used for new situations for which they were not designed. Alternatively the 'old wine in new bottles' syndrome may apply where new terms are constantly invented when there might be old ones that work just as well. In addition to this there is a level of analysis problem which centers on the question of how to analyze the different types of location in which sources of explanation can be found (Buzan, 1995). This is particularly the case in a complex multi-level polity like the EU, where national, supranational, and international institutions plus a range of NGOs operate within the multi-level polity.

If the concept of Europeanization is to be useful then it also needs to be distinct from others (concept intension) and be capable of specifying the events to be covered (concept extension) (Gerring, 1999). One example of intension could be the need to make a distinction from 'rights-based politics' such as that adopted by Hollifield (1992) or from Freeman's (1995) work derived from the politics of regulation. There are, however, grounds to suppose that the EU is distinct as a form of political association with no exact parallels or precedents (Ruggie, 1998). If the focus is on diffusion of EU practices and norms and concept extension, then it may be that there is already an existing body of work on policy transfer that could be used, whereby policies, institutions, and administrative arrangements in use at one time and/or place are used in the development of policies, institutions, and administrative arrangements in another time and/or place (Dolowitz and Marsh, 1996: 334). There may thus be scope for processes of Europeanization that are not linked to the EU. For example, Austria, Germany, and the Netherlands have been to the fore in pushing for links to be made between admissions policies and integration capacities (Groenendijk, 2004). These trends have been evident in other EU Member States too, and have even led some commentators to refer to a 'return to assimilation' (Brubaker, 2001). These trends may have pan-European dimensions, but may not necessarily be linked to the EU as a structure of governance.

The debate about Europeanization thus tends to center on adaptation in domestic politics to new patterns of EU governance. It is important to note that this need not entail convergence or harmonization. Europeanization does not mean the adoption of a one-size-fits-all EU template. Convergence and harmonization may be the outcomes, but it is equally plausible to suppose that there may be divergence. Also, adaptation may take various forms (Knill and Lehmkuhl, 1999). It could be 'coercive' with EU prescriptions, which is unlikely in the area of anti-discrimination given national sensitivities and the choice of directives as the legal instrument. Adaptation could be 'negative' in the sense that it creates new opportunity structures that empower domestic actors. It could be 'framing' (the softest forms of adaptation) where EU effects are more indirect through effects on the beliefs of domestic decision makers, which leads them to pursue different strategies. McCrudden (2005: 17) identifies two risks associated with reliance on an EU-directive model. These are, first, superficial consistency and, second, adaptation seen as sufficient rather than a necessary tool for future policy development. As stated earlier, it is too early to judge effects. What we can analyze is adaptation. We can also hypothesize that given the issue area and the legal instruments used; it is more likely that negative and/or framing integration will be the outcomes with effects on the opportunity structures in the area of pro-migrant politics, and on the mindsets of actors involved in these areas. We can now move on to explore adaptation in Britain and France.

The Law of 16 November 2001 covered the main points of the EU directives and their transposition into French law relating to employment and training, and introduced the concept of indirect discrimination into French law with enforcement remaining subject to the discretion of different magistrates 'recent case law does not appear to encourage them to apply it explicitly' (Kretzschmar, Ebermeyer and Dehoumon, 2004: 33). In April 2003, the *Conseil interministériel à l'intégration* defined government priorities regarding integration and combating discrimination. The first was centered on new migrants and integration for those that want it, with particular emphasis on French-language training. The next priority was to combat discrimination with emphasis on the urban dimension. The Perben Law of March 2004 stiffened penalties for discrimination to up to five years imprisonment and fines of up to €45,000 in provision of goods or services, in the normal exercise of any economic activity, in hiring, in the disciplining or dismissal of an individual, in employment, in applications for internships or in training in employment. Fines of up to €75,000 were authorized when discrimination was based on a refusal to provide goods or services in a public place, or with the aim of denying access to a public place. Law 2004–1486 creating the High Authority against Discrimination and for Equality (HALDE) completed the transposition of Directive 2000/43 and was adopted on 21 December 2004. This HALDE Law entered into force on 1 February 2005 and created an independent administrative body, the High Authority, with competence for all forms of discrimination forbidden by the laws of the republic, including that of race or origin. The High Authority will ensure the application of the principle of equal treatment and have the power to make recommendations on all issues relating to equality, identify and promote good practice, conduct studies and research, and investigate individual and collective complaints. The HALDE Law also created in Article 19 a general principle prohibiting direct and indirect discrimination on the basis of 'race' and origin and provides for the necessary shift in the burden of proof in civil and administrative cases as regards salaried workers, public agents, self-employed and non-salaried workers, and covers social protection, health, social benefits, education, access to goods and services, membership of, and involvement in, an organization of workers, professionals, or employers, working conditions and access to employment (Migration Policy Group, 2005: 49). In France, we can see the impact of EU governance through the introduction of the concept of indirect discrimination and the establishment of an independent body responsible for monitoring application of the law and combating discrimination.

For transposition of the anti-discrimination directives, the UK government chose to impose the measures by regulations introduced under the European Communities Act (1972) rather than by primary legislation. The effect of this has been to make the legislation in the United Kingdom 'more complicated, more confusing and less accessible than it had been before these amendments'. The reason for this is that the 1972 European Communities Act strictly limits the content of transposition regulations to the scope of the relevant directives. Thus, prior to the directives, the Race Relations Act offered protection on grounds of color, race, nationality (including citizenship), and ethnic and national origins. The Race Directive is concerned with equal treatment irrespective of racial or ethnic origin, which means that all the regulations introduced to implement the EU legislation apply only to racial and ethnic origins.

The key development in UK race relations occurred in the aftermath of the failed police enquiry into the racist murder of Stephen Lawrence. The 2000 amendment to the race relations legislation extended the scope to cover nearly all functions of public authorities and gave public authorities a statutory duty to promote race equality. Interestingly, one effect of this extension of the scope of the legislation has been to erode the British government's bottom line during the negotiation of the anti-discrimination directives. The UK government had been keen to ensure that the immigration authorities would be free to discriminate on the basis of racial or ethnic origin when targeting certain groups for purposes of immigration control. In a landmark case in 2004 this was ruled unlawful.[1]

The UK authorities had introduced pre-entry controls exercised inside Prague airport. It was found that Roma were 400 times more likely to be stopped at these controls. This was the first test of the 2000 Race Relations Amendment Act, which extended provisions to include public bodies. Article 19D of the 2000 legislation did permit discrimination on the grounds of nationality, or ethnic or national origin in relation to certain immigration and nationality functions where the act of discrimination was authorized by the minister. The Court of Appeal and the High Court had ruled that Roma were more likely to be seeking asylum and thus discrimination was justified. The House of Lords overturned these rulings from lower courts and argued that this was discrimination that contravened Section 1.(1)(a) of the Race Relations Act 1976. It was argued that direct discrimination could not be justified and that it was wrong to treat all members of the group in the same way on the basis of a stereotype rather than as individuals.

7.5 Conclusion

This chapter has explored the ways in which European integration now affects debates about anti-discrimination and immigrant integration in Britain and France. The focus was on both the development of EU competencies (European integration) and the scope for these emergent forms of European governance to affect domestic political processes in Britain and France (Europeanization). The chapter began by exploring the dynamics of inter-governmental negotiation surrounding the insertion of Article 13 dealing with anti-discrimination in the Amsterdam Treaty, and the subsequent negotiation of the June 2000 and November 2000 anti-discrimination directives. It was shown that particular conjunctural dynamics associated with the entry of Haider's Freedom Party into the Austrian coalition had an important effect on the negotiations. The opposition to the Austrian coalition drew from an anti-fascist frame that made it difficult for the French government to back away from the Commission anti-discrimination proposals.

These proposals did, however, reflect the ideas of a network of activists and NGOs that had been active in this field in the 1990s. While they were not present at the negotiating table, their ideas were. The understanding of anti-discrimination at EU level reflected an Anglo-Dutch paradigm. There was thus a good fit with existing British approaches, but grounds for supposing that there could be more implementation problems for the French authorities. The insertion of a derogation precluding the collection of data on ethnic origin did, however, ease the French position. The use of a directive as the preferred legal instrument also allowed for flexibility during the implementation process.

The chapter's discussion then moved on to explore the scope for Europeanization of the anti-discrimination politics in the two countries. A discussion of Europeanization demonstrated the scope for pressures to emanate from the EU but for there also to be scope for cross-border diffusion of ideas and practices concerning anti-discrimination and immigrant integration that are not necessarily linked to the EU. Different forms of adaptation to EU requirements were also identified. While it is still too early to judge effects, the discussion thus far suggests that the effects of EU anti-discrimination legislation are unlikely to be direct and 'coercive'. Instead, we are more likely to see 'negative' adaptation where structures of political opportunity may be reconfigured as a result of developing EU competencies or 'framing' effects where the mindsets of actors involved in these areas change as a result of European integration.

Note

1. R v. Immigration Officer at Prague Airport and another *ex parte* European Roma Rights Centre and others, 9 December 2004 (2000) UKHL 55.

References

Brubaker, R., 'The Return of Assimilation? Changing Perspectives on Immigration and its Sequels in France, Germany and the United States', *Ethnic and Racial Studies*, 24:4 (2001): 531–48.

Buller, J., and Gamble, A., 'Conceptualizing Europeanization', *Public Policy and Administration*, 17:2 (2002): 4–24.

Buzan, B, 'The level of analysis problem in international relations reconsidered' in Booth, K., and Smith, S. (eds), *International Relations Theory Today* (Cambridge: Polity, 1995).

Calvès, G., ' "Il n'y a pas de race ici": le modèle français à l'épreuve de l'intégration européenne', *Critique Internationale*, 17 (2002): 173–86.

Chopin, I., *Campaigning against Racism and Xenophobia: From a Legislative Perspective at European Level* (Brussels: European Network Against Racism, 1999).

Chopin, I., Cormack, J., and Niessen, J. *The Implementation of European Anti-Discrimination Legislation: Work in Progress* (Brussels: Migration Policy Group, 2004).

Danese, G., 'Transnational Collective Action in Europe: The Case of Migrants in Italy and Spain', *Journal of Ethnic and Migration Studies*, 24:4 (1998): 613–25.

Dolowitzm D., and Marsh, D., 'Who Learns What from Whom?' A Review of the Policy Transfer Literature', *Political Studies*, 44:2 (1996): 343–57.

Dyson, K., 'EMU as Europeanization: Convergence, Diversity and Contingency', *Journal of Common Market Studies*, 38:4 (2000): 645–66.

ECRI, *A Basket of Good Practices* (Strasbourg: Council of Europe, 1995).

Favell, A., *Philosophies of Integration: Immigration and the Idea of Citizenship in Britain and France* (Basingstoke: Palgrave Macmillan, 2001).

Foreign and Commonwealth Office, *Partnership of Nations: The British Approach to the European Union Intergovernmental Conference 1996* (London: HMSO, 1996).

Freeman, G., 'Modes of Immigration Politics in Liberal States', *International Migration Review*, 29:4 (1995): 881–913.

Geddes, A., *Immigration and European Integration: Towards Fortress Europe?* (Manchester: Manchester University Press, 2000).

Geddes, A., *The European Union and British Politics* (Basingstoke: Palgrave Macmillan, 2004).

Geddes, A., 'Getting the Best of Both Worlds: Britain, the EU and Migration Policy', *International Affairs*, 81:4 (2005): 723–40.

Geddes, A., and Guiraudon, V., 'Britain and France and EU Anti-Discrimination Policy: The Emergence of an EU Policy Paradigm', *West European Politics*, 27:2 (2004): 334–53.

George, S., *An Awkward Partner: Britain in the European Union* (Oxford: Oxford University Press, 1998).

Gerring, J., 'What Makes a Concept Good: A Critical Framework for Understanding Concept Formation in the Social Sciences', *Polity*, 31:3 (1999): 357–93.

Goffman, E., *Frame Analysis* (New York: Harper, 1974).

Groenendijk, K., 'Legal Concepts of Integration in EU Migration Law', *European Journal of Migration and Law*, 6:2 (2004): 111–26.

Guiraudon, V., 'European Integration and Migration Policy: Vertical Policy-Making as Venue Shopping', *Journal of Common Market Studies*, 27:2 (2001): 334–53.

Guiraudon, V., 'Immigration Policy and Politics', in A. Cole, P. Le Gales, and J. Levy (eds), *Developments in French Politics* (Basingstoke: Palgrave Macmillan, 2005).

Hoffman, S., 'Obstinate or Obsolete? The Fate of the Nation State and the Case of Western Europe', *Deadalus*, 95: 3 (1966): 862–915.

Hollifield, J., *Immigrants, States and Markets: The Political Economy of Migration in Europe* (Cambridge, MA: Harvard University Press, 1992).

House of Lords, *EU Proposals to Combat Discrimination* (London: House of Lords, 1999).

Knill, C., 'Cross-National Policy Convergence: Concepts, Approaches and Explanatory Factors', *Journal of European Public Policy*, 12:5 (2005): 764–74.

Knill, C., and Lehmkuhl D., 'How Europe Matters: Different Mechanisms of Europeanization', *European Integration On-Line Papers*, 3 (1999): http://eiop.or.at/eiop/texte/1999-007a.htm

Kretzschmar, C., Ebermeyer, S., and Dehoumon, M., 'Discrimination Based on Racial and Ethnic Origin: France' in Chopin, I., Cormack, J., and Niessen, J. (eds), *The Implementation of European Anti-Discrimination Legislation* (Brussels: Migration Policy Group, 2004).

McCrudden, C. 'Thinking about the Discrimination Directives', European Anti-Discrimination Law Review 1 (2005): 17–23.

Moravscik, A., 'Preferences and Power in the European Community: A Liberal Intergovernmentalist Approach', *Journal of Common Market Studies*, 31:4 (1993): 473–524.

Migration Policy Group, *European Anti-Discrimination Law Review*, 2 (2005).

Putnam, R., 'Diplomacy and domestic policies: the logic of two-level games', *International Organization*, 42: 3 (1988): 427–60.

Radaelli, C., 'Whither Europeanization: Concept Stretching and Substantive Change', *European Integration On-Line Papers*, 4:8 (2000): http://eiop.or.at/eiop/texte/2000–008a.htm

Ruggie, J., *Constructing the World Polity* (London: Routledge, 1998).

Sartori, G., 'Concept Misinformation in Comparative Politics', *American Political Science Review*, 64:4 (1970): 1033–53.

Singer, J., 'The Level of Analysis Problem in International Relations', in J. Roseneau (ed.), *International Politics and Foreign Policy* (New York: Free Press, 1969).

Tyson, A., 'The Negotiation of the European Community Directive on Anti-Discrimination', *European Journal of Migration and Law*, 3:2 (2001): 199–229.

8
Religious Discrimination: Muslims Claiming Equality in the EU

Valérie Amiraux

8.1 Introduction

Let's imagine a young woman queuing for her first visit to a job center. She has dark skin and wears a colorful headscarf. She is carrying a file on which her long oriental name is written. It is longer than the line she had to write it down on. Without following her through the complexities of job center administration, what do you think you would notice first as a 'white' non-Muslim spectator of the scene? Her gender, her different skin color, her ethnic origin, or her religious affiliation as indicated by the headscarf? Which is the most visible of these signs? Where is difference more striking? Let's now suppose that the dialogue with the job center officer is aggressive and ends up with the young girl crying and the officer yelling at her that she will never be accepted as a job seeker in Britain. What could be the motive? Her bad English? Not having correctly filled in the required forms? An arbitrary decision by the employee not to assist her for racist reasons? Let's now imagine that the young woman with the headscarf goes to court and claims discrimination, what would be the most efficient criterion to promote in her case: gender, race, ethnicity, religion? What would be the grounds for helping her to get reparation and for asking that justice be done? Is there any clear and distinguished reason at all for explaining the bad treatment of which she has been the victim?

This chapter is based on a project[1] that tries to deal with similar types of intricate situations in which nobody knows where boundaries are, how to classify the discourses and actions, or what categories to use to better describe the situation at stake. By looking at the emergence of 'religious discrimination', a new tool for the European Union (EU) since inclusion as one of the grounds of discrimination in the Employment

Directive[2] is a new avenue to help the promotion of claims for equality made by Muslims living in Europe, I try to figure out whether this concept of religious discrimination is of any relevance in the case of Muslims living in Britain and France. More largely, in the aftermath of 9/11, various surveys and studies conducted by institutions such as the European Monitoring Center on Racism and Xenophobia (EUMC) or the Open Society Institute have shown the development of anti-Muslim feeling (sometimes called Islamophobia or Muslimophobia) all over Europe. In a report released in March 2006, for instance, the International Helsinki Federation for Human Rights (IHF) examined the widespread negative attitudes toward Muslims in Europe (International Helsinki Federation for Human Rights, 2005). In this post-9/11 context, individually or collectively, experiences of discrimination and unequal treatment are being reported by Muslims and, in a few cases, even carried into the courts. However, religion as a criterion of discrimination has not yet been officially researched and applied to the situation of Muslims in the EU.

Religious discrimination results from the articulation of a variety of socio-economic and cultural processes. Broadly speaking, it describes the 'discrimination of people for belonging to a religion, for holding a belief or for manifesting it' (Grashorn quoted in ENAR, 2003: 11). It is new in the way social research has started to look at it, policy makers have been trying to comply with it in domestic law, and also in the way Muslims have started to use it to promote their interests and ask for recognition of their rights. Different levels of analysis are intertwined in conflicting experiences. such as the young veiled woman mentioned above, and I will limit myself in this text to assessing the value of referring to 'discrimination' in relation to two of these levels. The first relates to the articulation between Muslim group demands and liberal EU states' policies for accommodating religious differences in plural societies. The demands made by Muslims of EU states reveal problematic relationships that lead to requirements in terms of assimilative cultural demands (Statham, Koopmans, Giugni and Passy, 2005). How does the accommodation of differences in a regime of equality work when it comes to the specific case not of a racial or ethnic group, but of multiple communities of Muslim believers? The second level concentrates on individual inter-subjective experiences of racism supposedly motivated by the religious belief of the victim. Contrary to what has been done in most of the social sciences' Islam-in-Europe field of study, I privilege narratives of experiences of discrimination by individuals, independently of their eventual participation in associations or other activist organizations.

This chapter specifically addresses religious discrimination as a topic within a wider perspective questioning religious pluralism in the EU. It concentrates in particular on the various interpretations and uses of the European anti-discrimination provisions in various EU contexts. Far from being a sole by-product of migration to Europe, the presence of Muslims has to be shaped within the larger framework of the European integration process: how can pluralism become a value and be enacted as a practice when it comes to minority religions in Europe? What types of social dynamics are being carried out by an implementation of equality that relies on courts and trials as main sites for its construction? What does the discrimination repertoire bring to the discussion on Islam in EU Member States? How is it invested and used by Muslims, both individually and collectively?

The central hypothesis is the following: religious discrimination may be relevant in helping to map forms of inequality and injustice that some individuals (Muslims) are experiencing in certain sectors, in particular education and employment. On a pure academic level, introducing 'religious discrimination' may help us to see and say new things about the perception of Islam and the situation of Muslims in EU Member States. This reflection started, for instance, with two observations. First, religion is marginal and even absent from most of the reflection on anti-discrimination policies in EU Member States that concentrate rather on gender and race/ethnicity as a main variable.[3] Second, strong ideological distinctions between French and British so-called models of integration come together through Muslims (either individually or as members of associations) relying on non-national legal provisions to get their rights defended and protected, even to obtain compensation. Religious rights have entered the realm of cultural rights and human rights (Amiraux, 2004, 2005b), and the juridical repertoire has taken the lead on political and civic types of mobilization to claim equality. This process is based on the assumption that religious discrimination is something specific and distinct from ethnic and racial criteria, commonly referred to when dealing with discrimination. The line between ethnicity and religion when dealing with discriminatory practices is, however, not easy to draw.

This text opens with an overview of what I call the dominant narratives framing public discourses on Islam in Europe. A second part focuses on the differences between Britain and France in dealing with religious differences, with a special emphasis on their policies toward Muslim populations. What has the EU added to these national provisions? A third part examines the ways in which Muslims have tried to invest in these new legal provisions, both individually and collectively. Can the concept of religious discrimination help Muslims to achieve their claims?

8.2   Dominant narratives framing discourses on Islam in EU Member States

Many international events have damaged the promise of multiculturalism, or, to put it another way, expectations regarding multiculturalism have been affected following 9/11 in the United States, and also the murder of Theo Van Gogh in the Netherlands and the 7/7 bombings in London. In France as in Britain, contradictory attitudes have coexisted in the aftermath of September 11 (Bonnefoy, 2003). A double dynamic has taken place, on the one hand opening up a greater space for public speech on Islam and Muslims living in Europe, but on the other hand, closing down in the name of security almost all places where dialogue had taken place thus helping the emergence of more explicit expressions of hostility toward Muslims.[4] These global narratives have shaped the emergence of a series of dichotomies framing Muslims in clear-cut terms as good versus bad, loyal versus disloyal, playing off in particular 'our Muslims' versus Muslim 'others' (Werbner, 2004: 460[5]).

This double-headed Janus figure of trustworthy versus untrustworthy Muslims conditions public speech on Islam and Muslims in Europe. It has become the yardstick in the evaluation of Muslims' behavior in European societies. This trend has been very much sustained by the readiness of all types of citizens to offer information and opinions related to what Islam is ('a bad thing') and who Muslims are ('suspect citizens'). In the French context, for instance, 'being a Muslim' is framed by dominant narratives, some of them originating from Muslims,[6] that have slowly contributed to the mere simplification of public perceptions of the 'typical life of Muslims in France', feeding the multiplication of stereotypical representations of how Muslims think, sleep, eat, love, what they look like,[7]and so on. In a climate where the perceptions of Muslims in France and in Britain remain largely negative, it is said that they keep a distinct way of life and separate themselves from mainstream society (Pew Research Center, 2005). In this light, their alienation is seen as a direct result of the cultural isolation of some Islamic enclaves in the heart of Western Europe, of which young veiled women stand as the living embodiment.

The set of stereotypes that sustains racism against certain groups varies from one group to another. It more largely relates to a problem of typification. Berger and Luckmann put it quite clearly: 'If I typify my friend Henry as a member of category X (say, as an Englishman), I *ipso facto* interpret at least certain aspects of his conduct as resulting from this typification[8] – for instance his tastes in food are typical of Englishmen, as are his manners, certain of his emotional reactions, and so on' (Berger and Luckmann, 1971: 46) This relates to a central assumption of the promotion of equality in liberal societies: 'the chief mischief of discrimination is that a person is subject to detriment because she is attributed with stereotypical qualities based on a denigratory notion of her group membership' (Fredman, 2002: 16). However, the stereotypes attached to Muslim culture and traditions are relatively identical from one EU Member State to another: they cover demographic characteristics (Muslims have more children than non-Muslims), inequality between women and men (alienation), traditionalism, and anti-Semitism. What makes Muslims the ultimate 'others'? The public opinion sensitivity to the 'clash of civilizations' theme, regularly re-proposed as a grid for analysis is based on the assumption that Islam as a denomination and Muslims as believers constitute the ultimate cultural 'other' that will never be able to cope with democratic and liberal values. The historical process that led to this assumption is quite an old one, which started long before imperial expansion but which found new energy in it. Without falling into the trap of criticizing Orientalism, what makes Muslims so in-comparable to other believers, what makes Islam so specific (Dakhlia, 2005)? Relying on stereotypes, for instance branding all assertive Muslims as 'fundamentalists' (Modood, 1992),[9] is central to the process of essentialization of their cultural characteristics. Here religion and culture function as the equivalent of race.

The dynamism of their religious commitment, the fact that there is no distinction between politics and religion, the 'non-modern' features of Islam, its 'natural violence' and 'aggressiveness', are to be added to the list of grievances. But what makes Islam so specific is its own religious dynamic. Islam, in opposition to other religions (in Europe, Christian denominations and Judaism), is a dynamic religion fed by young people going back to religious practice, while churches and synagogues are deserted. This active membership, based on pure voluntary engagement – in the sense that there is no social coercion to be a Muslim in non-Muslim Europe – contrasts dramatically with the difficulty other denominations claim to face in secular Europe (Davie, 2002). Related to this idea of the particular vigor of Islam (with no evidence or data), comes the assumption that being a Muslim would automatically lead to a Muslim way of acting as citizens of EU Member States. The boundary between intimate spiritual life and participation in social life does not apply to Muslims and the causal link between religious belief and action is systematically presumed. This applies to falling in love as well as to becoming an activist. One good illustration of the perverted association of images and discourses that implicitly leads to a confusion between religious private belief and types of conduct is the multiplication of special booklets on 'What is Islam', 'Understanding the Koran', 'the history of Islamism since Muhammad', and so on by most of the national newspapers in Europe immediately after 9/11, as if the intimate knowledge of the Koran and of the Islamic civilization's history would enable a better understanding of contemporary politics in the Middle East. As pointed out by Alain Roussillon, one needs to be clear about the fact that being knowledgeable about Islamic law or Islamic theology does not help getting to the root of why Iran and Iraq went to war against each other for more than eight years, or to sort out the motivations of individuals committing suicide bombings: 'The risk lies here in contributing to the confusion between Islam as such, in its diverse historical trajectories with the use that actors make of religious references in producing meanings to understand the situation they are engaged in, *hic et nunc*' (Roussillon, 2001: 78–79). The idea that Muslims are subject to tensions deriving from conflicting loyalties is 'fed by public moral panics surrounding the danger of Islamic "terror" or "disloyalty", expressed in the speeches of politicians, newspapers columns, and global news reports' (Werbner, 2004: 452).

The role of Islam in the political participation of Muslims as citizens is largely overstated. In this general context, what makes a Muslim a Muslim? Who are they and where can they be seen? Since the introduction of the religious question in the British census (in England and Wales) in 2001, it has become easier to know the number of persons declared as Muslims.[10] This type of question is still not present in the French system which continues to infer religious identity of its citizens from the national origin of the prime migrants, even in spite of the fact that the Muslim presence in France is not discussed as a migration issue anymore, but rather as being tied to the politics of citizenship.[11] The legacy of the sociology of religion may have affected the qualitative look at Muslims (religious identification is an individual choice; Islam is experiencing an institutional deregulation; religious identities may change in a life course; you may opt out or convert, and so on), but not so much the way they 'count' them, or the way they elaborate on their practices. The task of identifying Muslims by their practices, however, remains as difficult as when relying on origins. For instance, basing the counting of Muslims on the regularity of their visits to mosques and places of worship remains a criterion stemming from a Christian standard (places of worship do not have the same theological status in all monotheisms). It excludes part of the female audience that cannot visit neighborhood mosques because they are not provided with a proper space. And it also means that those Muslims living in Europe who prefer to go to churches instead of mosques are not taken into account either (Amiraux, 2006).

Islamophobia has until recently been the catchword to subsume all this popular knowledge and all the stereotypes circulating about Islam and Muslims. Generally speaking, it describes a 'growing distrust and hostility' experienced by Muslims in Europe.[12] Over the past four years, all European countries have adopted new anti-terrorism legislation and policies, the scheduling, nature, and scope of these responses varying from nation to nation.[13] These provisions and the wider definition of terrorism have consequences, in many respects, for grassroots Muslims. The extension of the notion of crimes of association with terrorism has, in particular, given birth to a religious profiling of suspects among student populations, Muslims clerics, and regular visitors of mosques and places of worship (mosques have become the main targets of police forces in almost all EU Member States). Procedures such as the use of immigration and asylum laws as tools in the fight against terrorism are directly of concern to Muslims living in Europe. All over the EU, Muslims are certainly more exposed to racism than other groups of vulnerable peoples. Discrimination and criminalization have both contributed to the automatic suspicion of individuals on the basis of signs that could trace their adherence to faith in Islam. The word has become fashionable among Muslims in France and in Britain, but following different paths. In the post 9/11 context, V. Geisser distinguishes between an Islamophobia caused by security issues (as a consequence of terrorism for instance), and an Islamophobia of an ideological nature (Geisser, 2005).[14] Applied to the two contexts in focus here, one could say that Great Britain, as illustrated in the aftermath of both 9/11 and 7/7, is of the first type, while the French are more inclined to have 'structural national' difficulties in accepting Muslims, mostly in relation to the colonial legacy (Laurens, 2004). The post 9/11 security measures in Europe have certainly accentuated the anti-Muslim prejudice in security agencies, particularly in the police practices of control and ID checks.

Muslims in Europe are widely misrepresented. The question of the relation between Muslims conducting ordinary lives and radical movements and associations which may accept violence is troubled by the omnipresence of media coverage of those on the margins (Dassetto, 2003). But this highly visible segment of Muslims is not the biggest one. Terrorism, fanaticism, radicalism, and Islamism should not be underestimated, but they contribute to the blurring of public perception of grassroots Muslim citizens. What's more, has research really taken the opportunity to reverse this trend? Islam should not be perceived as belonging to the migration file. It is not a migrant culture anymore.[15] Islam no longer constitutes, in any of these contexts, the everlasting last chapter of integration policies, but has an existence on its own as an object of public policy. The use of the categorization in terms of generations is rarely used as it still inscribes individuals in a chain of migration. In social sciences literature, for instance, the study of Muslims in France changed status as an object of study. Being a Muslim in France is nowadays conceived as an individual choice, emancipated from any type of coercion, not simply as an inheritance.[16] As a matter of fact, self-identification as a Muslim does not end in reproducing static identities, but rather in helping the emergence and invention of multiple ways of its expression.

8.3   National patterns for dealing with discrimination and religious differences: what did the EU legislation bring in?

Religious discrimination belongs to several texts that define the juridical provisions for anti-discrimination policies in the EU. After its mention in Article 13 of the Amsterdam Treaty in 1997, it was included in the Employment Directive of November 2000, to be implemented in the member states by the end of 2003.[17] The existence of this specific ground does not make it easier to trace the line between what belongs to ethnic, racial, cultural, or strictly religious domains. Indeed, the question of a universally valid definition of religion is itself still open as none of the international legal provisions starts with a clear identification of criteria to establish what makes a religion (neither the UN Article 18, nor Article 9 of European Convention on Human Rights). As in any field of the social sciences, the methodological doubts are infinite when trying to come to terms with observing and analyzing the intimate beliefs of people and the way they affect the daily life of citizens in secular societies. It embraces practices, rites, and customs, but also refers to values, ideas, and spirituality. It has an institutional visibility that aims at reaching a community of believers and an intimate signification for individuals. In religion, beliefs manifest themselves not only as ideas and principles, but are embodied in ways of living that respect specific requirements and let them eventually exist independently of the dogmatic frame. The believer performs his religion 'according to religious rules and convictions in daily life' (Robbers quoted in ANAR, 2003: 13). It is up to him or her to make it visible or not, explicit or not in a context where the coupling of alleged racial identity with cultural markers is becoming the rule when dealing with security and defense issues.

The situation of Muslims in France and Great Britain is obviously not the same. The term 'Muslims' does not refer to similar populations in both contexts; neither is encompassed by the same terminology. In terms of chronology, the same steps can be found in both countries (first male, from ex-dominions or colonial territories, with rural backgrounds, then wives and children joining them in Europe for definitive settlement). In the British case, Muslims are mostly South Asian from former British imperial dominions.[18] Pakistanis became Asians then Muslims in British terminology. In the French context, Muslims also stem from the ex-colonized territories, mostly from Algeria, Morocco, Tunisia, and Senegal, then later from other countries such as Turkey or Bosnia. The current Muslims were French Muslims during the colonial administration of Algeria, who then became Algerians, then migrants, Arabs, and finally (back to religious categorization) they were once again Muslims. In both contexts, early racial violence took place in the 1970s, 'Paki-bashing' in Britain and the murders of Arabs ('*ratonades*') in Paris, both examples of postcolonial racist violence. Of course, public policies did not follow similar lines when it came to migration and integration (Geddes and Guiraudon, 2004).

Controversies and the nature of public passionate debate related to the settlement of Muslims also differ from one country to the other (Amiraux, 2005a). While French public opinion and policy makers started to be obsessed with headscarves in 1989 until a law passed in March 2004 banning ostentatious religious signs from public schools, the most important (if one excludes the discussions following the London bombings in July 2005) controversial public debate on Muslims and British citizenry took place when the campaign against Salman Rushdie started. Similar situations opposing young Muslim girls wearing headscarves and schools administrators have occurred in both contexts. But the English and French systems did not identically address the question of Islamic headscarves in public or private schools, even though closer analysis shows that the converse appears to be the case (Poulter, 1997: 44). Both countries have developed contrasting approaches toward the development of public policies in relation to the presence of religious and ethnic minorities on their territory (not to mention the contrasts in the educational systems). 'Muslim pupils are able to wear the hijab more confidently and freely in English schools, even though their technical legal rights are better safeguarded by French law' (Poulter, 1997: 74). Differences between the two contexts may continue, but the two so-called models are currently in turning phases: toward affirmative action in France and toward an inclusion of markers other than color in the race relations discussion in the British context. In that process, the notion of indirect discrimination is becoming central, as will be illustrated in the third section.

Race discrimination law in both contexts needs to be discussed while keeping in mind the corresponding provisions in EU law. Europe made the crime of 'religious discrimination' possible. 'Discrete areas of law – especially constitutional theory and discrimination law – have responded to the problems which arise when faith-based arguments are used by agents to justify beliefs and action' (Malik, 2000: 132). The British anti-discrimination provisions are much farther elaborated than the French ones. In that respect, the impact of the 2000 EU Council Directives[19] was stronger in the French case and extended the coverage of the anti-discrimination provisions in the British context, not to mention the impact of the incorporation into domestic law of the European Convention of Human Rights (Human Rights Act 1998, starting effect October 2000 in Great Britain). 'The result is a hierarchy of directives within EU law, with race and ethnic origin given the widest reach, followed by gender discrimination, which covers employment and social security on, and trailed by, discrimination on grounds of age, religion, sexual orientation, and disability' (Fredman, 2002: 70). Comprehensive laws exist in France and in Britain.

The change related to religious discrimination was drastic in the British case after the implementation of the European directives, especially the one on equality in employment. While discrimination on religious grounds, prohibited in Northern Ireland, was previously lawful in Great Britain, since December 2003 it has been a crime (see *Norwood v. DPP*, 2003). The anti-terrorism Crime and Security Act also contains an article dealing with incitement to religious hatred ('racially or religiously aggravated'). In the British context, the state sustains race relations as a legitimate tool for policy. Race is thus a legitimate category to think of difference among people. It does not, however, mean that all people are included in the elaboration of the typology of groups recognized as ethnic or racial ones. Muslims, for instance, do not belong to the classification (Poulter, 1998; Barry, 2001) and religion as mode of identification remains separate except in two cases, Sikhs and Jews, since 1983. Both these groups benefit from protection under the Race Relations Act (RRA).[20] For a long time, the legitimate British category for dealing with cultural difference was a definition of race mostly based on color. In the British context of the established Church of England, Muslims (among other religious groups) consider themselves as suffering a double discrimination as they are protected neither as a religious nor as a racial group. Religion does not belong to the definition of race as defined in the 1976 and 2000 RRAs. Blasphemy law in the British context is also not yet extended to Islam.[21]

The first move toward the introduction of religious elements in ethnic identity occurred when Sikhs asked for exemption from wearing a crash helmet when riding a motorbike (1976). Then in 1989 came permission for them to be exempted from wearing safety helmets on construction sites. In 1988, the Criminal Justice Act for Sikhs gave them permission to wear their daggers (*kirpans*) in public places without being guilty of offense. In 1983, the *Mandla* v. *Dowell Lee* decision allowing males to wear the turban at school was significant. The school administration defended its position by arguing that wearing a turban would accentuate religious distinction and eventually create problems in a multiracial school. During the court discussions, the debate centered on identifying whether Sikhs are or are not an ethnic group. The decision to grant Sikhs ethnic group status also stemmed from some members of the House of Lords defending the idea of Sikhs being 'more than a religious sect' (Lord Templeman, quoted by Poulter, 1997). The final result is a definition of ethnic origin that sets it apart from religion. Religious protection is not, however, comprehensive in Britain. It is directly related to the race legislation which creates difficulties, for instance, for 'white' converts who do not belong to a racial or ethnic minority. In 2006, Muslims have yet to be granted the position of a group defined by ethnic origins in Great Britain, with the clear consequence that they can hardly claim any protection for racial or ethnic discrimination related to the specificity of their experience in that domain. They still have to go for indirect discrimination on the grounds of race.[22]

The centrality of race (based on color) of the British system contrasts with the denial of race and ethnicity in the French context. But it does not mean that racism does not exist: 'If "there is no race here", there is nevertheless racism' (Calvès, 2002: 175). France is a proactive secular republic where race and ethnicity are not considered to be legitimate variables when thinking of differences between people, not to mention, of course, religion. France is color-blind; at least according to the first article of the Constitution. The constitutional principle of the unity of the French people (*l'unicité du peuple français*) explains the French government's refusal to ratify many European texts mentioning the notion of minorities (Calvès, 2002). Working as a politician or as an academic and using notions such as ethnicity or race to point out difference seems to be too offensive toward French ideology described as 'Jacobin' or 'Republican' (Brubaker, 1998; Chapman and Frader, 2004; Favell, 1998; Hargreaves, 1995). 'The use of the word "immigration" to encompass what are in many respects post-migratory processes is itself symptomatic of the difficulties experienced by the French in coming to terms – both literally and ontologically – with the settlement of people of immigrant origin.

In the English-speaking world, such people are commonly referred to as "ethnic minorities" or "minority ethnic groups", 'and a large part of what the French call "immigration" is commonly known as "race relations". In France, such terms are taboo' (Hargreaves, 1995: 1–2). Thinking of migrants and the public management of Islam in relation to the legacy of the colonial experience is a relatively recent development in France (Savarese, 2000). The Algerian crisis is central in that process (Branche, 2005; Ferro, 2004; Harbi and Stora, 2004), but not exclusive of other elements (Saada, 2006). On the one hand, this link between treatment of migrants and the colonial past is exposed in relation with the ambiguity of the Republican project (on the link with anthropology, see Colonna, 1995; Lucas and Vatin, 1975). This contradiction is exhibited in the tensions in a republican ideal represented by political figures able to defend, in the same discourse, equality for all French citizens and the legitimacy of classifying people according to their race and civilization. It is the signal that amnesia is no longer possible in the French context. For a long time, however, this contradiction has facilitated life, by considering as two distinct issues the history of migration and the historical process of constitution of the French nation (Blanchard and Lemaire, 2003).

Religious identification of citizens is no longer relevant in either context, in the sense that it does not condition access to politics for groups and individuals. However, this does not mean that all denominations benefit from equality of treatment or, better said, parity. They are not all alike (Lindohlm, 2004) and Muslims as a group of believers suffer misrecognition (Carens and Williams, 1998), which brings us to the broader analysis of the public position of religion in secular liberal and plural Western European democracies. Can religion be accepted as part of the definition of a group?

8.4 Forms of discrimination experienced by Muslims: what is religious, what is not?

In liberal democratic systems, religious beliefs are protected at different levels, mostly by constitutional provisions. Moreover, religion is on the EU anti-discrimination agenda thanks to the Employment Framework Directive, which has been transposed in both contexts: equal treatment should be irrespective of religion or belief (intended also as non-belief), enacted in France by the law 2001–1066 (16 November 2001), and in Britain by the Employment Equality Regulations of 2003.[23] Of course, the impact of the European directive cannot be considered identical when dealing with countries that have for a long time been considered so opposite in their public management of differences. In all EU Member States, both notions of direct and indirect discrimination are regulated by anti-discrimination legislation, but the notion of victimization that exists, for instance, in the British system of protection is not considered as such in the French one.[24] Direct discriminations are still considered to be easier to establish than indirect ones, but the relevance of the latter is crucial in the case of Muslims and Sikhs willing to sue France for the effects caused by the application of March 2004 law banning religious symbols in schools.[25] Indeed, without referring to particular ethnic or racial groups, or to religious communities, the exclusion from schools primarily touches members of religious minorities (Sikhs, Muslims) thus creating a disproportionate disadvantage.

As we have seen, different national traditions and political cultures map the competition between various institutional settings that organize the public existence of religion. In the French context, neither race nor religion can be said to benefit from a privileged position in the constitutional scheme. There is no admitted definition of religion, exactly as there is no juridical consistency for the notion of race (Calvès, 2002). In the British context, race and ethnic relations are the core elements of the entire anti-discrimination system. 'Racial equality began with colour, but by the 1980s had gone ethnic (decisively through the judgment of the House of Lords on *Mandla* v. *Lee* in 1982, which gave legal protection against discrimination to Sikhs; Jews, though white, were already covered). ... It is time to enact legislation outlawing religious discrimination to complement existing provisions on racial and ethnic discrimination' (Poulter, 1997: 73).

The question of the legitimacy of extending the scope of ethnicity to include Muslims is therefore accurate in the British context, while it is irrelevant in the French one.[26] The extension of the RRA to include a clause against incitement to religious hatred is constantly present in the discussion of the Commission for Racial Equality since the Rushdie Affair, with no success for the time being. In Britain, the settlement of disputes involving Sikhs or Jews under the RRA has generally been solved by the principle of reasonable accommodation, in particular when touching upon issues such as dress code. Muslims, even though not directly protected by the RRA have benefited from these types of solutions. French Republican values are embedded in a matrix articulating the secularization of society with the neutrality of the state (*laïcité*[27]). In some cases, such as in the headscarf controversies that started toward the end of the 1980s, it has been unable to solve the tension between two constitutional principles: first, the individual freedom of conscience, and, second, the state's neutrality. Differently, the British political setting hosts the established Church of England (with bishops, appointed by the sovereign with the approval of the Prime Minister, sitting in the House of Lords). In both contexts, religion being brought back into public debate is related to the settlement of minority religions and, in particular, to the controversies or conflicts involving Muslim citizens. In France, the headscarf controversies that regularly come to the front of the public stage have contributed to this dynamic, as well as the Northern England riots opposing Pakistani and Kashmiri youngsters against white British youngsters in 2001. In a more profound way, it questions the place of religion in liberal democracies where religion has played a central role in the past and has somehow left traces in contemporary societies, conditioning the criteria religious minorities have to meet if they want to be recognized.

The discussion on equality in plural religious societies cannot be driven without considering the potential conflict between equality and other values (neutrality, liberty, dignity) that are central kinds of moral values in the EU human rights discourse. It touches upon the tension between, on the one hand, a project of formal equality aiming at equal protection of individuals when confronted with similar situations, and, on the other hand, a project of substantive equality trying to achieve the equal representation of different groups by addressing the structural causes for inequality. The law is therefore a perfect field for observing how cultural pluralism (of which religious pluralism is a part) has begun to be taken into consideration in judgment. Talking about Muslims in European contexts, assessing their exposure to discrimination cannot but underline the necessity to cross it with other criteria such as language, color, or ethnic origin. Is discrimination against Muslims a specific type of race discrimination or can we identify elements that would help to distinguish it? If religious discrimination remains difficult to assess (in particular related to the modalities of defining ethnic versus racial or religious identities), what are the most frequent claims of religious discrimination by Muslims?

In the British as in the French contexts, similar issues come to the forefront that primarily concern rituals and worshiping. One thinks, for example, of the building of mosques (Cesari, 2005), the denial of leave to celebrate religious holidays (in particular for Aid el-Kabir), the possibility of having *halal* food in the workplace or in public schools, and the presence of chaplains in hospitals or jails, to quote a few. However common these cases seem to be, they nevertheless involve major problems for the judge, such as the necessity to estimate the degree of practice (i.e., in *Nyazi v. Rymans Ltd*) to identify for instance whether absence from work appears as a necessity according to the religious dogma. But in the case of Muslims requesting Blackburn Council that toilets no longer face Mecca, it was judged that this cannot be counted as a case for discrimination (quoted in Statham, Koopmans, Giugni and Passy, 2005).

At an individual level, many criteria overlap and coexist, leading to the reinforcement of discrimination. Religion and race have not only a cumulative effect, but complement each other when it comes to discrimination. For instance, Muslim women, who appear not only in the EU, but as universal targets for religious discrimination, lie somewhere in the interstices between the race criteria, the gender issue, and the religious variable. Following the headscarf controversies in France, Muslim women joined the usual cohort of the traditionally threatening Muslim men.[28] But still, can we claim specificity for the type of discrimination a Muslim woman would experience as compared with the type a non-Muslim woman would be subject to? Is there something specific in the fact that she is a Muslim? Should the different potential criteria of discrimination be treated separately?[29] Should being a Muslim and a woman (one could add other items such as being black, poor, handicapped, and so on) be considered as belonging to two categories of people who are potential victims of different types of discriminations? For instance, in the street stop-and-search procedures of police departments in the United Kingdom, only race and ethnicity are registered in the files. In France, discrimination on the grounds of belief or religion is almost always systematically classified as discrimination motivated by racial and ethnic origins. The overlap between race and religion is the main obstacle to the autonomy of religious discrimination in case law and it may even be unrealistic to think of disentangling one from the other.

These discussions have an obvious impact on the definition of political and cultural boundaries framing citizenry and delimiting what does or does not belong to politics. The current moment for Muslims in Europe is characterized by their quest for respect of their religious practices, asserting their differences in public, and not just behaving in reaction to hostility from European societies. The enforcement of the anti-discrimination law proceeds mostly by means of individual claims before a tribunal. Muslim individuals' or associations' investment in the field of discrimination does not, for now, appear as a means to value difference (limited to a reversal of the stigma, 'Islam is beautiful'),[30] but rather as a way to obtain symbolic recognition of the integrity of individuals' identity with a special emphasis on religion as a significant part of that identity. Certainly, the emergence of a new racism based on culture (including religion) rather than on race conditions this dynamic. Especially as cultural racism does not only produce a specific climate, but also leads to acts and practices of discrimination in the 'classical' areas of social life (employment, education, housing, health). All social sectors can therefore end up being sites of culture-blind indirect discrimination (Modood, 2005: 42), exactly as color-blindness in US affirmative action policy, even if ostensibly race neutral, singles out race for special treatment (Case, 2000). For instance, the omnipresent discussion on the compatibility between Islam as a set of values and European ones of liberalism and democracy makes it hard for Muslims to get large support in favor of their request to be treated alike. In some specific situations, it also contributes to the stigmatization of practices that in other contexts would not even have been noticed.

Cultural racism increases the social cost of declaring oneself to be Muslim. At the same time, talking about discrimination and racism in general remained just as difficult.[31] On that specific point, the move from a discourse on 'the right to be different' to one on non-discrimination appears to be used by Muslims more and more, both individually and as a group, to bring themselves within the established grounds of equality. This move invites one to consider the potentially liberating dimension of a positive self-definition of group difference, 'from an understanding of equality in terms of individualism and cultural assimilation to a politics of recognition, to equality as encompassing public ethnicity, that is to say, equality as not having to hide or apologize for one's origins, family, or community, but requiring others to show respect for them and adapt public attitudes and arrangements so that the heritage they represent is encouraged rather than ignored or expected to wither away' (Modood, 2005: 134). It should, however, clearly distinguish between exceptional demands (such as demands for exemptions beyond those granted to other groups) and parity demands for groups (asking for equal treatment compared with other groups) (Statham, Koopmans, Giugni and Passy, 2005).

One of the particularities of the discussion about Muslims in Europe goes beyond the idea of a specificity of Islam and lies in the difficulty, first, in thinking of religion as an integral part of people's lives in secular contexts, and, second, in assessing the impact of religious belief on the daily lives of individuals both at public and intimate levels. Faith may even encompass commitments associated with race, nationality, and cultural tradition which are important in the life of an individual (Malik, 2000). Here the notion of 'religiosity' to designate the intimate part of what links an individual to a religion (defined as dogmatic forms of piety) is useful as it emphasizes the role of the individual rather than of the community in giving meaning to his or her choice in the daily course of life. In a way, religiosity is what concretizes religion in society: it gives meaning to action, and it may help in the recognition of others, which a religion does not necessarily do (Roy, 2005). As a consequence, one may be entitled to ask whether religion belongs to culture. Is religion something specific? What links can it pretend to establish with politics in secular societies? What do laws do when the religious beliefs of some citizens conflict with social norms in certain contexts? If religion is a private matter, then why do states involve themselves in it? Liberty and equality are clearly competing and conflicting values. Are laws therefore necessary in the achievement of dignity, just because they make invisible things (religious identification and belief) visible?[32]

The question of equality when it comes to religious groups opens a Pandora's Box of discussion about whether religious rights should be equated with cultural rights, whether Islamic values contradict democratic ones. The securitization of the debate over Islam in Europe has to be taken into consideration in assessing the impact of the 'making visible' dynamic. In the aftermath of 9/11, in EU Member States religious profiling is emerging that makes invisible people newly visible through the highlighting of certain characteristics. Equality before the law achieves important objectives, but never suffices. Equality of treatment is based on an abstract idea of justice that, for instance, does not fully consider important differences in terms of distribution of power and wealth. These are opposed to another conception of equality based on a conception of justice correcting misdistribution, thus starting with an assessment of the equality of results. 'The choice between different conceptions of equality is not one of logic but of values or policy'

(Fredman, 2002: 2). It cannot be limited to the legal repertoire and the sphere of law-making.

8.5 Concluding remarks

Historically, the relationship between EU Member States and Islam has never been a balanced one. The current moment is not a new one. 'We want Muslims to love us for our values. But we refuse to countenance the thought of loving them for their values' (Bulliet, 2004: 116). Nowadays, public mistrust toward Muslims is expressed on many levels. It involves inter-religious comparison: why do Muslims in Europe continue to believe and ask for recognition in public while Christians do not? Thus, animosity toward Muslims is not strictly dependent upon inter-religious dogmatic conflicts anymore, but on the representation of Islam as a dynamic faith compared with others. The mistrust toward Muslims in EU non-Muslim contexts relates also to the complex history of the relationship of secular society to God. Moreover, in a postmigratory context, the difficulty in raising a proper public discussion on Islamophobia in France, for instance, can be related to the difficulty in thinking of the limits of the Republican principles. Cases of religious discrimination reveal conflicts between types of religiosity that occur in a 'disenchanted world' and oppose civic spheres to religious ones. Can this be labeled racism or is it more of a civic versus religious sphere fight? Religion, faith, and beliefs are hard topics because of their invisibility and their intimate resonance. Consequently, 'decisions, beliefs and actions of the faithful can often appear unjustifiable, obscure and irrational to those who do not share this faith' (Oliver, Scott and Tadros, 2000: 3).

Co-presence seems to be the new framework for describing interactions between people that do not share much beyond a common space, a single territory for political participation. The complex nature of the problem becomes clearer when the issue of recognition comes to the forefront. Recognition is reported as the response to the moral suffering coming from individual experiences of discrimination for religious reasons. Various politics of recognition and identity politics coexist in the EU, depending upon multiple factors linked with each national trajectory. Knowing and giving credit to the existence of others in public is the dominant question on the political EU agenda related to the presence of Muslims: what forms of recognition of religious pluralism would have preference? Until now, the institutionalization of Islam has been the path chosen by most non-Muslim states to cope with Islam and

Muslims, albeit relying on different modalities to identify the structure and the leadership. 'There is, after all, a profound difference between the will to understand, for purposes of co-existence and enlargement of horizons, and the will to dominate for the purposes of control' (Saïd, 2003, in Laurens, 2004). Institutionalization appears as a limited recognition of the stability of Islam as worship in European public spaces, without properly opening space for discussing the long-term presence of Muslim European citizens and the related recognition of their religious distinction. Recognition is something you do commonly everyday. You recognize your child. You recognize a friend passing in the street. It also belongs to more abstract mechanisms of interrelation with the world surrounding you: how do institutions address plural and diverse audiences at cultural, economic, social, and religious levels? Religious pluralism somehow has another, broader, significance than a pure inter-religious institutional one. If finding the way to answer social and cultural diversity is not a new challenge in the EU, the current situation is appealing to a 'reasonable pluralism' that cannot be addressed only as a juridical question.

Notes

1. Entitled 'Religious Discrimination of Muslims in the European Union: Experience of Injustice, Fight for Recognition, and Implementation of Equality in a Plural Society' (DISCRIMUSMIN, Marie Curie Fellowship, European Commission), this project aims at comparing the situation of Muslim populations and Islam in four member states of the European Union (France, Germany, Italy, United Kingdom from a religious discrimination perspective.
2. Religious discrimination fits Article 13 of the Amsterdam Treaty (1997).
3. Things are slightly different at the European level. It was, until recently, at best an added variable to a list of criteria for discrimination, beside language or origin. For an attempt to formulate the entire discrimination issue in terms of religious discrimination, see Sharf, 2003.
4. A recent statement by Michel Houellebecq exemplified this. He declared in an interview that 'Islam is really the most idiot religion' (*Magazine Lire*, September 2001). Even more recently, Brigitte Bardot stated during a TV show what she had written in her book (*Un cri dans le silence*, 2003) that 'Islam is disgusting', and she made an explicit connection between Aid el-Kebir celebrations and the 9/11 terrorist attacks in the United States. She was sentenced for 'incitement to racial hatred' and had to pay a €5000 fine (in addition to a further €5000 fine to the publisher 'les éditions Durocher'), plus one symbolic euro to the MRAP and LDH, two anti-racist associations which had sued her (Paris Correctional Tribunal, 10 June 2004). Houellebecq was sued by four Islamic associations. The Paris Correctional tribunal ruled that he had not incited racial hatred, discrimination or violence by his 2001 declarations. For a similar case related to the Italian context, see Allievi, 2006.

5. Germany introduced a test reserved exclusively for Muslims applying for German citizenship in the Land (region) of Bade Württemberg. The Muslim test is a set of 30 questions that the civil servant in charge of interviewing the applicant is free to ask if he/she feels a doubt about the interviewed Muslim. The set of questions includes women and men relations, homosexuality, and so on.

6. On this specific anti-Muslim discourse by Muslims in the French context, see Geisser, 2003. For the British situation, see Runnymede Trust, 1997; and the Parekh report (Commission on the Future of Multicultural Britain, 2000).

7. See the developments of aesthetic comments on the beauty of good and bad Muslims that I have described elsewhere as Orientalist (Amiraux, 2006; Roy, 2005: 1).

8. Right after the bombings in London in July 2005, when learning about Shehzad Tanweer's lifestyle (one of the protagonists), the British public opinion showed surprise upon discovering that he was conducting a silent and normal life plus practicing cricket. How could such a young guy be at the same time a regular practitioner of cricket and a terrorist? Cricket is, in fact, often wrongly perceived as a sanctuary for patriotic links with the country, while in most of the neighborhoods where South Asian populations live, cricket courts are arenas for confrontation between conflicting communities (see Werbner, 1997; Arnaud, 2001).

9. Talking about stereotypes about Asian men, Modood explains: 'until the *Satanic Verses* affair, Asian men were stereotyped as unassertive, over deferential, and docile, not able to stand up for themselves. Within a few years, the prevalent stereotypes of Muslim men (in Britain the majority are Asians) included the idea that they were inflexible, always demanding something, fanatical, and aggressive' (Modood, 2005: 14).

10. Of the population in England and Wales, 72 percent said they were Christians (37 million people out of 52 million) as a confirmation of the difference between declaring one's faith and practicing it (church attendance, for instance, indicates that 4 million people go regularly to church). The 6 percent belonging to the other religions encompasses 1.5 million Muslims, 600,000 Hindus, 300,000 Sikhs, 300,000 Jews, 150,000 Buddhists and 300,000 others, a total of 3 million; 15 percent (8 million people) said they had 'no religion' (against the 40 percent estimated in the 2002 British Social Attitudes Report); 4 million (7 percent) did not answer the question, which was on a voluntary basis.

11. A question about religion was asked in the French census for the last time in 1872.

12. That there is European concern about Islamophobia is without a doubt. See the reports by institutions such as ECRI, Raxen, and also the three round tables organized in Brussels by Anna Diamantopoulou in 2002.

13. It includes the EU Common Positions and Framework Decision on combating terrorism passed December 2001 (incorporated in domestic laws in June 2002). In France, the 15 November 2001 law on security has been completed by other security measures since the London bombings. One of the identified targets of this series of measures is the so-called sensitive mosques. In Britain, five anti-terrorism laws have been enacted since 2001 of which the Comprehensive Terrorism Act (2000), entered into force in February 2001, is the central piece.

14. The notion of Islamophobia first popped up in the British context when the Runnymede Trust published its first public report on this notion in 1997 (Runnymede Trust, 1997). The entry of the notion of Islamophobia in the social science discourse followed different paths but remains highly ideological in the French context for instance. While it is admitted by most EU institutions as a notion encompassing religious intolerance, racism toward Muslims, and more largely toward migrant populations, the French context still refers to Islamophobia in a quite controversial manner, in particular on the basis of the hypothesis that Islamophobia would be an invention to promote Islamism in France (see Geisser, 2005). Rather than one uniform Islamophobia, European countries are deploying national Islamophobias.

15. The designation of Muslims interviewed in the various countries includes '*les enfants de migrants*' (people from migrant origins) or 'British Muslims'.

16. This corresponds to what other studies of different populations of believers also identify as major change, in Europe and beyond (see Laermans, Wilson and Billiet, 1998).

17. Religious discrimination belongs to Article 13 of the Amsterdam Treaty (1997). Even though not legally binding, the Amsterdam Treaty constituted a platform for anti-discrimination policies that directives later put into form.

18. There is a big difference between directness and indirectness of the experience of otherness (Berger and Luckmann, 1971). France and Britain have in common a past colonial experience and a direct historical experience of Islam in policy. How did both contexts treat Islamic law during the colonial experience? The British in India allowed the development of Muslim family law with its own separate courts.

19. Council directives 2000/43/EC (29 June 2000); Council directive 2000/78 (27 November 2000).

20. Leading decision is *Mandla* and *Anor* v. *Dowell Lee* (1983) in which Sikhs were considered to be an ethnic group because of their distinctive cultural and religious traditions, common ethnic origins (not a racial group as no immutable characteristics). Jews were already one ethnic group since *Seide* v. *Gillette* (1980). How is the difference between Jews and Sikhs envisaged to justify that the former are an ethnic and the latter a racial group? See McColgan, 2000: 403–45.

21. John William Gott, in 1922, was the last man sent to prison for blasphemy (nine months hard labor) because he compared Jesus with a circus clown. The last public prosecution for blasphemy in Scotland was in 1843. In 1977, a private prosecution was brought against Gay News for publishing a poem, 'The Love That Dares To Speak Its Name', depicting a centurion's love for Christ. As Salman Rushdie published his *Satanic Verses*, some British Muslims unsuccessfully called for him to be tried under the law. But the law only recognizes blasphemy against the Church of England (1883); 1977 is the last year the blasphemy law was used. In the context of the *Satanic Verses* controversy, the proposal by the Commission for Race Equality to abolish it was not consistent with race equality.

22. Interestingly, the public debate on the right to publish the Danish cartoons in the British press in February 2006 was an occasion to bring to the forefront the discussion of the necessity to extend the blasphemy law to denominations other than the Anglican established Church.

23. The insertion of the Amsterdam Treaty Article 13 in the EC Treaty in 1999 has expanded the legal competence of the EU in the field of anti-discrimination. Moreover, this also expanded the list of criteria for the origins of discrimination. Beforehand limited to sex and nationality, the EU recognized after 1999 'sex, racial, or ethnic origin, religion or belief, age, disability and sexual orientation'. Then came the birth of the two directives mentioned earlier.

24. Religiously aggravated offenses were introduced in November 2001 in the United Kingdom.

25. See 'Loi relative à l'application du principe de laïcité dans les écoles, collèges et lycées publics' (15 March 2004) published in *Journal Officiel de la République Française*, n° 65 (17 March 2004): 5190.

26. Ethnicity here refers to the subjective and objective features of a group, and to the membership of a group, primarily defined by descent (Modood, 2005: 22).

27. Defining *laïcité* is almost an impossible mission. The French Constitution states that France is a '*laïque*' republic, but there is no legal definition of it and the notion is defined in a multiplicity of texts that establish the distinction between civil and religious authorities.

28. Vincent Geisser speaks of a 'radical hijabophobia' (Geisser, 2005: 76).

29. See, in the United States, the 'sex plus' approach: the court addresses the racial and sexual discrimination of Black women separately and the claim comes categorized as one of sexual discrimination with a secondary category of racial discrimination.

30. As beautifully stated by Modood, for Britain, dignity may be achieved through the rediscovery of Islam and while '*Cassius Clay is the name of a mode of oppression; Muhammad Ali is the name of the mode of being*' (Modood, 2005: 107).

31. 'We did not talk much about racism at home. There was a shame about talking about such things, and we did not see ourselves as victims' (Modood, 2005: 3).

32. In the British context, this is more or less the position adopted by the Commission for Racial Equality.

References

Allievi, S., *Niente di personale Signora Fallaci* (Reggio Emilia: Aliberti, 2006).

Amiraux, V., 'Expertises, savoir et politique. La constitution de l'islam comme problème public en France et en Allemagne', in Zimmermann, B. (ed.), *Les sciences sociales à l'épreuve de l'action* (Paris: EHESS, 2004), pp. 209–45.

Amiraux, V., 'Representing Difference', *Open Democracy: Free Thinking for the World* (15 November 2005a): http://www.opendemocracy.net/democracy-resolution_1325/difference_3026.jsp

Amiraux, V., 'Discrimination and Claims for Equal Rights Amongst Muslims in Europe', in Cesari, J., and Mac Loughlin, S. (eds), *European Muslims and the Secular State* (Aldershot: Ashgate, 2005b).

Amiraux, V., 'Existe-t-il une discrimination religieuse en France?', *Maghreb-Machrek*, 183 (2005c): 67–82.

Amiraux, V., 'Speaking as a Muslim. Avoiding Religion in the French Public Space', in Jonker, G., and Amiraux, V., *Politics of Visibility: Young Muslims in European Public spaces* (Bielefeld: Transcript, 2006).

Arnaud, L., 'Sous le maillot, la race? Idéologie et discours sportif dans les politiques d'intégration des "minorités ethniques" en France et en Grande-Bretagne', *Politix*, 14:56 (2001): 165–83.

Barry, B., *Culture and Equality: An Egalitarian Critique of Multiculturalism* (Cambridge: Polity, 2001).

Berger, P., and Luckmann, T., *The Social Construction of Reality: A Treatise in the Sociology of Knowledge* (Harmondsworth: Penguin, 1971).

Blanchard, P., and Lemaire, S., *Culture coloniale. La France conquise par son Empire, 1871–1931* (Paris: Autrement, 2003).

Blanchard, P., and Lemaire, S., *Culture impériale. les colonies au coeur de la République, 1931–1961* (Paris: Autrement, 2004).

Bonnefoy, L., *La stigmatisation de l'islam et ses limites dans les discours et pratiques des institutions publiques en France et en Grande-Bretagne après le 11 septembre 2001*, Master thesis, IEP Paris, 2003.

Branche, R., *L'Algérie: une histoire apaisée?* (Paris: Seuil, 2005).

Brubaker, R., *Citizenship and Nationhood in France and Germany* (Cambridge, MA: Harvard University Press, 1998).

Bulliet, R. W., *The Case for Islamo-Christian Civilization* (New York: Columbia University Press, 2004).

Calvès, G., 'Il n'y a pas de race ici. Le modèle français à l'épreuve de l'intégration européenne', *Critique internationale*, 17 (2002): 173–86.

Carens, J., and Williams, M., 'Muslim Minorities in Liberal Democracies: The Politics of Misrecognition', in Bhargava, R. (ed.), *Secularism and its Critics* (Oxford: Oxford University Press, 1998).

Case, M.-A., 'Lessons for the Future of Affirmative Action From the Past of the Religion Clauses?', *Supreme Court Review*, 325 (2000).

Césari, J., 'Mosques Conflicts in Western Europe', *Journal of Ethnic and Migration Studies*, special issue, 31:6 (2005).

Césari, J., 'L'islam dans l'immigration: un bilan de la recherche', *La Pensée*, July–September 1994, pp. 59–68.

Chapman H., and Frader, L. L. (eds), *Race in France: Interdisciplinary Perspectives on the Politics of Differences* (Oxford and New York: Berghan Books, 2004).

Colonna, F., 'Islam in the French Sociology of Religion', *Economy and Society*, 24:2 (1995): 225–44.

Commission on the Future of Multicultural Britain, *The Future of Multicultural Britain* (London: Profile Books, 2000).

Dakhlia, J., *Islamicités* (Paris: Presses Universitaires de France, 2005).

Davie, G., *Europe: the Exceptional Case* (London: Darton, Longman & Todd, 2002).

Dassetto, F., 'After September 11th: Radical Islamic Politics and European Islam', in Maréchal, B., Allievi, S., Dassetto, F., and Nielsen, J. (eds), *Muslims in the Enlarged Europe: Religion and Society* (Leiden: Brill, 2003).

ENAR, *Belief and Exclusion: Combating Religious Discrimination in Europe. The First ENAR Approach* (Düsseldorf: ENAR, 2003).

Favell, A., *Philosophies of Integration: Immigration and the Idea of Citizenship in France and Britain* (Basingstoke and New York: Macmillan, 1998).

Fekete, L., 'Anti-Muslim Racism and the European Security State', *Race and Class*, 46:1 (2004): 3–29.

Ferro, M., *Le livre noir du colonialisme XVIème-XIXème siècle: de l'extermination à la repentance* (Paris: Pluriel éditions, 2004).

Fredman, S., *Discrimination Law* (Oxford: Oxford University Press, 2002).

Geisser, V., 'L'islamophobie en France au regard du débat européen', in Leveau, R., and Mohsen-Finan, K. (eds), *Musulmans de France et d'Europe* (Paris: CNRS éditions, 2005).

Geddes, A., and Guiraudon, V., 'Anti-discrimination Policy: The Emergence of a EU Policy Paradigm Amidst Contrasted National Models', *West European Politics*, 27:2 (2004).

Harbi, M., and Stora, B. (eds), *La guerre d'Algérie. La fin de l'amnésie (1954–2004)*, (Paris: Robert Laffont, 2004).

Hargreaves, A., *Immigration. 'Race' and Ethnicity in Contemporary France* (London: Routledge, 1995).

International Helsinki federation for Human Rights, *Intolerance and Discrimination against Muslims in the EU: Developments since September 11* (IHF, March 2005): http://www.ihf-hr.org.

Küçükcan, T., *Politics of Ethnicity, Identity and Religion* (Aldershot: Ashgate, 1999).

Laermans, R., Wilson, B., and Billiet, J., *Secularization and Social Integration* (Leuven: Papers in honor of Karel Dobbelaere, Leuven University Press, 1998).

Laurens, H., *Orientales II: La IIIe République et l'Islam* (Paris: CNRS, 2004).

Lindholm, T. *et al.* (eds), *Facilitating Freedom of Religion and Belief: A Deskbook from the Oslo Coalition* (Leiden: Martinus Nijhoff Publishers, 2004).

MacColgan, A., *Discrimination Law: Text, Cases and Materials* (Oxford and Portland, OH: Hart Publishing, 2000).

Malik, M., 'Faith and the State of Jurisprudence', in Oliver, P. (ed.), *Faith in Law: Essays in Legal Theory* (Oxford: Hart Publications, 2000).

Modood, T., 'British Asian Muslims and the Rushdie Affair', in Donald, J., and Rattansi, A. (eds), *Race, Culture and Difference* (London: Sage, 1992).

Modood, T., *Multicultural Politics: Racism, Ethnicity, and Muslims in Britain*, (Minneapolis: University of Minnesota Press, 2005).

Oliver, P., Douglas Scott, S., and Tadros, V. (eds), *Faith in Law: Essays in Legal Theory* (Oxford: Hart Publishing, 2000).

Open Society Institute, *The Situation of Muslims in France in Monitoring the EU Accession Process: Minority Protection*, vol. II (Budapest: OSI, 2002).

Pew Research Center, 'Support for Terror Wanes Among Muslim Publics. Islamic Extremism: Common Concern for Muslim and Western Public', *The Pew Global Attitudes Project, 17 – Nation Pew Global Attitudes Survey* (Washington, DC: The Pew Forum on Religion and Public Life, July 2005).

Poulter, S., *Ethnicity, Law and Human Rights: The English Experience* (Oxford: Clarendon Press, 1998).

Poulter, S., 'Muslim Headscarves in School: Contrasting Legal Approaches in England and France', *Oxford Journal of Legal Studies*, 17: 1 (1997): 43–74.

Riley, A., 'Headscarves, Skull Caps and Crosses: Is the Proposed French Ban Safe from European Legal Challenge?', *CEPS Policy Brief*, 49 (April 2004).

Roussillon, A., 'Islam et mondialisation: état des lieux (provisoire) des débats suscités en France par les attentats du 11 septembre', *Monde Arabe*, n° 174 (2001): 75–89.

Roy, O., *La laïcité face à l'Islam* (Paris: Stock, 2005).

Runnymede Trust, *Islamophobia: A Challenge For Us All?* (London: Runnymede Trust, 1997).

Saada, E., *Les Enfants de la colonie: les métis de l'Empire français entre sujétion et citoyenneté (1890–2000)* (Paris: La Découverte, 2006).

Saïd, E., 'Preface to Orientalism', *Al-Ahram Weekly*, 750 (7–13 August 2003).

Savarese, E., *Histoire coloniale et immigration. Une invention de l'étranger* (Paris: Séguier, 2000).

Scharf, M., *Belief and Exclusion: Combating Religious Discrimination in Europe. A First NGO Approach* (Düsseldorf: ENAR, 2003).

Statham, P., Koopmans, R., Giugni, M., and Passy, F., 'Resilient or Adaptable Islam? Mutliculturalism, Religion and Migrants' Claims-making for Group Demands in Britain, the Netherlands and France', *Ethnicities*, 5:4 (2005): 427–59.

Vatin, J.-C., and Lucas, P., *L'Algérie des anthropologues* (Paris: François Maspéro, 1975).

Weller, P., Feldman, A., and Purdam, K., *Religious Discrimination in England and Wales* (London: Home Office Research Study 220, February 2001).

Werbner, P., ' "Our blood is green": Cricket, Identity and Social Empowerment Among British Pakistanis', in MacClancy J. (ed.), *Sport, Identity and Ethnicity* (Oxford: Berg, 1997).

Werbner, P., 'Theorising complex diasporas: purity and hybridity in the South Asian public sphere in Britain', *Journal of Ethnic and Migration Studies*, 30:5 (2004).

Part III

Discriminations in French and British Contexts

9
Societal Framework in Britain and France: Muslims in Prison

Jim Beckford and Danièle Joly

9.1 Introduction

This chapter developed from a project we designed to research populations of Muslim background in French and British prisons. Prior to
undertaking the actual research, we set out to establish the two differing
societal contexts which preside over the question of Muslims in prison
and its pertinence. This chapter explores a wide range of contexts that
bring issues about Islam and prisons to the fore in particular – and distinctive – ways. Beginning with England and Wales, the argument attrib-
utes special significance to the history of church–state relations and the
role of the Church of England as a 'broker' for other faiths in the public
realm. The second half of the chapter examines how the French
Republic's constitutional doctrines of *laïcité* influence the treatment of
Muslim prisoners. It also emphasizes the consequences for the treatment
of Muslims that can be traced back to France's colonial ventures in Africa
and the perception that is widespread in many sections of French society
that Muslims are associated with political extremism, or even terrorism.

9.2 The research context in England and Wales

The treatment of Muslims in prison is not the kind of topic that has
often been newsworthy or high on the agenda of British politicians. Nor
is it located in a clearly demarcated field of academic research. In fact,
there have been few investigations of this topic in England and Wales.
By comparison, interest in the incarceration of Muslims has been much
higher in the United States – mainly because of controversies surrounding the conditions in which 'Black Muslims' or members of the sepa-
ratist movement, the Nation of Islam, have been imprisoned. These

controversies have given rise to numerous court cases and a substantial literature in legal studies. No echoes of these legal questions have been heard in the United Kingdom, although a small number of prisoners in England and Wales have associated with the Nation of Islam. In short, the reasons for conducting an intensive study of the treatment of Muslim prisoners may not be immediately self-evident.

Nevertheless, questions about the treatment of Muslims in prison have taken progressively clearer shape in recent years. The questions take many different forms and they emerge from a variety of contexts. Each context generates its own formulation of the issues that concern the conditions in which Muslims are incarcerated. No single context is more influential than the others. It is the conjunction of these different contexts that makes the research timely and important.

9.2.1   State and Church

In the absence of a written constitution in the United Kingdom there is a general assumption that freedom of religion nevertheless exists. In fact, the Human Rights Act 1998 incorporates the European Convention on Human Rights into English and Scottish law, so the protection of religious freedom now has some substance in law.

The legal scholar, Anthony Bradney (1993: 158), argues that the idea of religious freedom in Britain rests on the assumption that the country is homogeneous in religious terms:

> It speaks of a country where all are essentially the same, where there are 'our traditions' which unify 'us' and divide 'us' from other nations. 'We' know there is religious freedom because 'we' can follow our religion (which 'we' take lightly) and if others are different they are different in no significant way. If the religious beliefs of others vary in any important manner, altering the way in which they view the family or children or education or whatever, then this indicates that their beliefs take them outside the magic circle of acceptable standards; this, in itself, justifying their different treatment.

The Church of England, in particular, has been enjoying privileges and responsibilities that derive from its status as 'established in law' since the sixteenth century. Other churches are nowadays 'tolerated' in the sense of being implicitly permitted to function in Britain without explicit legal or constitutional legitimation. As Bryan Wilson (1995: 101) has pointed out, however, tolerance is a much weaker form of protection than a legal guarantee of religious freedom.

The growth of religious diversity since the 1950s, especially in England, has helped to reopen debates about the 'establishment' of the Church of England and about the advantages that mainstream Christian churches enjoy in public life. The increase in the number of Buddhists, Hindus, Muslims, and Sikhs in Britain has moved questions about equal opportunities in religion higher up the public agenda. The issue of the individual citizen's 'right' to hold religious beliefs is not really at stake. But issues about the public recognition of the main faith traditions have come to the surface of political life – aided, no doubt, by the linkage that exists in some cases between religion and ethnicity. These issues are particularly acute in prisons for a variety of reasons. The issues flow from the fact that certain Christian organizations have enjoyed either de jure or de facto privileges in their relation with prison authorities. In British prisons, Christian chaplains have acted as brokers for other faiths but also as gatekeepers (Beckford and Gilliat, 1998). However, the British government currently supports and encourages all faith communities to engage with the processes of public policy-making (O'Beirne, 2004).

9.2.2 Muslims in Britain

Estimates of the number of Muslims resident in England and Wales have varied between about one million and two millions. The 2001 Census puts the figure at roughly 1.6 million or 3 percent of the population. Most British Muslims are either migrants to the United Kingdom from Pakistan, India, Bangladesh, and East Africa or descendants of these migrants. With the exception of asylum seekers and refugees from the former Yugoslavia, Somalia, Afghanistan, Iraq, and some parts of the former Soviet Union, relatively few Muslims have been permitted to enter the United Kingdom for the purpose of settlement since the 1980s. Nevertheless, the Muslim population of England and Wales is increasing because its birth rate is higher than the national average. In addition, Britain has perhaps as many as 10,000 white and African Caribbean converts to Islam.

The geographical distribution of Muslims is not even in England and Wales. Most of them live in the major conurbations and cities of England, with dense concentrations in parts of the North West, the Midlands, and London. Nevertheless, the fact that the number of mosques, Muslim organizations, and *halal* food businesses continues to increase in many other parts of the country suggests that a process of internal redistribution is beginning to take place. A small minority of British Muslims have already achieved high levels of prosperity and material security, while the majority still struggle to achieve parity with their white compatriots.

As legislation and administrative practice in England and Wales place so much emphasis on monitoring and penalizing the 'racial' or 'ethnic' basis of unfair discrimination, it is difficult to identify the separate effect of religious factors. Outside prisons, there is no requirement in law to guard against discrimination on purely religious grounds; there are numerous grounds on which British Muslims can claim, with justification, that their position tends to be inferior to that of other sections of British society. Their sense of relative deprivation and injustice is particularly strong in relation to housing, education, employment, policing, and generalized discrimination (Anwar and Bakhsh, 2003; Commission on British Muslims and Islamophobia, 2001; Weller, Feldman and Purdam, 2001).

Turning points in the development of a sense of marginalization and social exclusion among British Muslims include the 'Rushdie affair' in 1988; the mounting hostility toward asylum seekers beginning in the 1990s; the large-scale disturbances in Oldham, Burnley, and Bradford in the Summer of 2001; and the aftermath of Al-Qaeda's attacks on aircraft and buildings in the United States on 11 September 2001. This aftermath includes the introduction of new anti-terrorist legislation, the Anti-terrorism Crime and Security Act 2001, and the detention in custody – without charge or trial – of about twelve foreign nationals suspected of involvement in terrorism linked to radical currents in Islam. This figure was augmented after the 7 July 2005 suicide bombs on the London bus and underground. Moreover, 30 percent of respondents to an ICM opinion survey conducted by telephone interviews with a sample of 500 British Muslims (generated by a two-stage process of random sampling and 'snowball' sampling) in November 2001 reported that hostility or abuse had been directed against them or a member of their family as a result of the events in America on September 11.[1] According to a second survey of 500 adult Muslims conducted in March 2004 by ICM Research, 33 percent of respondents reported that they or members of their family had experienced hostility or abuse from non-Muslims because of their religion.[2]

Moreover, the anti-Islamic, anti-Muslim, and anti-Asian machinations of movements and parties on the extreme right wing of British politics show no signs of declining in strength or frequency in the early twenty-first century. On the contrary, extremist ideologues are now targeting Muslims directly in the former mill towns of Lancashire and Yorkshire, thereby provoking serious anxiety, unrest and, on occasion, violence among young Muslims in particular. No doubt, these considerations weighed on the minds of the 51 percent of respondents to an opinion poll commissioned by the BBC in 2001 who agreed with the statement that Britain was a 'racist society' (ICM poll for BBC News).

9.2.3 Increase of Muslims in prison

The fact that the number of Muslims, male and female, serving prison sentences in England and Wales has nearly trebled since 1991 from 1959 to 5865 in 2003 – whereas the total prison population has grown by about one-third in the same period – gives rise to many concerns. Muslim prisoners have increased as a proportion of the prison population from 4.49 percent in 1991 to 8.05 percent in 2003. They have also become more diverse in terms of their national origins and reasons for being in the United Kingdom. For example, civil war in Somalia and the former Yugoslavia, genocide in Central Africa, warfare in Afghanistan and Iraq, and economic hardship in parts of Central and Eastern Europe have all raised the numbers of Muslim asylum seekers, refugees, and other actual and would-be migrants to the United Kingdom in recent years. Inevitably, some of these foreign nationals have ended up in prison, thereby adding to the diversity of the Muslim inmate population. In fact, foreigners amounted to 24 percent of all South Asian sentenced prisoners and 31 percent of all Black sentenced prisoners in 2003.

In addition to being diverse in terms of their nationality, Muslim prisoners come from a wide variety of ethnic backgrounds. In fact, the ethnic background of Muslims in the general population is sharply different from that of Muslims in prison.[3]

Again, ethnically South Asian Muslims constitute only 29 percent of all Muslims in prison, whereas people of South Asian descent amount to 74 percent of all Muslims in the United Kingdom.[4] The stereotypical image of the Muslim prisoner as of South Asian or British-Asian origin is therefore misleading. Claims about the over-representation of this stereotypical Muslim prisoner in the prisons of England and Wales should be scrutinized carefully (see also Matthew and Francis, 1996: 144). There is certainly an over-representation of Muslims in the inmate population, but many of them are foreign nationals and/or from backgrounds other than South Asian.

It is evident, however, that the Prison Service of England and Wales (PSEW) has faced a significant change in the religious composition of the people whom it is required to hold securely and safely. The training of prison staff, the design of diets, the configuration of chapels and chaplaincy centers, and the appointment of Visiting Ministers of 'other faiths' (called 'sessional chaplains' since 2003) have all undergone changes intended to accommodate a growing proportion of prisoners from religious backgrounds other than Christian.

These changes have had a particularly significant impact on the provision of facilities and opportunities for Muslims to practice their religion in prison. First, the recently retired Chief Inspector of Prisons, Sir David Ramsbotham, emphasized the contribution that appropriate facilities for religious practice could make toward his vision of 'a healthy prison'. Second, the Chaplain General of the PSEW who took up his appointment in the summer of 2001, the Ven. William Noblett, had previously established the chaplaincy at HMP Full Sutton on a thoroughly multi-faith basis. His policies and practice had set new standards for cooperation between chaplains and Visiting Ministers. There was a clear expectation that his appointment to a position of leadership at the prison service headquarters would herald major advances in the recognition that Muslims, as well as the followers of other faiths outside the Christian category, should be better integrated into prison chaplaincy at all levels. Third, the creation and filling in 1999 of a new post of Muslim Advisor to the PSEW was also evidence that the prison service intended to give more voice to Muslim opinion and to establish a more satisfactory basis on which imams could be selected, trained, inducted, and remunerated for their services as Visiting Ministers, sessional chaplains[5] – or, more radically, as full-time Muslim chaplains.

9.2.4   Voluntary organizations for the welfare of Muslim prisoners

The history of links between the PSEW and representatives of Islam in the United Kingdom is lengthy, but formal cooperation did not begin until the early 1980s. For most of the 1980s and 1990s the Islamic Cultural Centre, based at the London Central Mosque, took the responsibility of looking after the interests of most Muslim inmates.[6] One senior administrator, Bashir Ebrahim-Khan, acted as the main point of reference for questions about the religious, cultural, social, and dietary needs of inmates. In his capacity as Prison Affairs Coordinator, he negotiated with governors of prisons as well as with staff at prison service headquarters. Indeed, he was one of the compilers of a radical plan for the overhaul of the Prison Service Chaplaincy that was presented to the Secretary of State at the Home Office in a meeting at the House of Commons in March 1996.[7]

High on the list of Mr Ebrahim-Khan's priorities were two particular issues. First, he sought an improvement in the ways in which Muslim Visiting Ministers were appointed, trained, and reimbursed for their services and expenses. Second, he argued as early as 1992 for the creation of a new salaried post of Muslim Advisor to the prison service. The proposal was that such an Advisor, with the status of an Assistant Chaplain General, would assume responsibility for the recruitment, training, and working conditions of Muslim Visiting Ministers as well as for the day-to-day issues affecting the religious obligations of Muslim inmates.

Ironically, the Islamic Cultural Center's success in pressing for the appointment of a Muslim Advisor to the prison service heralded the loss of its position as the body mainly responsible for nominating Muslim Visiting Ministers. The prison service reallocated this function to a new organization, the National Council for the Welfare of Muslim Prisoners (NCWMP), which was supported by the Iqra Trust, an independent, charitable organization with expertise in Islamic education and programs of educational outreach in the United Kingdom and the United States. The NCWMP, formed in 1999, represented a number of prominent national Muslim organizations. In other words, there was a history of successful collaboration between the Iqra Trust and the prison service, including the Prison Service Chaplaincy, before the first Muslim Advisor took up his post in the summer of 1999.

In a sense, the NCWMP and the Muslim Advisor were also competing with each other for the support and patronage of powerful Muslim interest groups including the Muslim Council of Britain and the handful of Muslims who had reached the highest echelons of parliament and of political parties. Moreover, the Muslim Advisor, as a civil servant, was accountable to senior managers in the prison service and was therefore subject to a certain amount of indirect political constraint. Some of the issues with which he dealt on a virtually daily basis were politically sensitive. For example, the furore that surrounded the so-called Shoe Bomber, Richard Reid, threatened to be highly damaging to the interests of Muslim inmates and Visiting Ministers. Reid was convicted of attempting to use explosives concealed in his shoes to blow up an airliner *en route* from Paris to Miami in December 2001. Some journalists and program makers claimed that he had converted to Islam in prison whilst serving sentences in the early 1990s and that, by implication, English prisons were a breeding ground for Islamic extremism. Another potentially destructive controversy developed in the wake of the attacks by Muslim extremists on New York and the Pentagon on 11 September 2001. Again, there were allegations that Muslim Visiting Ministers had fermented dissidence in prisons by preaching radical forms of Islam. Press reports claimed that two Visiting Ministers had been suspended from duties on suspicion of circulating 'inflammatory anti-American literature' (*Guardian*, 29 December 2001) to Muslim inmates. One of them was reinstated after an investigation; the other's suspension turned out to be unconnected to extremism (*Muslim News*, 3 January 2002).

The crucial question is, therefore, whether the appointment of a Muslim Advisor and the progressive increase in the number of full-time Muslim chaplains in prison will eventually weaken the direct involvement of Muslim voluntary organizations such as the Iqra Trust, the Muslim Council of Britain, and the NCWMP in the monitoring and guidance of the prison service's treatment of Muslim inmates. By the end of 2004, it was clear that the full-time Muslim chaplains were making very little use of the NCWMP. In fact, some of them were quite critical of its alleged failure to deliver services or Islamic literature to prisoners.

9.2.5   Ethnicity

Muslims in England and Wales, whether in prison or not, constitute not only a religious minority but also an ethnic minority. This means that most of the 1.6 million Muslims who voluntarily answered a question about their religion by categorizing themselves as such in the 2001 Census of the UK's population come from social, national, and cultural backgrounds different from those of the majority of Britons. They were either born in countries such as Bangladesh, India or Pakistan, or raised in the United Kingdom by parents who had originally come from these countries. Roughly 60 percent of today's British Muslims were born in the United Kingdom, but their families and communities are still likely to observe social and cultural norms that are different in some respects from those shared by the majority in Britain. Moreover, the collective and individual identities of most British Muslims retain varying degrees of association with South Asian ways of life – remembered, adapted, or invented. This means that Muslims in the prisons of England and Wales have access to distinctive notions of such things as morality, loyalty, solidarity, shame, cleanliness, and propriety. They are not 'ruled' in any deterministic sense by these notions, and British ways of life have influenced their outlooks. Nonetheless, many British Muslims still honor and reproduce distinctive patterns of thought, feeling, and action that reflect the ethnic origins of their parents and grandparents. The treatment of Muslim prisoners gives rise, therefore, to questions about the extent to which prisons magnify, challenge, or repress ethnic distinctiveness.

9.2.6   Racism in a postcolonial setting

An investigation into Muslim inmates also helps to explain the continuing, but changing, nature of relations between Britain – as the former colonial power in most of South Asia – and its former colonial subjects and their descendants who are now resident in the United Kingdom. Indeed, prisons – as symbols and instantiations of the power of the state – could be considered as sites where the tensions and grudges of a postcolonial order would be at their most severe. Racism, in the sense of prejudice and discrimination aimed at people defined by their skin color and other phenotypical characteristics, could also be expected to flourish in settings like prisons where the routines of official categorization and discipline are backed by the threat and the reality of legitimate physical coercion. Social class and gender are further dimensions of the postcolonial context that have a bearing on the way in which Muslim inmates experience custodial sentences. Many of these issues come to a head in perceptions, discussions, and denials of racism.

9.2.7 Islamophobia

Allegations that British Muslims were the victims of Islamophobia began to surface in the late 1980s, at roughly the same time as some commentators started to argue that racism was no longer a matter of biological differences, but was assuming a new form based on cultural differences. This was part of a political strategy to keep the categories of 'Black' and 'Asian' separate in order to reflect more faithfully their different experiences of racism in Britain. Researchers have subsequently assembled more arguments in support of the claim that hostility to Islam and to Muslims has increased significantly in recent years. Meanwhile, evidence has also come to light of a growing willingness of British Muslims to identify themselves as 'Muslims' first and foremost in many situations – in preference to identification as, for example, 'Asians', 'Pakistanis', or 'Bangladeshis'. The British public first became aware of this movement toward the assertion of distinctively Muslim interests and identities in the course of the controversies that enveloped Salman Rushdie's novel *The Satanic Verses* in 1988, the hostility that it evoked among Muslims, and the *fatwah* issued by Ayatollah Khomeini. Just over a decade later there was additional evidence of the salience attaching to 'Muslim' identity in the civil disturbances that broke out in various cities of Northern England, beginning in Oldham in May 2001 and continuing in Bradford in July 2001. It is no accident that political movements on the extreme right wing of British politics now target 'Muslims' as well as 'Asians', thereby helping to reinforce the very identity that these movements seek to undermine.

9.2.8 Islam and extremism

The context in which our research on Muslims in prison was conducted changed dramatically on 11 September 2001, when Al-Qaeda terrorists launched a series of coordinated attacks on targets in the United States. The loss of several thousand lives aboard hijacked aircraft and on the ground in New York City, Washington, DC, and Pennsylvania has done more than any other event to suggest associations between extremist Islamic beliefs and serious criminal conduct. The UN-backed military campaign against the Taliban regime in Afghanistan, attacks on American embassies and a warship in Yemen, the widely publicized murder of an American journalist in Pakistan, the arrest and conviction of a Muslim convert for planning to blow up an aircraft with explosives concealed in his shoes, and the bombing of a nightclub patronized by Western tourists on the Indonesian island of Bali have led to suspicions that extremist currents in Islamic thinking are only the most visible symptoms of a deeper incompatibility between Islam and modern Western democracies, cultures, and economies. This is a theme much publicized by Huntington's 'Clash of Civilizations' book. Particularly controversial is the fact that some of the Muslims charged with criminal offences are believed to have converted or reverted to Islam during previous spells in prison. Journalists therefore raise questions about the likelihood that prisons have become 'breeding grounds' of Islamic militancy.

9.2.9 Prison problems

It would be a serious mistake to assume that the topic of Muslims in prison was timely simply because of links between Islamic extremism and acts of terrorism. Another aspect of the context for our research is equally important: that is, the well-publicized problems faced by the PSEW. Even before the rate of increase in the prison population began to accelerate sharply in the early 1990s, prisons were often in the news for reasons that had nothing to do with Muslims.[8] By 2002, the incarceration rate for England and Wales had reached 139 per 100,000 of the population. This was the highest rate in Western Europe. At the same time, the prison service reported that it had failed to achieve six of its 15 'key performance indicators', thereby acknowledging that the system was operating in a far from satisfactory manner. Any consideration of the treatment of Muslims in prison must, therefore, take this context into account.

9.3 The research context in France

The most salient feature of the relation between religion and society in France is the set of secular, republican values and institutions known as *laïcité*. It was forged during and after the French Revolution and even more specifically during the Third Republic after 1871. The principal result was a law separating State and Church in 1905 that still governs the relationship between the state and religion in France today (see Baubérot, 1997, 2000; Boepflug, Dunand and Willaime, 1996; Poulat, 1987; Willaime, 2004).

9.3.1 *Laïcité*

Laïcité, or republican secularism, contrary to appearances, has many shades of meaning. Historically, at least three of these meanings have been operative during different periods of the French Republic. One meaning sets religion and the state in an antagonistic and mutually exclusive relationship; another makes no concession to religion in institutional terms but, in practice, it shows flexibility toward religious rights; and the third meaning interprets *laïcité* as a kind of neutral or agnostic attitude of the powers-that-be toward religion. It holds that all faiths are supposed to be on a par, and the state recognizes many of them if they respect public order, pluralism, and the exclusion of religion from the institutions of the Republic – especially state-run schools. On the other hand, as Jean-Paul Willaime (2004: 296, 330–3) emphasizes, the degree of actual – as distinct from ideological or legal – separation of Church and State is open to various interpretations. For example, the public culture of France has remained predominantly Catholic; the French state's centralized and hierarchical structures seem to be modeled on those of the early modern Catholic Church; the Republic still finances extensive religious activities in the Alsace-Moselle region as well as in some overseas territories; state funds go toward the cost of maintaining church buildings forming part of the national cultural heritage. *Laïcité* is therefore nothing if not elusive, ambiguous, and still potentially contentious. The 2003 Stasi report's revival of hard-line *laïcité*, nonetheless, makes an explicit reference to the need of imams (*aumoniers*) in prison.

Historically, the Catholic Church was opposed to *laïcité*, but progressively (and particularly since Vatican II) it came to make compromises; the old animosity against the French Republic has given way to a new attitude which appreciates the neutrality of the state and finds comfort in the autonomy of the Catholic Church, and of Christian churches in general, from the state.

Given the background of French *laïcité*, it is not surprising that chaplaincy is a relatively modest aspect of the prison system in France. There is only one official at the prison service headquarters with responsibility for chaplaincy provision across the entire system. In addition, Regional Directors decide, in conjunction with prefectural officials, whether to accept or reject proposals that come from directors of individual prisons for the appointment and payment of chaplains. In effect, then, directors enjoy qualified discretion about the resources allocated to religious, spiritual, and pastoral care of prisoners.

Nevertheless, according to Thiébaud (2000), the criminal law Code specifies that prisoners should be informed, on arrival in prison, of the opportunity to meet a representative of their religion and to attend religious services (Article D.436). Other chapters in the Code state that prisoners must be able to meet their religious, moral, or spiritual obligations (Article D.432); to write to their chaplains in confidence (Article D.438); to keep religious artifacts and books (Article D.439); and to talk to chaplains in privacy, even when they are in punishment cells (Article D.437).

The number of unpaid and remunerated chaplains in post in January 2001 was 635,[9] of whom only 45 (7 percent) received payment for full-time work and 249 (39 percent) for part-time work. The remaining 341, or 54 percent of the total, served as voluntary chaplains. In addition, 190 voluntary chaplaincy auxiliaries helped chaplains with their group work. Roman Catholic chaplains amounted to 47 percent of all chaplains; Protestants 34 percent; Jews 10 percent; and Muslims 6 percent. Other chaplains included three from Orthodox Churches and two Buddhists. The proportions of chaplains paid by the prison service vary by faith community. Thus, 57 percent of Catholic chaplains, 32 percent of Protestant chaplains, 48 percent of Jewish chaplains, and 50 percent of Muslim chaplains received payments. The total budget for chaplains in 2000 was 2 million French francs.

The end of the 'war between the two Frances' (Poulat, 1987) and the relatively peaceful relationship between the Republic and the Church in recent decades have removed the tension that used to galvanize French society (Gauchet, 1998). However, this declining tension between state and religion does not apply to controversial new religious movements – widely vilified in official discourse as 'cultic excesses' (*dérives sectaires*) – and, more importantly, Islam. As a newcomer to French society on a massive scale, Islam faces many problems in the French public sphere

(Geisser, 2003). Three sets of problems can be identified:

(a) Islam is mainly the religion of North Africans or of their offspring; Turks, although economically excluded to the same extent as young people from North African origin, do not come from former French colonies and are not yet perceived as radicalized. Even after two generations or more, the *'Islam des banlieues'* ('Islam from the deprived suburbs') still bears the painful marks of the colonial legacy and the painful decolonization of Algeria in the early 1960s. A significant proportion of Muslims in France consists of Algerians or of people of Algerian descent (about 1.5 million) (Amiraux, 2002). The return of about one million French people from Algeria after independence gave rise to resentment on their part toward the Algerians who came to France to work in industry.

(b) In Algeria, radical Islamists have been nurturing anti-French feeling, among other things, which in turn has given further ammunition to the French extreme right in their struggle against Muslims or 'North Africans'.

(c) Islam is a religion that seems to represent a more radical challenge to *laïcité* and to the customary French separation between the public and private spheres than does any other religion. The dominant institutions of France are resistant to recognizing any kind of community other than the national one. Islamic communities are perceived as a threat to the pattern of individual citizenship, which has shaped French history over the last two centuries. All these problems are aggravated by the current trend toward Islamic radicalism in the world. The trend includes the Iranian revolution (1979); the radicalization of the FIS (Front Islamique du Salut) in Algeria after the refusal of the Algerian military rulers to recognize their right to govern the country in 1992 when they had obtained a majority in parliament; and the Al-Qaeda phenomenon, particularly after 11 September 2001.

9.3.2 Particular problems for Muslim prisoners

The French prison system, in comparison with its English counterpart, is distinctive for holding prisoners indicted for being members of 'associations of criminals involved in terrorism' (*'association de malfaiteurs en relation à une action terroriste'*). A few hundred of them were arrested in the 1990s, and the trend, after 11 September 2001, is toward more arrests, convictions, and long prison sentences. They form a category of 'Muslims' that, until 2002, were not represented in English prisons at least on the same scale as in France.

Another distinctive feature of the French prison system is that many prisons that are close to the so-called *banlieues* (deprived suburbs), where many Muslims live, have a much higher proportion of Muslim inmates than elsewhere. According to prison officials, the proportion of Muslim inmates can be as high as 70 or 80 percent. This is not the case in Britain (see the statistics in Beckford and Gilliat, 1998; Guessous, Hopper and Moorthy, 2000). Yet, unlike the situation in the prisons of England and Wales, Islam is very weakly institutionalized in French prisons, partly because of *laïcité* but also because of the fear of having inmates claim rights that might be used against the *status quo* within the prison.

9.3.3   The independence of prison directors

In addition to these factors, another important feature of the French prison system is the extensive independence enjoyed by prisons in terms of how they interpret *laïcité* and put in place their own rules in line with the preferences of their directors. In one prison, for instance, we were denied access to prisoners because, as we were told afterwards, the Director, an elderly man awaiting retirement, was not looking for 'trouble'. In another prison, by contrast, the director was a 'liberal' who did everything he could to facilitate our research. In the third prison, one of the largest in Europe, we were denied entry to the prison for some time, in spite of the authorization that we had received from the Minister of Justice and the prison administration. After a few months, however, and with the cooperation of one of the leading officials who happened to be of North African origin, we were given generous access to the prison to do our research.

The extensive autonomy of each prison director to interpret *laïcité* in his or her own way can be provocative to inmates who realize that the rules of the game are largely dictated by the prison administrators rather than by central regulations. This might seem to be contradictory to the French state system, which is well known for its Jacobin tradition and centralism.

9.3.4   Statistical uncertainty

Another difference between the French and the English prison systems concerns statistics. In England, people admitted to prison are asked to declare their religious identity so that they can receive appropriate religious support, including their dietary requirements. In France, since the second half of the 1990s, it is illegal to ask someone to declare his or her religious faith, and there are no official data concerning the religious or ethnic identity of French people in general, and of those in prison in particular. It follows from the lack of official data about ethnicity and religion in the French prison population that official commentary on these phenomena is virtually non-existent.[10] The result is that otherwise excellent analyses of the demographic evolution of the French prison population can take no account of changes in its ethnic or religious composition (see, for example, Tournier, 2000). It would also be unthinkable in France to conduct any official investigation along the lines of the National Prison Survey carried out in 1991 by the British Home Office (Walmsley, Howard and White, 1992).

The only statistical data which might give some clue as to the number of Muslims in French prisons are those which distinguish between nationalities. But this is of very limited help since it would fail to distinguish between French people of North African origin who happen to be Muslims and other French citizens. The only information that is more or less certain to identify Muslim inmates is their name. But in some cases (in few cases as a matter of fact) Muslims have French names. On the whole, the lack of statistical data on religion makes it difficult to be precise about the number of Muslims within the French prison system.

Official statistics on the number of Muslims or of people from any other religious or ethnic background in French prisons do not exist, but unofficial estimates suggest that the *percentage* of Muslims in prison is between 50 percent and 60 percent of the inmate population. Yet, Muslims constitute roughly 7 percent of the population of France, assuming that they number somewhere between 4 and 5 million.[11] If it is indeed true that 50 percent of the French prison population of 50,000 is Muslim, they are seven times over-represented. In some prisons – two out of the three we studied – the proportion of Muslims appeared to be even higher than 50 percent. According to some Prison Officers who were directly in touch with the inmates, the rate on some wings is close to 70 or 80 percent.

9.3.5 The ambiguity of *laïcité*

Each prison seems to interpret *laïcité* to suit itself and to reflect its own history and social setting. The problems arising from the practice of Islam within prison that result in some tension with *laïcité* include

- daily collective prayers
- prayer mats (it is forbidden to carry them in prison)
- meals during Ramadan
- *halal* meat requested to be on sale in prison shops
- the provision of *halal* meat from outside

- daily prayers and the practice of prison staff entering cells during prayers
- meeting the imam (the Muslim minister)
- the provision of a compass (a metallic object that cannot be received by post or handed over in prison) for determining the direction of Mecca when making daily prayers
- the performance of religious obligations (mainly the daily prayers) during working hours in prison
- the provision of *The Qur'an* in prison libraries
- female Muslim inmates wearing head scarves.

French prison officials seem to have no explicit solutions to these problems. Many refuse to discuss them formally, hiding behind *laïcité* and the necessity of having a secular public sphere in prisons.

This policy has its limits, however, and with many prisons filled with Muslims, the problem of new patterns of conduct within prison is becoming more and more salient. In a way, French *laïcité* has actually been based on a double standard: firmness in the declaration of principle, but some degree of flexibility in its actual application. In the school system, for example, the principle of *laïcité* was firmly asserted against the Catholic Church, but chaplaincies were established in state schools (*écoles publiques*). In the same fashion, the day for the weekly holidays was chosen to be the same as the Catholic one, Sunday (Baubérot, 2000). The protagonists of a 'defensive *laïcité*' tend to refuse compromise and to insist rigidly on the rules of the French system in schools, prisons, and the public sector in general. The outcome is a refusal to accept cultural diversity and the display of any religious symbols (especially Islamic ones) in the public sphere. In prisons, Islam tends to be treated as 'nonexistent' since prisons are public institutions and therefore compelled to follow the public rules of *laïcité*. But reality imposes the need for some flexibility: how to tackle the problem of food, how to cope with prayers and religious radicalization?

The last problem is common to many European countries, but an aggressive interpretation of *laïcité* in the French case, due to the cultural crisis within French society and the refusal to recognize some Muslim principles considered contrary to *laïcité*, make the situation more tense than in many other European countries. The failure to recognize that any community, other than the nation, stands between the individual and the state places some of the most vulnerable people in difficult situations. That is why those Algerian groups, who do not really amount to a community, pose the most 'communitarian' threat to the French state.

They do not form a community in contradistinction to the so-called Chinese or the Portuguese or Turks. The 'communitarianism' of North African young people, particularly those who are economically excluded, socially stigmatized, and confined to the disadvantaged suburbs, arises from the fact that they do not receive sufficient economic support from the state[12] and they cannot count on any community assistance (the Algerians are the least socially organized people among the North Africans in France). 'Islamization' in disadvantaged French suburbs operates as much as a religion substituting for non-existent communities, and that is why this process is most widespread in the *banlieues*. By becoming active Muslims, these socially disaffected people are seeking some form of community that could compensate for the lack of any social group capable of giving them a sense of dignity and identity within a society where they count for very little (*'quantité négligeable'*). But since any visible community in France is regarded with suspicion and as a potential threat to national identity, Islamization meets with hostility. This hostility has increased because of the actions of radical Muslims in the Southern Mediterranean region and because of the historical links between France and Algeria.

The paradox of the French situation is that where real communities exist, they have no public visibility; and where 'communitarian' visibility is highest, there is a lack of community except in a symbolic sense. On the other hand, since public visibility is denied to communities, whenever a potential community begins to look for legitimacy (like the newly constituted Islamic communities), they are forced into some kind of radicalization because they are automatically treated as 'fundamentalist' or 'extremist'.

Cases in point include the issue of headscarves in women's prisons, collective prayer, or even *halal* food for Muslims. These cases are treated by most of the prison authorities as something that goes against *laïcité* and, therefore, as illegal. To wear a headscarf in prison is regarded as incompatible with *laïcité* by prison managers; permission for Friday prayers is refused; Muslim ministers are not recruited for fear of radicalism and fundamentalism. In turn, all of this pushes Muslim inmates toward more radical and more rebellious attitudes vis-à-vis a management that denies them the basic right to practice their religion (which, incidentally, is formally recognized by the laws of *laïcité* that provide for religious freedom).

Throughout the Western world Islam represents a new challenge whose multiple social and cultural dimensions are yet to be understood, tackled, and somehow translated into the terms used in democratic traditions. But in France, Islam is even more of a challenge to society because the public sphere is defined in a way that radicalizes the part of the Muslim population that feels more stigmatized than in many other European countries.

A comparison between France and England, in so far as prison rules and tolerance thresholds for Muslims are concerned, provides a clear example of these problems. In British prisons, it is acknowledged that Muslim inmates have the right to *halal* food as a condition of complying with their religious obligations. This right is not recognized as such in France: greater or lesser degrees of tolerance exist toward it in different prisons. The minimal requirement is met that an alternative food is available when pork is on the menu. But there is no recognition of the right to appropriate food on religious grounds, neither for Islam nor for Judaism. In the prisons of England and Wales, the right to collective prayers is also recognized. In practice, there is no such provision in France. Friday collective prayer took place in only one out of the three prisons that we studied (hereafter referred to as Prison A, B, C); and this was due in part to the director's favorable attitude toward religious matters and his open interpretation of *laïcité*, which contrasts with the rigidity that we found in the other prisons.

The *hijab* is accepted in the prisons of England and Wales, whereas in France it is simply prohibited except in cells. For the Director of the women's section of Prison B, the question of the veil was handled like this: 'the rule is that they can wear it in their cells but not when moving about the prison or during classes or sport or walking time. The rule of *laïcité* is: no veil.' The Director seems to be unaware of the fact that the *hijab* is mainly intended to be worn in the public sphere and that, in the private sphere, it is useless, at least among wives, other women, husbands, and children. Social and cultural diversification is denied for the sake of a mythically homogeneous nationhood that refuses to acknowledge the existence of minority groups as a way of defending universality.

The only practical way that the French prison system has found to cope with the problem of Islam is to recruit prison officers from North African backgrounds who have a much better understanding than do the other officers of the cultural needs of Muslim inmates. For example, the Assistant Director of Prison C believed that the problem of the Muslim prisoners could be partially solved by appointing new staff from the 'Dom Tom' (*Départements d'outre-mer*) or overseas French territories and from the families of former immigrants. This solution to the problem of relations between prison managers and Muslim prisoners is satisfactory in many respects, but it still does not solve the major problem of accepting Islam as a fully fledged religion – which is the religion of the majority in some prisons – in many French prison establishments and of getting prisons to adjust to this fact.

The major problem in French prisons is to see how *laïcité*, as it is interpreted and applied by management, is received, reworked, and reinterpreted by prisoners. For our purposes there are roughly three types of prisoners:

(i) Foreigners with no real experience of French culture (for instance, illegal immigrants). Many of them do not speak French or speak it only in a rudimentary fashion.

(ii) Foreigners from former French colonies in North Africa or Black Africa. They include people from the Maghreb who went to France to work illegally without necessarily having close relatives there.

(iii) French citizens of African origin (Black as well as North African), who are second- or third-generation immigrants. Most of them live in the disadvantaged suburbs or *banlieues*.

The understanding that prisoners have of *laïcité* does not necessarily reflect their cultural background, their social origin or their age. They display many types of attitude toward *laïcité*, its rejection, or its internalization.

Another problem is that in many cases even those who react against French *laïcité* and reject it can find that they are directly influenced by it. It is impossible to understand their views of religion and their relation to themselves as well as to their other 'brothers in religion' without taking account of how they internalize *laïcité* (in a positive or negative sense).

In any case, those prisoners – and they are the absolute majority in the prisons that we studied – who are French of Maghrebin descent or North Africans who share a similar culture, have a religious view of reality that does not seem to depend significantly on whether or not they have French citizenship. This is particularly true of those whom many French sociologists and journalists call 'young people from the disadvantaged suburbs' ('*les jeunes des banlieues*').

9.4   Conclusion

This chapter has argued that the topic of Muslims in prison carries widely different significance in the two settings of France and Britain. In fact, questions about Muslim prisoners arise in sharply different forms. Discourse about them is also patterned differently. Our argument is that these differences are far from accidental. They are actually conditioned – though not determined – by complex sets of factors that, in turn, have been shaped by centuries of tension, struggle, and compromise between the forces of religion and politics. Again, our evidence indicates that policies and practices conform to the logic of each country's mode of accommodating religious and ethnic minorities.[13]

Notes

1. The survey was commissioned by BBC Radio 4: http:www.bbc.co.uk/radio4/today/reports/archive/features/muslimpoll.shtm (accessed 19 March 2003).
2. http://www.icmresearch.co.uk/reviews/2004/guardian-muslims-march-2004.htm (accessed 30 May 2004).
3. For example, roughly one-third of prisoners registered as Muslims in England and Wales are Black, whereas the 2001 Census showed that only 2.2 percent of the general population was Black. People who identified themselves as of 'Chinese or other' ethnic identity in the Census amounted to only 1.3 percent of the population, but this category accounted for 26 percent of Muslim prisoners. The proportion of Muslim prisoners who are white is 12 percent, whereas white people constituted 91 percent of the population according to the 2001 Census.
4. Census, 2001, England and Wales.
5. Representatives of faith communities – other than mainstream Christian churches – who conducted religious services, teaching, study groups, and pastoral support in prison were called 'Visiting Ministers' until the Prison Service Chaplaincy decided in 2002 to refer to them all by the more inclusive title of 'sessional chaplains'.
6. In addition, the Al-Khoei Foundation began looking after the religious interests of the small number of Shi'a Muslim inmates in 1994.
7. Online document at: http://www.angulimala.org.uk/Religion%20in%20Prisons%20(Disc%20Paper).pdf (accessed 3 September 2003).
8. There have been many allegations of, and inquiries into, such things as overcrowding, lack of time permitted for association with other prisoners, lax security, racism, brutality, high rates of suicide, poor nutrition, inadequate health care, inhumane treatment of female prisoners giving birth, and the failure to prevent illegal drugs from circulating among inmates.
9. According to the '*Administration pénitentiaire: rapport annuel d'activité 2000*' online at http://www.ladocumentationfrancaise.fr/BRP/024000162/0000.pdf (accessed 10 September 2003).
10. For example, annual reports of the prison service's work make no references to ethnicity and only brief observations about religion such as the number of paid and unpaid chaplains, the budget for chaplaincy, and the duties prescribed for chaplains and their auxiliaries by the Penal Code sections D432 to D439.
11. Boyer (1998) estimates the number of Muslims in France to be around 4,155,000. He categorizes them as follows: 2.9 million of North African descent, among whom 1.55 million from Algeria, one million from Morocco,

and 350,000 from Tunisia. In addition, there are 315,000 from Turkey and 250,000 from Black Africa. A further 100,000 are from the Middle East and about 350,000 are political asylum seekers.

12. Most of them have not had the kind of employment that would have given them entitlement to benefits; and those below the age of 25 are not entitled to the minimum monthly unemployment benefit.

13. We are grateful to the Economic and Social Research Council for generously funding the project entitled "Muslims in prison: a European challenge" (R000 23 8528) between 2001 and 2004. Jim Beckford and I were the co-directors of the project. Farhad Khosrokhavar took charge of the research in French prisons.

References

Amiraux, V., 'The Situation of Muslims in France' in *Monitoring the EU Accession Process: Minority Protection*, vol. 2 (Budapest: Open Society Institute, 2002).

Anwar, M., and Bakhsh, Q., *British Muslims and State Policies* (Coventry: University of Warwick, Centre for Research in Ethnic Relations, 2003).

Baubérot, J., *La morale laïque contre l'ordre moral* (Paris: Seuil, 1997).

Baubérot, J., *Histoire de la Laïcité* (Paris: PUF, 2000).

Beckford, J. A., and Gilliat S., *Religion in Prison: Equal Rites in a Multi-Faith Society* (Cambridge: Cambridge University Press, 1998).

Boepflug, F., Dunand, F., and Willaime, J.-P., *Pour une Mémoire des Religions* (Paris: La Découverte, 1996).

Boyer, A., *L'islam en France* (Paris: Presses Universitaires de France, 1998).

Bradney, A., *Religions, Rights and Laws* (Leicester: University of Leicester Press, 1993).

Commision on British Muslims and Islamophobia, *Addressing the Challenge of Islamophobia: Progress Report 1999–2001* (London: Uniting Britain Trust, 2001).

Gauchet, M., *La Religion dans la démocratie, parcours de la laïcité* (Paris: Gallimard, 1998).

Geisser, V., *La nouvelle islamophobie* (Paris: La Décourverte, 2003).

Guessous, F., Hopper, N., and Moorthy, U., 'Religion in Prisons 1999 and 2000', in *National Statistics Bulletin HOSB 15/01* (London: National Statistics, 2000).

Matthews, R., and Francis, P. (eds), *Prisons 2000: An International Perspective on the Current State and Future of Imprisonment* (London: Macmillan, 1996).

O'Beirne, M., 'Religion in England and Wales: Findings from the 2001 Home Office Citizenship Survey', *Home Office Research Study 27* (London: Home Office, 2004).

Poulat, E., *Liberté, laïcité, la guerre des deux France et le principe de la modernité* (Paris: Cerf/Cujas, 1987).

Stasi, B., *Rapport de la commission de réflexion sur l'application du principe de laïcité dans la République* (Paris: la Documentation Française, 2003).

Thiébaud, J.-M., *Prison et Justice: Mode d'Emploi pour les Détenus et leurs Familles* (Paris: L'Harmattan, 2000).

Tournier, P., 'Apports de la démographie à l'étude du changement dans l'univers carcéral (1978–1998)', in Veil, C., and Lhuilier, D. (eds), *La Prison en Changement* (Paris: Erès, 2000).

Walmsley, R., Howard, L., and White, S., *The National Prison Survey: Main Findings* (London: HMSO, 1992).

Weller, P., Feldman A., and Purdam, K., 'Religious Discrimination in England and Wales', *Home Office Research Study 220* (London: Home Office, 2001).

Willaime, J.-P., *Europe et Religions. Les Enjeux du XXIe Siècle* (Paris: Fayard, 2004).

Wilson, B. R., 'Religious Toleration, Pluralism and Privatization', *Kirchliche Zeitgeschichte*, 8:1 (1995): 99–116.

10
Ethnicity, Islam, and Allegiances in the French Military

Christophe Bertossi

10.1 Introduction

How can the needs of ethno-cultural and religious diversity be accommodated within the French *République*?[1] Formally, the ideological project of French citizenship provides a sharp solution: the transformation of individuals into *universal* citizens parallels the melting of social, cultural, and religious identities into a common *national* identity. In other words, French citizenship has been founded on the fiction that equality is possible insofar as it is based on a common belonging to the post-revolutionary nation and it erodes all forms of ethnicity pre-existing the nation-state (Gellner, 1983).

It is no accident that the soldier was given a very peculiar place in the iconography of the French nation-state. At the end of the eighteenth century, the 'citizen-warrior' became the emblem of what a real and good citizen 'should be', that is, absolutely dedicated to his nation and ready to give his life for it (Castles. Chapter 2 in this volume; Schnapper, 1998). Consequently, there has been a connection between the nation and the soldier that did not belong to what Durkheim calls the 'profane' world. Victorious at Valmy in 1792, the new modern nation returned to the very foundations of French republican thinking on cohesion among equal citizens (Feld, 1977; Peled, 1998: 17). This explains why the military institution has always been center stage of this model, particularly after conscription became universal in the last third of the nineteenth century and concerned all male citizens over the age of 21 (Lagache, 1989). The French military exemplified national morals and provided the *République* with an institution of integration complementary to the school system, able to produce 'genuine' citizens. This is why ethnicity and the military have been mutually exclusive: ethnicity was not a relevant question as far as the French nation and its citizenship were concerned.

However, a completely new picture emerged after conscription was abandoned in 1996.[2] The 'blood tax' that had been part of the civic duties for all (male) citizens changed as military service became voluntary. This transition toward a professional military implied, in turn, a diversification of recruitment, particularly where conscripts were essential for its functioning, that is, in the extremely labor-intensive forces such as the Army and the Navy. Some of these new recruits were to be found in areas where youngsters had to face particularly high unemployment rates. In these areas, the French armed forces enlisted members of minority groups who otherwise struggled to gain employment, notably because of the 'racial' discrimination they faced; volunteering for the French armed forces became a way to escape this discrimination. Consequently, the military had to find a way to accommodate its new 'ethnic' recruits.

Of course, the issue of ethnicity within the military was not totally new, since France had been a *république* within its metropolitan center but an empire in its colonies. Colonial troops participated in the extension of the French Empire after the beginning of the conquest of Algeria in 1830. Natives volunteered in 1841 and 1845 to new colonial regiments such as the Algerian *'tirailleurs'* or the *Spahis*. All but a few exceptions, such as Algerians after 1912, were volunteers. Their contribution was considerable during World War I and II. Nonetheless, they were not fully fledged soldiers as they could not progress to the rank of captain or above in the Army. The presence of Muslims within the French military was again felt during the Algerian War of Independence by the so-called Harkis, Algerian auxiliary soldiers of the French Army who were repatriated after 1962 (Jordi and Hamoumou, 1999; Roux, 1992;). At the time, 'ethnicity' within the French military had no link with the question of French citizenship or the nation. 'Ethnic' soldiers were second-class military in the same way they were second-class citizens in the later developments of the French colonial empire.

By contrast, ethnicity in the military today fits a very different context that is directly connected to citizenship and, consequently, to discrimination. After the suspension of conscription and the increasing recruitment of populations originating from migration, some of them practicing Islam, ethnicity has become the focus for new attitudes in the French military toward these new recruits. These recruits have been questioned, by their military peers and superiors alike, as to their motivation for volunteering, the actual level of their allegiance toward the

French state when most of them are dual citizens, the quality of their integration into French society, and the compatibility between their being Muslim and their French citizenship. At the end of the day, these new French soldiers are often treated as if they cannot be trusted because of their family names, their customs, or the religion they practice. This is conducive to discrimination.

This chapter's objective is to understand this process. How is ethnicity generated within a republican integration institution like the military? How does this result in tensions and conflicts crystallized in ethno-cultural and religious identities? How does this pave the way for discrimination?

10.2 French ethnic soldiers?

The first article of the 1958 French Constitution outlaws all forms of ethnic statistics (Amiraux, Chapter 8 in this volume). As a result, it is impossible to say how many 'ethnic' soldiers have volunteered for the French armed forces since it has become a professional body. Another element is directly related to this: no significant category is used to label them. Who are they? The only notion available to encompass the new manpower issues related to ethnicity in the military is that of 'populations from migrant origins'.

There is much to say about the limits of this notion. Its vagueness is obvious. Who are we talking about? All of them are French citizens but they have accessed French citizenship through different gates, ranging from descent to naturalization. If they somehow share a common experience of migration, this experience is highly diversified, and does not correspond to a common background that would embrace them in a generalized way. Most of the interviewees met during this research were born in France to parents who were born in a former French colony (Morocco, Algeria, Tunisia, Niger, Ivory Cost, Senegal, and so on) and had migrated to France in the 1960s and 1970s. A different kind of migration is that of the descendants of the Harkis who left Algeria in the aftermath of Algerian independence in 1962. Some interviewees descended from political migration, their parents having arrived in France as refugees, notably from Laos and Vietnam during the 1970s and 1980s. A minority of the military we met were born abroad and arrived in France when they were children.

This so-called migratory origin fails to inform us about the identity that individuals so labeled have developed through these different types of economic, political, and colonial migrations, particularly when they were born in France and self-identify as French. This blurred boundary between *de jure* French citizens and their 'origins' is made even more complicated when it interferes with the different types of histories these 'servicemen from migrant origins' find in the military, notably the colonial legacy of the French armed forces and the involvement of their parents and grandparents as colonial soldiers during the twentieth-century's wars (World War I and II, decolonization wars). As a consequence, the notion of 'populations originating from migration' erases these multi-leveled distinctions and critically withdraws the postcolonial dimension which is at stake when these populations are addressed by the military.

This loose notion is equally limited on other levels. Labels matter in social life: qualifying these populations as 'migrants' suggests that they are not French in the same way that so-called native populations are. This induces an ethnic bias in the universal tropism of republican politics of citizenship. This bias is embodied in the notion of 'integration'. Because they are 'from migrant origins' (even after several generations) their problem 'must be' their integration into French society. The problem is that no one is clear about what these new French citizens are expected to do in order to conform to this integration imperative. At the end of the day, whereas the French *République* claims a basis in universal principles, these principles are contradicted by the permanent stigmatization of the so-called encumbered identities (Islam, second citizenship, and so on) of supposed 'migrants', even when these identities are not those which are used by these French citizens when defining themselves.

This integration bias finds special vividness within the military. The chief of staff of the Army summarizes the military's pro-integration stand when he emphasizes that 'the Army is a factor for integration. I am not convinced that investigating issues of ethnicity within this institution is relevant. If you had asked me what I think about this question, I would have told you that this ethnic-orientated approach makes no sense because our principles are grounded on the very principle of integration.'

It is no accident if our interviewees reacted strongly to the very notion of integration. Integration, so they say, does not concern them. A corporal in the Army explains this reaction: 'I'm not originating from migration. This is a mistake. ... I've asked nothing of no one: France is my country. I got French nationality by birth, just like my father did. Now, anyway, I'm put in the same basket. Whatever I'll tell you, I'll be treated the same way: "immigrant", this is a label stuck on my back.' This contributes to the creation of a common fate for those soldiers 'from migrant origins': they are expected to disappear, but at the same time they are systematically confronted with discourses challenging them because of their alleged ethnicity, or their 'visibility' due to a first or family name, a religious practice, or simply a diet. To put it briefly, there are ethnic soldiers in the French military because servicemen of migrant origins are perceived as ethnic. The question is now how this ethnicity is generated in what has been considered for the last two centuries as the holy temple of integration in France.

10.3 Ethnicity from within the military identity

Certainly, the *République* as a set of grand principles (such as equality, universalism, and the nation) has an influence on the way people think of themselves and understand the question of integration of minority groups within that common belonging. But using the *République* as such an explanatory framework is far from satisfying if we want to understand how an egalitarian philosophy accommodates the material inequalities and prejudices that are directly connected to membership in a minority group (see Favell, 1998; Hargreaves, 1995). From that perspective, the military and its relation to ethnicity helps us to appreciate how all this functions. The question here is less the niche or resources ethnicity may find in an institution like the French military than the mutual inter-relationship between two different forms of identity, namely ethnic identities and the military identity. The latter is center stage for the feelings that members of the military develop vis-à-vis their role in French society. It also has an impact on ethnic identities.

To highlight this relationship, one must turn to how membership in the military is defined by its members. On a poster hung in a corridor of an Air Force basic training center, one can read the following message:

From now on you are *soldiers*. You decided to serve and you have chosen, by a freely subscribed contract, the armed profession ... You have chosen to be *military*!

This imposes *duties* on you.

Because being in the military cannot be reduced to wearing the uniform!

You will be military if you have the will and the conscience of belonging to a community that respects and cultivates traditional *values* of *discipline, solidarity, honor,* and *loyalty*.

Disciplined soldiers, you will be the ones on whom *one can count*. *This implies that you will be exemplary at all times and in all places.*

Your rights as citizens and your daily comfort must not make you forget this ... You are now in the service of your country. Deserve it and be proud of it. (original emphases)

The call is clear. Being a member of the military is not a profession: it is a mission that places soldiers within a constellation of values that, in turn, creates a community, based on the consciousness that every member has of belonging to the group. What is this community? To find elements of the answer, one must address two notions that have been forged by sociology to deal with identities, and that can be applied to the armed forces. These are Weber's notion of 'communalization' (Weber, 1968) and Goffman's notion of 'total institution' (Goffman, 1961).

Let's go back to the poster: the soldier, it is said, is neither an individual nor an ordinary citizen. Someone is a soldier insofar as he or she has the 'conscience of belonging to a community that respects [some] traditional values'. The notion of 'community' refers to one of the fundamental problems of sociological theory, which concerns the classical distinction between 'society' and 'community'. Ferdinand Tönnies formulated this dichotomy but Max Weber deepened it through the concepts of 'sociation' and 'communalization' (Rex, 2002: Tönnies, 1974; Weber, 1968). For Weber, communalization is a social relation grounded on the 'subjective feeling of the parties whether affectual or traditional, that they belong together' (Weber, 1968: 40). By contrast, 'sociation' describes a rational sort of social relation, which is typical of institutions and emerged with the development of the modern nation-state.

At this stage it seems contradictory to speak of a 'military community'. Would the military, institution *par excellence* of the modern nation-state, also be a community? Weber gives a very simple answer to this apparent paradox: when individuals live together and ground this experience in shared consciousness, they have something in common, 'every sociation – even when it is created on a pure rational mode – attracts a conscience of community that extends as a personal fraternization' (Weber, 1968). Weber's sociological theory bridges the gap between the type of rational social relations one finds in a modern institution and the affective belonging its members feel toward it. This applies to the military.

What is even more striking is that, when Max Weber describes how sociation can shift into a community, he does not have in mind any type of institution: he applies his definition to *ethnic* institutions, which in his theory refer to institutions prior to the modern nation-state. These few pages of *Economy and Society* still remain the founding inspiration for an important literature on ethnicity and provide us with a precious clue about what we have to deal with when we address ethnic, cultural, or religious identities within the military.

The notion of communalization shows that the ethnic issue in the military does not only concern the actual acceptance or not of some sorts of diversity, be it ethnic or religious, in an institution that is grounded in the group cohesion of soldiers. Rather it outlines the coexistence of two forms of solidarity relations that are mechanically concurrent: the military identity and ethnicity. It may be difficult to belong simultaneously to both, that is, being seen as another member of the group (fellow military) and as a member of other groups (ethnicity). The multiplicity of memberships of that sort is reduced because of the intense feelings of allegiance and loyalty that the military inspires. Allegiance to the State is primarily seen as an allegiance to the military community. Soldiers of migrant origin who would make claims about their ethnicity as soldiers would not be perceived as genuine members of the institution by their peers. Ethnicity is made into an issue of loyalty.

At this stage, one must scrutinize not only the different types of social relations of solidarity within the military, but also the singularity of the military as an institution. To do so, the notion of 'total institution' is particularly relevant in the way Erwing Goffman developed it after his research on the life of inmates in a psychiatric hospital. Goffman defines a total institution as 'a place of residence and work where a large number of like-situated individuals, cut off from the wider society for an appreciable period of time, together lead an enclosed, formally administrated round of life' (Goffman, 1961: xiii). This definition, Goffman argues, does not concern only hospital institutions but also prisons, caserns, merchant- and warships.

The key aspect of this notion is that it highlights 'the initial effects of institutionalization on the social relationships the individual possessed before he became an inmate' (Goffman, 1961: xiv). Life in a total institution constitutes a rupture from 'normal life' for several reasons that belong to the peculiarity of the total institution: first, individuals are submitted to a single authority that organizes the entirety of daily life, including their privacy; second, they live in conditions of extreme proximity with all those who belong to the same institution, and obey the same rules and constraints; third, all activities are scheduled along a strict program that plans and structures everyday life in advance. Goffmann concludes:

> it is characteristic of inmates that they come to the institution with a 'presenting culture' (to modify a psychiatric phrase) derived from the 'home world' – a way of life and a round of activities taken for granted until the point of admission to the institution. ... Total institutions do not substitute their own unique culture for something already formed; we deal with something more restricted than acculturation or assimilation. If cultural change does occur, it has to do ... with the removal of certain behavior opportunities. (Goffman, 1961: 12–13)

Among those removed behavior opportunities, some are connected to ethnicity. That is, for new recruits, entering the institution does not correspond simply with their endorsement of the very values that form the institution's identity. It constitutes a transformation of the type of relationship they form with the group they join; it involves their loss of contact with the society they leave. This creates a tension between the inside and the outside world; between a closed environment and the rest of society; between the new community of which they become a member and the individuals they once were. It is at the intersection of these two dimensions that one can understand the very social dynamics at play when ethnicity enters the military.

The analysis of the notions of 'communalization' and 'total institution' calls for further comment. What the case of ethnicity in the French military provides us with is a sociological reading of the way the republican apparatus impacts diversity: it is not enough to place the sensitive relationship between ethnicity and citizenship in the French context solely in the hands of the republican tradition as such, usually conceived as the foundation of a political culture. Or, to put it more precisely, if the *République* 'in itself' cannot be held accountable for the position ethnicity may be allocated within the armed forces (the same could be said for other institutions such as schools or prisons), it plays a structuring role in social representations individuals develop on ethnic issues, for example when soldiers discuss Islam, secularism, and the Muslim headscarf, or even the war in Iraq and the second Intifada.

This generates a further social signification that must be added, that is, the relations of solidarity members of a group have with other members of the same group and with members of other groups. To put it in a Weberian way, the meaningful intelligibility of others' social activity is a fundamental of a community's formation. As a result, the *République* certainly participates in this meaningful intelligibility that social actors give to their own actions. But all this exists within the peculiar constraints of social existence and gives more or less resources to ethnic, cultural, or religious identities. The point here is that the *République* has several social meanings, which do not function as the initial source of attitudes or behaviors but as legitimating principles behind these attitudes or behaviors. Republican reasoning can be mobilized for justifying anti-ethnic and racist behaviors, just like it can be the basis for claims of recognition made by individuals 'from migrant origins'.

To illustrate this point, the next sections will focus on how the 'military from migrant origins' we met understand their place in the French armed forces, and successively address issues of ethnicity, allegiances, Islam, and discrimination.

10.4 The place of ethnicity in the French professional military

The first finding of this research is that ethnicity does not impact on the way French military 'from migrant origins' envisage their membership in the military community, their motivation to enter the military or, once they have become soldiers, their attitude toward their chosen profession. These are no different from what recent surveys have shown, where the whole French Army is concerned (Benoit-Guilbot and Pfirsch, 1998).

The unique variations that emerge from ethnicity are only indirectly connected to membership in minority groups. These are shaped by the social environment members of minority groups face in civil society. The experience of discrimination is particularly quoted as a motivation for entering the armed forces, perceived as a place where prejudice and discrimination are less patent that in civil society. They envision it as an equality-based institution where the only distinctions are those of rank and not on race, which explains why some show such an enthusiasm vis-à-vis the armed forces.

They mention how they perceive the military as a 'right', 'straight', 'disciplined' and 'just' social sphere. One young woman in the Army sees it as 'a place of truth'. Entering the military can be conceived as a way to become 'invisible'. As a sergeant of the Army explains: 'when I leave the uniform, I am seen as a *Maghrébin* like the others.' Volunteering for the military is often seen as an opportunity for escape from the prejudices found in the rest of society.

If volunteering is a way to escape discrimination and an opportunity to access training and professional experience, some of these soldiers also insist on the military's devotion to cherished values as an important part of their French identity. For those who have witnessed it, however, the military's professionalization has paralleled the loss of most of the important values that were part of the military identity. Of course, this identity varies in intensity, but variations do not depend upon their belonging to a minority group, rather they depend on the kind of missions and specializations they are involved in. The warrior identity is stronger for people working as commandos or for those who embark on ships than for administrative clerks in the Air Force, for example. Another variation goes along a generation line: people who enlisted after 1996–97 appreciate the new atmosphere they have found in the military, while their elders regret it. The youngest recruits seek adventure, travel, the practice of sport, and also a stable job, while the older ones emphasize the 'service we (as soldiers) are supposed to provide to the nation'.

In the same way that they show diverse attitudes to the military identity, servicemen do not conceive ethno-cultural and religious identities within the military from a single perspective. Three different attitudes can be outlined.

The first attitude is rooted in the desire to become invisible upon joining up. For those who share this stance, in the community of soldiers all forms of idiosyncrasy must disappear: individual identity must be left outside the barracks. Most of the time, this type of discourse is justified by operational considerations aimed at the proper functioning of the institution to which they belong. For such functioning, soldiers must all be alike. This position also identifies feminization as a challenge to military cohesion and shows no support for the fight against gender discrimination in the armed forces. Some extend this conception about uniformity to the whole of French society, and argue about the importance of 'assimilating in adopting the French way of life'. In this particular case, military identity is considered as a cultural understanding of its place in the *République* at large. This prolongs traditional conceptions from a Durkheimian perspective of the military as an integration institution.

Sometimes, however, it is less for the sake of the institution than for their own individual situation that soldiers want to keep ethnicity outside the realm of the military community. As a young *gendarme* puts it: 'I don't think that one can be different in the military. We are all dressed the same. We do the same job. I want to show the least difference I can. Being the most discrete, passing as invisible, melting myself among my colleagues.'

The second type of discourse rejects assimilation as a flattening cultural process, leading to the extinction of ethno-cultural diversity in the institution. Cultural diversity constitutes a resource for the military, including from a purely operational perspective. Linguistic skills, cultural knowledge, and special sensitivity in situations involving 'minority' populations: all these contribute to the value recruits 'from migrant origins' bring to the military. In this discourse the military should be more tolerant vis-à-vis ethno-cultural and religious diversity. The French military's professionalization constitutes a niche of opportunity for such tolerance to emerge: 'there will be a diversity that previous generations have not known. They are obliged to merge with it and create a team spirit. [Officers] are here not only to command but also to create cohesion.' Here is the real challenge that the military community must deal with: it does not concern the ethnicity of the new recruits, but the ability of the military community to adapt to its new sociological situation.

In this context, most of the soldiers we met shared something that echoes the last comment. Whereas new recruits are accused of refusing integration into the very military identity because of their so-called ethnicity, these soldiers 'from migrant origins' point to another kind of community they see as challenging the very principles of republican universalism: officers are perceived as being disconnected both from the actual sociological reality of today's French military population, and from the universalistic values of French citizenship. An Army officer of Algerian origin, who started his career as a private, relates what he found at the Army's Officer School in Coëtquidan:

> that's a mold of Judeo-Christian culture. Not even Judeo-Christian: Catholic! ... I didn't know those boys ... They're nice boys, you see? But that was too much to me. ... There are Patron Saints all the time. ... There is a constant higher bid on religious beliefs. We went to the mass. Ok, cool. ... But some felt obliged to fall on the chapel's floor with their body in the shape of a cross, to show they believed more than their buddy behind! ... I believe I'm profoundly *laïque* and republican, but this is not. ... Among themselves, they feel good. Once they arrive in the regiment, what do you know?

Lastly, a third type of attitude sees no contradiction between the sphere of ethnicity and that of the military. These soldiers do not consider themselves members of a specific community, members of the armed forces. Instead, they feel they are doing an ordinary job and that there is very little difference between the military and the civil world of work. Professionalization has brought a new context in which the private realm can be protected from the institution, where authority extends only to professional activities and 'normal' everyday life is left untouched. The military is no longer a 'total institution'. Thus, the peculiar institutional and social form of the military has vanished, and ethnicity is not an issue. As Yacine, a young non-commissioned Army officer, puts it, 'one can be different in the military, particularly now. We are not really required to fulfill our duties 24/24. It is rather 8am/5pm. When evening comes, you can do whatever you like. That leaves enough time for exercising your beliefs, and all what goes with them. Personally, I am a Muslim. That is not visible. I keep it for me. One does not show it.'

However, these three attitudes toward the position of ethnicity in the military share an additional characteristic: all the military we met have felt a stigmatization from their peers who 'have no origins' and, sometimes also, from their superiors. This stigmatization incorporates them into a type of ethnic identity to which they do not feel they belong. Whatever they think about the right place of ethnicity in the military, they are subject to an ethnicization process that multiplies the levels of direct or indirect exclusion within the institution. As a consequence, their induction into the military has not only modified some of their conceptions about the articulation between identities and the *République*. It has also imposed on them a kind of ethnicity they do not identify with, but which is constantly used by others to identify them.

This fits the distinction made by social anthropology between the way individuals define themselves and the way they are defined by members of out-groups (including the mainstream society) (Rex, 2002). The former kind of identity is aggregative, or can be mobilized: it can create a feeling of belonging 'for itself' (Rex, 1986). The latter is attributed by others, and ethnicity becomes a category used in this context to label members of minority groups which are perceived as 'inferiors' most of the time (Wieviorka, 1994). Being ethnicized often parallels the experience of racial and religious discrimination. It paves the way for ethnicity to be used as a resource for attaining citizens' equality, claims based on what has become, through that process, a 'scorned' identity of the stigmatized group (Giraud, 1998).

What is striking is how some of our interviewees never felt such an ethnicization *before* their entry in the military. A young Corporal in the Army expresses it clearly: 'that was the very first time during my basic training I was insulted, I was called a "dirty Arab". That was the first time, really. At the time, I was shocked because I had never been called something like that. Afterwards, I thought I didn't want to fight about it because, in the end, I was scared I would be the one who would be rejected.' This is not an isolated experience and other interviewees stated similar feelings. That is, they felt they had become ethnic *by* entering the institution that they initially considered as an egalitarian and republican institution *par excellence*.

This 'becoming ethnic' is based on different factors which are often intertwined one with the other. The 'visible difference' is the first factor of ethnicization. A non-commissioned officer in the Army explains: 'people see you: you are Black or dark-skinned. Identity is immediately made. ... When people look at me, I don't feel I'm Belgian or German. I am Black. So, when you ask them about people from migrant origins, that's obvious. I'm not from migrant origin since my father and grandfather were French (and fought with the French colonial troopers).'

But phenotype is not unique in leading to ethnicization. A second factor can be the family name, even when the first name does not sound 'ethnic'. In this case, the family name functions as a stigma, irrespective of the actual origin or religion. This is the case for Mathieu, lieutenant in the Army. Only his paternal grandfather was a Berber originating from Algeria, and married to a Polish migrant. His maternal family has its roots in a rural region of France. From this quite distant Algerian origin, he has kept only the family name. He says: 'I don't have the *Maghrébin* type. I have the origin but not the type. [However] all [my colleagues] asked me about the origin of this name. Not necessarily at once, but when I had what is called the "annual" or "evaluation interview"; whether I was originating from the *Maghreb*; whether I was Muslim, because nobody is supposed to know your religion. They asked me if I was Muslim and then ... they made amalgams between the origin of the name and the religion.'

The third factor of ethnicization found in our interviews concerns the sort of social capital which is attributed to individuals perceived as ethnic. This is twofold. On the one hand, when soldiers are identified as 'from migrant origins', they are attributed a low social capital, a *banlieue* culture, and all that that is supposed to imply: no academic degrees, no professional training, asocial comportment, or the use of drugs. Joudi, an able-seaman in the Navy, describes how other non-commissioned officers talked to him during the first months he was in the military: 'they go: "hey, so you come from the *banlieues*, ya-Djamel-buddy?" Above all, [it happened] when they saw me talking with the junior seamen. I just feel somehow they saw I was talking to a *Maghrébin*, and they immediately put me in the same mold as them. ..."And you're brothers then?" That's what they said.' This, however, not only concerns the lower ranks: officers from migrant origin may also face similar treatment. An acting sub-lieutenant remembers the very first time he met his colleagues: 'somehow they were expecting to find someone fitting the kind of profile they had imagined. But in the end, they were quite surprised I had graduated from the University'.

On the other hand, ethnicity can also be directly inferred from one's social background. When soldiers are perceived as having low social skills, their social origin is immediately transformed into an ethnic identity. Toufik remembers the weeks during which he embarked on a submarine and how 'the buddy who was with me in the same office, he didn't like Arabs at all. For example, I used to listen to *Skyrock* (a popular radiobroad-cast) in the office when I was alone. They play hip-hop music there. He told me he didn't like that at all, that it was shit music, music for Arabs.' On a more general level, most of the junior ranks are often designated under the single label of '*cassos*' which stands for the contraction of '*cas sociaux*' (socially disadvantaged persons). '*Cassos*' is equated with '*ban-lieues*' and *Maghrébins*. In the Air Force, junior ranks are called MTA (Air Technical Military). In the first years of professional recruitment in the military, MTA was commonly translated as 'Moroccans, Tunisians, Algerians'. This equation between the new waves of recruitment after the end of conscription and the ethnic profile of the new recruits can be found in all forces. In the Navy, those recruits designated as EICD are sub-ject to a similar ethnicization process grounded in their status in the mil-itary. As Ziad relates it, 'I was a leading seaman. I saw how EICDs were treated ... they had a pat on the back and they were immediately in their bad books: good-for-nothing, "*cassos*" as they called them.'

Finally, ethnicity is made an even more complex issue when it crosses the hierarchical structure of the French military. Our interviewees all agreed on the importance of this hierarchical structure that is, for many of them, the guarantee of a color-blind institution differentiated only on the grounds of military rank. What they contest, however, is the way the hierarchy parallels a cultural gap between officers and the rest, be they privates or non-commissioned officers. Officers as so far removed that they are seen as 'belonging to another planet'. One of the issues raised in this context is the ability of young officers to command youngsters from diverse origins they consider as '*cassos*' and 'ethnic soldiers'. This, in turn, deepens the gap between officers and the lower ranks, and puts the cohesion of the military community into question.

10.5   Allegiance and loyalty

Another issue raised by the military where 'ethnic soldiers' are con-cerned deals with their allegiances when most of them have two or more nationalities. To whom do these dual citizens belong? How do they combine their second nationality with their engagement in the French military?

Issues of dual citizenship have been center stage in the politics of integration in France since the 1980s. When the nationality law was finally revised in 1993, it was the result of a debate about the exclusiveness of national citizenship. By then, the question had become of how it is possible to be a member of two polities at the same time (Bertossi, 2001: 129–34). These questions particularly focused on military service, which was still compulsory in France and concerned young men who had to choose between doing their service in France or in the country of their second nationality. Bilateral conventions on this issue were signed between France and Tunisia (1982) and Algeria (1983). As a matter of fact, it was clear enough that few of them chose to serve in their country of origin (Tribalat, 1995: 209).

After the shift from conscription to professional armed forces, this issue disappeared from the debate on integration, and was replaced by other issues such as Islam and French secularism (Bertossi and Mohsen-Finan, 2006). At the same time, however, new recruits to the French armed forces have been obliged to justify themselves on the issue of dual nationality, particularly after the end of the Cold War and in a context where international conflicts are seen as relating to Islam (Chechnya, post-9/11 wars in Afghanistan and Iraq, the 'war on terror', second Intifada, and so on). The attacks in London on 7 July 2005 renewed these concerns as they involved British citizens as perpetrators. As such, being a Muslim is immediately connected to a kind of allegiance that may challenge liberal citizenship in European countries. This amalgam between practicing Islam and issues of loyalty concerns members of the French military in the most striking way. This section focuses on how the problem of loyalty involving dual citizens is constructed in the French armed forces and how these new dual-nationality soldiers understand the conjunction between both.

The first level of analysis of the dual citizenship issue in the military goes back to Goffman's stand on how a total institution may remove opportunities for its members when entering it. As a matter of fact, most of our interviewees described how they initially felt uneasy about their second nationality when they applied to the military. Some of them had anticipated that they could not retain this nationality once in the armed forces, though there is no legal obligation of that sort due to the French liberal tradition on dual citizenship. What is particularly striking is the low level of awareness they shared on this question. One of our interviewees was unaware that possessing the national identity card of her country of origin meant she had kept the citizenship of her parents. Their initial interview at the military recruitment center is a moment when the issue is first raised, and when they are invited to renounce their second citizenship if they intend to become soldiers. Azzam relates it: 'I had to choose French citizenship. I was not informed I could keep my Algerian citizenship. French citizenship was imposed on me, that's all. I think that helped me somehow because at the bureau of information of the Air Force [when I applied], I was told: "you were born in Algiers? So you have dual citizenship? You know that you cannot have two nationalities when integrating into the French Air Force?" So, naïve as I was, I said "OK". And now I am in the military and I meet many people who are dual citizens.'

A second level concerns the connection between nationality and belonging to an extended family (Rex, 2002). Their second citizenship was rarely perceived by our interviewees as being an issue for allegiance or loyalty, which only concerned their French citizenship. It concerns rather their membership of a transnational private sphere. Their country of origin is primarily the country of relatives who remained there. Dual citizenship is an ordinary condition that becomes useful when one returns for summer holidays in Algeria, Tunisia, or Morocco and visits grandparents, cousins, or friends. There is also a very concrete aspect to this: holding an Algerian, Tunisian, or Moroccan passport makes travel easier when crossing the border. An Army non-commissioned officer says: 'in everyday life, (dual citizenship) is indifferent. The plus is when I decide to go back to Algeria to see the rest of my family, because I still have my grandmother living there. The customs officer is less regarding, I think, than if I arrive with my French passport [which would be more difficult]. On my Algerian passport, my military condition is not stated. It only says "employee". ' This also is connected to the way nationality legislation in the *Maghrébin* countries makes it impossible to renounce their citizenship even for the descendants of migrants who were born and raised abroad. When crossing the border, as Rania says, 'we are obliged to show our Moroccan ID card, but again I'm not sure that is something which has anything to do with dual citizenship.'

From that perspective, allegiance is an issue that only concerns their French citizenship, their patriotism toward the French state, their belonging to the French nation. They claim they have no divided loyalties because they feel they proved their clear allegiance toward France when they decided to volunteer for the French military: 'I signed. And when you become an officer, you pledge an oath. They [other officers] pledged an oath and we became equals. I cannot understand why one is asked this question. ... Such an engagement is not neutral. I have not signed to enter the French Postal Service!'

The military 'from migrant origins' are not trusted as other soldiers: their comrades and their superiors suspect them because of their national origins which are superimposed with their ethnic and religious identities. As for ethnicity, there is a sharp contrast between the allegiances attributed to them by their peers and their superiors, and the way they themselves view the different belongings connected to their dual citizenship. While few of our interviewees insisted on the level of trust and responsibility they were afforded by the military, most of them recounted the opposite. The first reaction to this suspicion was incomprehension. A Harki's son serving in the Army explains his confusion: 'because with my origins. ... I still have family in Algeria ... they [the military] may fear that I speak with them, that I give them professional secrets, confidential things. It's absurd. It is my profession; this [France] is my country. ... why don't they start to speak to me, to see who I am, what my skills are? This is weird'. This approach to the issue of their origins and loyalty has been reinforced after 9/11, making these origins even more problematic. Mounia is sure of that: 'it is since 9/11 ... I think what scares people is they realize there are people who seem perfectly integrated, but who can suddenly turn against them.'

Our interviewees found it particularly difficult to accept that being considered 'good soldiers' was linked with the way others perceived the level not only of their integration as 'ethnic soldiers' but as dual citizens carrying problematic belongings. This is an issue which is stigmatized by the hierarchy in the field: a colonel in the Air Force reduced the issue of these new recruits to questions of challenged allegiance, fearing 'the worm in the fruit' or 'the sick bee in the hive'. But this discourse makes no sense to those it concerns. This disconnection, between the attribution of problematic allegiances due to migrant origins and the very loyalty they testify toward the French nation, is strikingly clear when their relatives' reactions vis-à-vis their joining the French military are addressed. Parents and friends have fully accepted and even welcomed this volunteering, which was generally perceived as a process of social mobility and a good opportunity. This is also the case for individuals whose parents fought for independence in the 1960s. Imad insists: 'my father has fully accepted my decision. The most striking in this is that my grandfather was a *Mujahid* during the Algerian war. He died in the war. And his grandson volunteers in the French Army after this! I think if he [my father] had resentment against France, he would never have come here to find a job.'

When the question is asked about their willingness to be involved in a conflict with their parents' country, answers relate less to conflicts of loyalty than to a global dilemma involving a whole generation of young professional soldiers who believe it is easier to die for the nation than to kill for the state. Killing people is a possibility these youngsters prefer not to think about. The French government's decision not to intervene in Iraq in 2004 reinforces this statement. As Hisham, a French Army trooper puts it, 'if France had gone to Iraq, I would have followed. I would have achieved my mission as any other soldier. It's true, though, that I wouldn't have been at peace with my conscience.' And further, Souad, a Navy officer attests: 'irrespective of the origins, this is a matter of conscience. Any military, when there is an operation somewhere and if he's involved in it, irrespective of his origins, he can question the moral aspect of the French intervention and his own intervention. That is, this is a matter of personal ethic and moral duty.' A young Army private confesses he once had a discussion with one of his fellows on this issue, 'a French native, he was born in France. He told me that if, for example, there was a war in France, he said, he'd leave the Army and he'd go help his family.'

As a result, young soldiers from migrant origins do not address issues of killing or dying in war any differently than their entire generation does. They would not refuse to be involved in a war against their country of origin, but this would crystallize the ethical dilemma others feel on the issue. This hypothesis, however, is a particularly theoretical scenario as they have difficulty imagining a conflict between France and a *Maghrébin* country. Such a situation is inconceivable and does not worry them. Instead, they fear that they would be challenged by their French military fellows in a conflict with a country perceived as Muslim. In other words, whereas the military institution seems to have doubts as to their loyalty and may see them as a 'Trojan horse', they fear becoming themselves victims of such a conflict because they are not trusted as ordinary French soldiers. Souad makes it very clear: 'because our own home ... here [in France], you can't say ... I tell you: even if I believe this is my home here, this is not. So, where is my place?' She hopes that no war will occur to force her to make this choice.

10.6   Islam in the military

The sensitivity to Islam in the French *République* has its roots in the colonial period (Fregosi, 1998). After postcolonial migrants definitely settled in metropolitan France in the mid-1970s, Islam became a focus for the

French politics of integration (Leveau, Mohsen-Finan and Wihtol de Wenden, 2002). It was an important line in the debates about a restrictive reform of the French nationality code in the 1980s–1990s, and Islam started to be seen as irreconcilable with universal republican values. Referring both to an ethnic issue connected to civic and cultural integration, and to an allegiance matter connected to 'genuine' loyalty and reciprocal trust (Bertossi, 2001: 204–17), integration politics concerning Muslims have recently become a challenge to the concept of *laïcité*. This is one element of the Europeanization of citizenship politics in EU countries (such as France, the Netherlands, or the United Kingdom), and the focus of their integration framework's crisis (Bertossi and Mohsen-Finan, 2006). In the post-Cold War era, Islam has been seen as a 'total identity', founding parallel and enclosed communities, refusing integration into European country citizenship, and producing gender discrimination. Muslims' identities have emerged as the main challenge to a 'liberal' conception of membership of a polity.

Logically, in this context, the emergence of collective claims by Muslims in the French armed forces has been feared ever since the military became professional and lost its societal role as integrator of French society. Such claims, however, existed before the end of conscription, particularly linked to the respect of dietary restrictions and Ramadan (Biville, 1990). In 1992, a Defense Ministry circular allowed *halal* food to be served to Muslim conscripts, although it was inconsistently implemented.

As far as religious management was concerned, Catholic, Protestant, and Jewish religions were represented by 176, 37 and 20 civilian and military chaplains, respectively. Nothing similar was provided for Muslims. Evidence was systematically given by the Defense institutions that no claim by Muslim soldiers was made on this issue (Ternissien, 2005). This situation was a breach in the *laïcité* principles that imply both neutrality of French institutions vis-à-vis religious identities and equal treatment for all religions, especially in enclosed institutions such as boarding schools, prisons, or the military. This unbalanced treatment between Islam and other religions was generally negatively assessed by our interviewees, who concluded that the military does not respect one of the founding principles of the *République*.

This situation, however, evolved after 2002 because of the conjunction of two main factors. On the one hand, institutionalization of representation for French Muslims led to the creation of the French Council of the Muslim Religion (CFCM) in the aftermath of the Nainville-les-Roches agreement between religious associations and the Ministry of the Interior in December 2002. On the other hand, the professionalization of the armed forces paralleled the reform of military chaplaincies. This reform resulted in the creation of a military chaplaincy for Muslims, which consultations with the CFCM made possible. The first nomination of a Muslim Chief Chaplain was made in March 2006.

This nomination, however, does not constitute a 'liberal hour' of religious diversity in France in general, and the French military in particular. It has not resulted in any global consensus on the legitimate place of Muslims, and members of the military still challenge this decision. The fear that 'more recognition of Islam in the armed forces will bring more religion into the barracks' is particularly shared and it constrains Muslim soldiers to be discrete about their religion if they do not want to be stigmatized as 'bad' soldiers. Our interviewees insisted that they did not want their practicing Islam to become encumbering or visible in their military lives. This creates a difficult arena for Muslim soldiers. On the one hand, the military has been reluctant to provide them with facilities provided to members of other religions. On the other hand, anticipating that they would be stigmatized if they made claims for such facilities, Muslim soldiers have been reluctant to systematically demand non-pork meals or a place for worship in their workplace. A practicing Muslim senior seaman argued that 'the military is not ready to accept Muslim chaplains. It could create more prejudices against Muslim soldiers.'

This leads us back to Goffman's statement on the way entering a total institution removes behavior opportunities. It is clear that this removal finds its dynamic both in the lack of opportunities afforded by the institution and in the way members of the institution internalize the types of opportunities they can obtain. What was obvious with ethnicity becomes even more striking with religious identities: becoming a soldier involves concessions Muslims must make in their military lives. Some of our interviewees said that they stopped practicing Islam when they joined the military. Others indicated that they had to give up practices they saw as unsuitable in the armed forces, such as the five daily worships or a strict respect of their dietary restrictions. This, in turn, impacts the way they consider themselves as 'genuine Muslims'. As Khadija, a young female *gendarme* says: 'I wouldn't say I am a practicing Muslim. If I said "yes, I am", then I would need to worship five times a day. I do fast during Ramadan but otherwise, it's no more. I don't eat pork. But it's true I make concessions about the meat.'

Variations in the intensity of religious practice are assessed differently by their religious peers. If some justify these necessary concessions, others challenge the faith of their comrades when the latter are seen drinking alcohol, for example. Some Muslim soldiers even accuse their fellow

Muslims of using Islam as an alibi. A corporal of Algerian origin declares: 'there are many people who claim they're Muslim. They insist on their *Maghrébin* identity to abuse the [military] system and I don't like it. If you're Muslim, you must be Muslim all the way'.

This understanding of what it means to be a Muslim is made even more complex when it involves non-Muslim 'native' soldiers. The latter make assumptions between the national origin, the social background, the cultural identity, and the membership of a religious group of soldiers identified as 'from migrant origins'. But labeling all soldiers 'from migrant origins' as 'Muslims' – irrespective of their actual religious identity – parallels the judgment non-Muslim servicemen make about what they see as inconsistent religious practices, and their conviction that Islam is only an excuse for not fulfilling obligations implied by membership in the military community. In other words, practicing Muslims are seen as a challenge to military cohesion, Muslims with irregular practices are seen as abusing the system, and even those who are not practicing Islam at all are put in the same category of 'Muslim soldiers'.

This situation can become critical when a large number of Muslim soldiers are gathered in enclosed situations (such as embarked for weeks on a ship) and are given no opportunity for accommodating their religious practices. The case of the aircraft carrier *Charles-de-Gaulle* illustrates this point. Estimates show that about 150 Muslims are serving on board. The systematical refusal of the command of the ship to afford Muslims a place of worship has generated a strong feeling of frustration. This exemplifies identity conflicts, and the restrictive management of Islam in such an enclosed social context jeopardizes attitudes of Muslims toward republican principles. If all our interviewees showed a very individualistic conception of their being practicing Muslims and their endorsement of liberal values, even so their feeling of discrimination could lead to collective mobilizations based on a resulting 'scorned' Muslim identity.

10.7 Conclusion

This chapter has aimed at achieving a better understanding of the relationship between ethnic and religious identities, and that of an institution of majority society, namely the French military. Paraphrasing Eugene Weber, this institution has been for over two centuries the main site of integration of individuals 'into Frenchmen' (Weber, 1976). To fully understand such a relationship between members of minority groups and an institution of the dominant society, one has to scrutinize at least two different levels: the characteristics of the institution and its relationship with the whole society, as well as the type of social relationships involving ethnicity, religious identity, and the feelings of members of that institution.

This approach illustrated how far the ideological understanding of republican principles was constrained by social reality. It showed that analyzing the opportunities provided to members of minority groups only from the perspective of the ideological stance of the *République* on ethnicity and Islam is far from sufficient. On the contrary, if we want to understand the relationship between ethnicity and the French politics of citizenship, it is necessary to have a more sociological approach.

Similarly highlighted here, is how it is possible to understand the citizenship dilemma this book is addressing: starting from the critical gap between the principles of universalism, equality, and color-blind inclusion on the one hand, and the social functioning of ethnicization as the first step on the way to discrimination and unequal treatment of members of minority groups on the other.

This argument has demonstrated the circularity of factors leading to direct or indirect exclusion of members of a minority group: in our case, soldiers perceived as 'from migrant origin' are successively seen as *Maghrébins*, Arabs, Muslims, and, eventually, people that cannot be trusted. Discrimination against formal citizens is not based on a single factor but is rooted in the complexity of social existence. Furthermore, not only are discrimination-generating factors plural, but the dimensions they refer to are multiple: in the post-Cold war context, ethnicity is closely linked to what is perceived as religious identity, and merges diverse concerns about cultural integration and conflicts of allegiance.

As a result, the institution's interpretation of its membership of populations 'from migrant origins' is not adequate. On the contrary, in our case, French military forces originating from migration show no 'ethnic behavior'; they do not mobilize on any ethnic or religious collective identity. When they are practicing Muslims, they endorse the principles of institutional neutrality in religious matters; they show no conflicts of allegiance or loyalty. They are just ordinary soldiers. The only difference that can bring them together is their feeling they are being discriminated against, and that they always must prove their loyalty, allegiance, and their status as 'good' soldiers. Here is the dilemma that erodes citizenship. A young sergeant in the Army, Karim puts it clearly: 'they will understand everything the day they understand we are French.'

Notes

1. This chapter is based on a research project on the French military from migrant origins, carried out in France between October 2003 and July 2005. The author conducted 62 in-depth interviews with members of the four French armed forces (Army, Navy, Air Force, and *Gendarmerie* – or Police Force) in 23 different sites in all French regions. For the methodology and a definition of the sample used for this research, see Wihtol de Wenden and Bertossi, 2005.
2. The initial decision to abandon conscription was taken in 1996, but the French armed forces only became constituted of professional servicemen in 2002.

References

Benoit-Guilbot, O., and Pfirsch, J.-V., *La décision d'engagement volontaire des militaires du rang: l'armée de terre* (Paris: Centre d'études en sciences sociales de la défense, 1998).

Bertossi, C., *Les frontières de la citoyenneté en Europe. Nationalité, résidence, appartenance* (Paris: L'Harmattan, 2001).

Bertossi, C., and Mohsen-Finan, K., 'La confessionalisation du débat sur l'islam', *Confluences Méditerranée* (Spring 2006).

Biville, Y., *Armées et populations à problèmes d'intégration* (Paris: Centre d'études sur la sélection des personnels de l'armée de terre, 1990).

Favell, A., *Philosophies of Integration: Immigration and the Idea of Citizenship in France and Britain* (Basingstoke: Macmillan – now Palgrave Macmillan, 1998).

Feld, M., *The Structure of Violence: Armed Forces as Social System* (Beverly Hills, CA: Sage, 1977).

Frégosi, F., 'Les problèmes d'organisation de la religion musulmane en France', *Esprit* (January 1998): 109–36.

Gellner, G., Nations and Nationalism (Oxford: Blackwell, 1983).

Giraud, M., 'L'ethnicity comme nécessité et comme obstacle', in Ferréol, G. (ed.), *Intégration, lien social et citoyenneté* (Lille: Presses Universitaires du Septentrion, 1998).

Goffman, E., *Asylums: Essays on the Social Situation of Mental Patients and Other Inmates* (New York: Doubleday, 1961).

Hargreaves, A., *Immigration, Race and Ethnicity in Contemporary France* (London: Routledge, 1995).

Jordi, J., and Hamoumou, M., *Les harkis, une mémoire enfouie* (Paris: Autrement, 1999).

Lagache, S., *Sélection et allocation de la ressource humaine dans les régiments de l'armée de terre: réflexions sur la conscription* (PhD Dissertation in Political Science, IEP in Paris, 1989).

Leveau, R., Mohsen-Finan, K., and Wihtol de Wenden, C., *New European Identity and Citizenship* (Aldershot: Ashgate, 2002).

Peled, A., *A Question of Loyalty: Military Manpower in Multiethnic States* (Ithaca, NY and London: Cornell University Press, 1998).

Rex, J., *Race and Ethnicity* (Buckingham and Philadelphia, PA: Open University, 1986). Pluto Press, 2002).

Rex, J., 'The Fundamentals of the Theory of Ethnicity', in Malesevic, S., and Haugaard, M. (eds), *Making Sense of Collectivity: Ethnicity, Nationalism and Globalisation* (London:

Roux, M., *Les harkis* (Paris: Editions La Découverte, 1992).

Schnapper, D., *Community of Citizens: On the Modern Idea of Nationality* (New Brunswick, NJ: Transaction, 1998).

Ternissien, X., 'Le ministère de la défense prepare l'armée à se doter d'une aumônerie musulmane', *Le Monde*, 21 January 2005.

Tönnies, F., *Community and Association* (London: Routledge & Paul, 1974).

Tribalat, M., *Faire-France. Une enquête sur les immigrés et sur leurs enfants* (Paris: La Découverte, 1995).

Weber, E., *Peasants into Frenchmen: The Modernization of Rural France, 1870–1914* (Stanford, CA: Stanford University Press, 1976).

Weber, M., *Economy and Society: an Outline of Interpretative Sociology* (New York: Bedminster Press, 1968).

Wieviorka, M., 'Ethnicity as action', in Rex, J., and Drury, B. (eds), *Ethnic Mobilizations in a Multicultural Europe* (Aldershot: Avebury, 1994).

Wihtol de Wenden, and C., Bertossi, C., *Les militaires français issus de l'immigration* (Paris: Centre d'études en sciences sociales de la défense, 2005).

11
Refugees, Gender, and Citizenship in Britain and France

Khursheed Wadia

11.1 Introduction

This chapter[1] explores the question of citizenship-building processes in relation to women asylum seekers[2] and refugees[3], and their civic participation not only in discrete refugee[4] women's community associations but also in (longer established) migrant women's community associations.[5] Its aim is fourfold: first, it discusses the relationship between the question of citizenship, refugee women, and their associations; second, it presents an overview of the establishment and development of refugee women's associations in Britain and France; third, it examines the forms of activities and activism in which refugee women engage; and finally, it asks what conclusions can be drawn about these forms of activities/activism in terms of drawing this section of the population into a more inclusive model of citizenship.

The question of citizenship is highly relevant to the case of asylum seeking and refugee women who, along with children, are among the most vulnerable groups in conflict situations, having been subjected not only to family and community dislocation but often also to gender related discrimination, violence, and exploitation at various stages of their flight from countries of origin, to countries of reception, and eventual settlement.

Among the reasons that may be put forward as to why citizenship is an important issue for asylum seekers and refugees generally and for women more specifically, are the following:[6]

First, because asylum seekers and refugees suffer a loss of citizenship rights, including that of residence, as well as threats to their human rights in their country of origin. However, asylum seeking and refugee women may suffer added persecution and loss of political, socio-economic, and human rights due to their position as women, either through law or because of social and religious norms; for example, restrictions on dress styles, on access to public places, on the right to earn a living, or on political enfranchisement. They may also be subjected to gender-related forms of harm (rape or genital mutilation) or harm for the reason of being a woman (being flogged for not wearing the veil).

Second, issues of citizenship are pertinent because the entry, settlement, and integration of asylum seekers and refugees in the reception country are strictly controlled by the rights that they are granted or denied. For the large numbers of women who arrive as dependants,[7] these rights are gained or denied depending on the immigration status of the male head of family of which they form a part. For those who lack autonomous legal status, access to political and other resources and structures can be severely restricted or denied altogether. For example, in cases where a woman's relationship with the male head of family breaks down, she may find herself deprived of some of the most basic rights in the country of reception.[8]

Third, as far as Europe is concerned, the idea of a European as opposed to national citizenship has been firmly placed on the political agenda as the European Union (EU) has expanded and the pace of political integration stepped up. Throughout this process, concern over the free movement of certain categories of the population residing in the EU has increased. Thus, citizenship rights (and their transferability) within Europe are marked by an overwhelmingly racial categorization between EU citizens (the majority of whom are representative of a white, 'modern', Judeo-Christian culture) whose socio-economic and political rights are unquestioned, so-called Third Country Nationals (mainly from the developing world) with formal residence status who have access to certain civic rights, and migrants (including asylum seekers) with greatly reduced rights. This racial categorization, combined with the 'male bread winner' and 'marriage' principles (see Lutz, 1997: 105) which underpin the immigration laws of most EU countries means that women migrants, including asylum seeking and refugee women, become particularly symbolic of 'non-Europeanness' and therefore as undeserving of European citizenship rights.

Fourth, if citizenship is about human agency and participation in a variety of political spaces as much as it is about the possession of certain legal rights (as argued below), then at a personal level, it is important for asylum seeking and refugee women to be able to develop the Self and gain control over their lives by carrying out actions to change not only their immediate situations but also the world beyond their doorsteps.

11.2   Citizenship

Before going on to utilize the concept of citizenship and to demonstrate how citizenship-building processes work in the context of refugee women's community associations, it is useful to outline how citizenship is understood here. Let us begin by stating what it is *not* understood to be. Citizenship is not understood in its traditional sense as a purely state-centered institution founded on the organizing principles of nationality (tied to a specified geographical territory) and popular sovereignty (as vested and legitimized in the political authority of the state). Second, in terms of the civil, political, and social rights that are claimed and granted, the practice of citizenship is not limited – as in the Marshallian conceptualization (Marshall, 1950; 1964) – to the public domain of human action and activity. Third, although the conceptualization of citizenship as it is used in this chapter (see below) rejects the split between the private and public domains (whereby mainly masculine models of action/activism to obtain 'needs' are legitimated within the public sphere and 'wants'-related action/activism is relegated to a delegitimized and depoliticized private domain), it does not align itself with new Right or neo-liberal thinking on citizenship.

New Right conceptualizations of citizenship advocate the private sphere as an important space for the social activity and contribution of the family and community, which are seen as the main social resources of citizenship and as the principal mediating institutions between the individual and the state. The family and community, on behalf of the individual, are urged to make an active contribution to the construction of the socio-economic and political order which the state safeguards through its authority and legal framework. Hence, by advancing 'active' or 'contributory' citizenship of this kind, practiced in a convenient space between the state and the market, new Right thinking seeks to relieve the state of its many responsibilities, especially in the area of social welfare. Moreover, this space can become neutralized as so-called contributory actions and individual responsibility come to replace an activist or participatory politics.[9] Based on this thinking, some of the most conservative of governments and international agencies have promoted active or contributory citizenship.[10]

The conceptualization of citizenship used for the purposes of this chapter is a left-feminist one which draws upon the pluralist participatory model put forward by feminist political scientists such as Anne Phillips (1991, 1993), Chantal Mouffe (1986, 1992a, 1992b), and Mary Dietz (1992). As lack of space precludes a fuller discussion of the diverse feminist conceptions of citizenship which reflect the main philosophical traditions in political science, the interested reader should refer to the literature in this field of study.[11]

Common to all feminist approaches to citizenship is the argument that citizenship both in its liberal and republican conceptions, and contrary to claims about its neutrality, is a highly and deliberately gendered concept which has prevented women from gaining a range of rights or of exercising rights gained, in public spaces, on an equal level with men. While radical feminists have dismissed rights as an expression of patriarchal values and power, there are others who have whole-heartedly accepted reform programs based on the extension of rights (liberal feminists). A third category (mainly feminists on the Left) maintains an ambivalent attitude in which there exists considerable skepticism about the individualistic character of rights, but where, in contrast with traditional Marxist thinking, rights are not rejected outright as a bourgeois sham but are seen as a potentially useful instrument in the protection of women's needs and as a counterweight to socio-economic inequalities. It is within this third group that the attempt has been made to conceive of a broader range of rights[12] including the right to political participation as a fundamental right (Gould, 1988). Thus citizenship becomes not only about legal status, but also about political practice. However, in traditional political science, participation refers to a narrow range of political activity in which little if any room is made for informal resistance or disruptive politics at the community level, practiced most often by those at the bottom of the socio-economic pyramid.

Consequently, feminist theorists have sought to extend the parameters of political participation by redefining the political ('what constitutes politics?' and 'how is it done?'). The redefinition of the political has led to a rejection of the distinction between the informal and formal arenas of politics, which has served to conceal activism at the grassroots (community) level and thus the activism of women (and other disadvantaged groups). It has also led to the repudiation of the division between the public domain where so-called universal rights have historically been fashioned and claimed by men, and the private domain to which women have been traditionally tied and where activity is considered non-political. The recognition of a dynamic, collective (and often informal) politics as part of the core substance of citizenship has informed the work of feminist theorists such as Phillips, Mouffe, and Dietz, and of Young (1989), who advocate a feminist pluralist participatory model of citizenship. While these theorists agree about the goal of a pluralist participatory citizenship, there exist differences between them on how to reach that goal (see Siim, 2000: 36–8). However, for our purposes, key elements drawn from this model, which will be borne in mind when discussing asylum seeking and refugee women's participation in associations, are that

- Citizenship-building takes place through political participation which may be increased through political equality strategies and rights.
- Women's multiple political roles (as parents, workers, and citizens) are recognized through the plurality of spaces in which politics is undertaken.
- The importance of sub-groups in terms of race, ethnicity, and gender is recognized through the development of solidarity politics aimed at securing equal rights.

Citizenship is therefore defined not only as a legal status reflecting the possession of certain formal rights but also as a practice which is independent of such a legal status. As access to legal rights is not always guaranteed by the mere possession of legal citizenship status, the independent practice of citizenship through political participation becomes an important component of this concept.

11.3 The study of refugee associations and citizenship-building

There now exists a significant body of literature on migrant associations in Europe within which, only in recent years, attention has turned toward refugee associations. Several works have examined the development, role, and functions of migrant community associations in Europe.[13] More recently, studies of refugee community associations include works by Joly (1996), Salinas, Pritchard and Kibedi (1987), Wahlbeck (1998), and Zetter and Pearl (2000).

Studies of migrant associations in Europe over the last 30 years, and those of refugee associations more recently, have mainly examined the role that such associations play, identifying the following as important functions performed: overcoming isolation; acting as 'tribune' of the communities from which they emerge; providing information about the country of reception; promoting country of origin culture and language; creating community-based welfare structures to plug gaps in state social service provision; maintaining links with the country of origin. Hence, migrant (including refugee) associations have been seen as negotiators of identity and as vehicles for the integration of the particular communities from which they emerge. As the creation of conditions in which formal citizenship status is eventually acquired is considered the most positive and important outcome for all migrants, then their settlement and integration has been raised as the dominant paradigm in the study of associations. However, political participation as an important right and as a means of citizenship-building and becoming part of a wider political community unbound by principles of legality and nationality has been insufficiently emphasized.

The question of refugees and citizenship-building may be considered through the study of participation in a number of public arenas (and at different levels) such as political parties, trade unions, non-governmental organizations (NGOs), and other public governance institutions. However, what defines such spaces, often referred to as 'invited spaces' (see Cornwell, 2002), is that they are shaped and dominated by resource-bearing agents who are external to refugee communities. These agents make decisions on which grassroots actors to invite in or keep out, and therefore risk marginalizing the very people they wish to 'consult' and involve. In contrast to these are refugee community associations which may emerge organically given the common interests and concerns of their members. Such associations constitute what we can call 'autonomous spaces',[14] and offer their members a more real means of legitimizing their own concerns, of gaining confidence to articulate those concerns, of making links with other social movements, voluntary and statutory agencies, and therefore of increasing their participation. Such associational spaces can also constitute sites of activism in a way that invited spaces cannot. As far as refugee women's associations are concerned, they represent an autonomous space at the very base of the participation pyramid in which asylum seeking and refugee women can get involved more easily as a means of escaping isolation, of developing coping strategies, and of challenging authority as a means of shaping a political and social identity for themselves. It is for this reason that they deserve to form the focus of our study in citizenship-building here. The information presented below (in Sections 11.4 and 11.5) is based on semi-structured interviews carried out with 20 associations in London, Birmingham, and Paris between October 2002 and October 2004. These were supplemented by in-depth interviews with 20 individual activist members of associations during the same period of time in the three cities mentioned.

11.4 The establishment of refugee women's associations in Britain and France

Asylum seeking and refugee women's participation in discrete refugee women's associations or in migrant women's associations does not have a long history in either Britain or France. The majority of refugee women's associations were established from the late 1990s and early 2000s, following increased refugee migration into the EU (mainly from East and Central Europe, the Middle East, Africa, and South Asia) and more specifically, the rising numbers of women asylum seekers.[15] However, a very small number of associations were set up during the 1970s and 1980s following the arrival of Chilean refugees in the early to mid-1970s, Iranians in the late 1970s and early 1980s, and Moroccans and Algerians (to France) in the early and late 1980s respectively. The overwhelming majority of refugee women's groups and associations are based in and around Paris and London simply because these cities are home to long established migrant populations. They also constitute the base for the most important public institutions of governance from which support is sought and given and they offer the best opportunities, such as they exist, for refugee migrants to make a success of their situation. In Britain, however, refugee women's associations are emerging in other major cities where refugee populations have grown as a result of New Labour's dispersal policy, set down in the 1999 Immigration and Asylum Act.[16] Thus Birmingham is second to London as far as the density of refugee community associations is concerned.[17]

Most of these associations emerged from loosely established collectives or networks of asylum seeking and refugee women sharing a common ethnic background and/or interests. There are several reasons why refugee women's networks and groups, whether undeclared or legal, have been set up. One is the desire among asylum seeking and refugee women to organize separately from their main community associations. While most of the literature on refugee associations presents an unproblematic view of the relations between the associations and the communities they emerge from, the reality is that they can be riven with tensions resulting from ideological, tribal, inter-generational, or class divisions, or because of unequal power relations based on gendered roles.[18] It is this last tension that has pushed some asylum seeking and refugee women to organize themselves separately from men, especially where such tension is imported from political associations and parties in the country of origin. This has been the case with some of the oldest networks, groups, or associations of Moroccan (Les Marocaines en

France, formed in 1978), Chilean (Collectif des Femmes Chilliennes – COFECH – established in 1979 in France), and Algerian women (le Groupe Femmes Algériennes formed in 1977), who felt that after long years of being pushed to 'prioritize' liberation goals or the like, they wanted to think of their own needs and rights. As far as recent refugee migrants are concerned, Afghani and Somali women have also spoken of tensions within their main community associations (between men who want to retain the strict gender roles as they operate in the country of origin and women who see their arrival in Britain or France as an opportunity for self-development) as a reason for organizing separately.

The trigger for setting up refugee women's networks, groups or associations can also often lie in the most mundane of events, such as coffee mornings organized by women from a particular community wishing to talk about common problems. This was certainly the case of the Midlands Refugee Women's Association (MRWA) and the Birmingham-based Arab Women's Association, or the many small African refugee women's groups located in and around Paris.[19] Alternatively, associations have emerged from campaigning against particular injustices or in favor of particular rights. For example, apart from feeling unrepresented by their main community association, Chilean women in France set up the Collectif des Femmes Chiliennes in 1979 also in solidarity with women comrades fighting dictatorship in Chile. More recently, the Paris-based Rajfire (Réseau pour l'autonomie des femmes immigrées et réfugiées) first emerged in 1996, in the wake of the *sans-papiers* protests.[20] It met regularly as an undeclared association from 1998 and did not become a legal association until 2002. In Britain, one of the most recently established associations, Mothers against Mistreatment of Asylum Seekers (MAMAS), was set up in 2004 to campaign specifically for the fair treatment of asylum seekers.

The pressure for networks and groups to form associations has resulted from the expansion of refugee women's activities and the concomitant need for funding. In France, a further impetus for the formation of associations proper is the Association Law of 1901 which stipulates that any network or group that wishes to organize along more formal lines (in terms of accessing funding, employing staff, or engaging with national or sub-national state and civil society institutions) is obliged to declare itself an association.

However, refugee women's associations together with migrant women's associations, whether undeclared or legal, form a small part of the migrant association landscape, due to a shortage of funds.[21] It should be noted that general migrant groups, including refugee migrants, have found it easier to organize and form associations in Britain than in France. This may be explained by the different histories of migration and related legislation in the two countries. While it is not possible to go into the details of this explanation here, two points are worth highlighting. First, large-scale non-European immigration to Britain, which began in the 1950s, brought in New Commonwealth citizens from the Caribbean and South Asia who were entitled to unrestricted entry (until 1962), British citizenship, and the political rights attached to it. Consequently, armed with political rights, immigrants from the New Commonwealth found it relatively easy to establish a thriving association culture which subsequent generations have continued. In France, on the other hand, immigrant communities have been unable to lay strong foundations for an active associative culture due to the fact that early generations from France's ex-colonies, with the exception of Algerians until 1962, were denied certain civil and political rights. Hence, more recently arrived groups have found it difficult to build on this poor legacy. Moreover, although immigrants obtained the right to form legally registered associations in accordance with the Socialist law of October 1981, this was not accompanied by other political rights (such as the right to vote) and in fact it may be argued that the October 1981 Association Law served to disincentivize refugee and other migrant groups from civic and political participation. Second, the term 'association' has been used very loosely in Britain and can refer to various groupings of people: from church groups and leisure circles to workers' welfare groups or overtly political organizations. In France, only a body recognized by the law of 1901 and which, at the very least, requires a formal constitution is termed 'association'. Hence, it is possible to publicly acknowledge many more associations in Britain than in France. However, in both countries, it is impossible to even roughly estimate the number of refugee women's associations in existence. The fact that many are undeclared and suffer a chronic lack of resources means that there is a continual process of association demise and renewal.

11.5   How do refugee women's associations contribute toward citizenship-building?

Let us turn to the question of asylum seeking and refugee women's participation in associations and what associations do. Refugee women's associations engage in activities that fall into two main categories: first, activities designed to inform reception society of the presence of asylum seeking and refugee women and make known their needs, opinions, culture, and customs; and second, activities which offer asylum seeking and refugee women a better understanding of reception society and which plug gaps in state and NGO provision of services to this group of women. In establishing and maintaining an interaction with reception society through the two categories of activities mentioned, the majority of refugee women's associations aim to empower their members, counter oppressive practices against their members, fight for equality, equity, and diversity, and improve their members' quality of life in the reception country.

The associations questioned for this research engage in a variety of activities through which reception society can learn about the circumstances in which asylum seeking and refugee women have fled their countries of origin and the situations that they encounter in western reception societies. Such activities include

- Public meetings, demonstrations, and other one-time events, often in conjunction with other social movements or progressive NGOs. For example, on 1 May, International Women's Day, International Refugee Week. More recently, associations and their members have participated in rallies and demonstrations against the war in Iraq.
- Campaigns against racism, deportations, female genital mutilation (FGM), forced marriage, and honor crimes against women.
- Lobbying political decision makers through petitions and letters. This kind of activity is undertaken by all of the bigger associations, often in conjunction with refugee NGOs and with the support of the smaller ones.
- Provision of witness accounts by individuals to sympathetic journalists – normally through personal contacts between individuals in associations and in the media.
- Cultural evenings, open to the public, organized (separately or jointly) by refugee women's associations and NGOs supporting refugee migrants.

The second category of activities, aimed at increasing knowledge and understanding of reception society, consists of providing asylum seeking and refugee women with some basic education, practical skills and help, and recreational space and experiences. They include, for example,

- Workshops on effective communication and assertiveness.
- Leadership training through inclusion of members in agenda-setting and decision-making within the association's own structures.

- Clinics on health (e.g., HIV awareness, trauma and depression, drug misuse, contraceptive advice) and related issues (domestic violence), good parenting skills.
- 'Sign-posting' services on behalf of public institutions that deal with asylum and refugee issues.
- Language classes and some employment-related training such as acquisition of IT skills, preparation of CVs and interviews.
- Cultural visits and outings (to theatres and museums for instance) for women and their children.
- Seminars on reception country history and culture.
- Legal advice and advocacy vis-à-vis asylum claims or debt issues.
- Child-minding and homework clubs for school-age children.
- Interpreting services for women who need to consult with health-care, education, and housing professionals.

Both these sets of activities in which refugee women's associations engage can be said to contribute toward citizenship-building. The first set of activities gets asylum seeking and refugee women directly involved in a number of political participation options, ranging from the conventional (lobbying politicians) to the informal (discussion of political and social issues in spaces provided by the association) to the more militant (demonstrations and even occupations as in the case of the *sans-papier* movement in France supported by associations such as Rajfire and ASFAD (Association de Solidarité avec les Femmes Algériennes et Démocrates). Their direct involvement in political action has a number of impacts.

First, asylum seeking and refugee women are generally more likely than women from labor migrations to experience increased awareness of political issues and to become familiar with the political structures and cultures that operate in the reception society. Many of the associations consulted during this research stressed the fact that, in their experience, a large proportion of asylum seeking and refugee women have higher levels of formal education, qualifications, and work experience than women who arrive as part of labor migrations and that this equips them with the tools to participate politically in the country of reception.[22]

Second, the women inevitably come across other social actors and associations with whom they can network. Being part of a larger collective which includes some high profile organizations can create a sense of empowerment and of making one's voice heard. In this respect many refugee women's associations work on a regular basis with each other, with some of the longer established migrant support organizations, feminist organizations, and NGOs. For example, among the larger refugee women's associations in France, Rajfire collaborates with ASFAD, Amnesty International (French section), and is a part of the CADAC (*Coordination des Associations pour le Droit à l'avortement*), whereas ASFAD has a regular connection with GAMS (*Groupe Femmes pour l'Abolition des Mutilations Sexuelles*), ELELE (a Turkish association the vast majority of whose members are women), and GISTI (*Groupe d'Information et de Soutien des Immigrés*). In Britain, refugee women's associations such as the Sudan Women's Association, the Horn of Africa Somali Women's Organization, and others are often brought together under the umbrella of organizations such as the Refugee Women's Resource Project (RWRP),[23] Action for Refugee Women (AFRW),[24] or Amnesty International's women's section in campaigns over issues of common concern such as FGM, sexual violence, 'honor' killings, and the fight against racism and injustices in Europe and elsewhere.

Third, direct involvement enables asylum seeking and refugee women to bring the political experience and know-how that many have gained in their countries of origin to political arenas in the reception country. Refugee migrant women arrive in EU countries as political exiles either in their own right, because of family links with anti-government or radical movements in their countries of origin, or because they form part of a persecuted ethnic group. Hence, unlike labor migrant women, and for that matter reception society women generally, many are schooled in forms of radical action which others have only heard of or witnessed through media reports.[25] This, for example, has certainly been the case of Palestinian women who were involved with movements such as the PLO or Hamas and who participated in or were influenced, through family or friends, by the women's demonstrations of the first Intifada.[26] The political know-how that many refugee women bring with them adds to the resources and perspectives of the associative and social movements of which they form a part.

The activities falling into the second category described above fill a crucial gap in service provision by statutory and voluntary agencies by teaching asylum seeking and refugee women about reception society. It is in this sense that the second set of activities fits in with the integration paradigm that dominates mainstream studies of refugee community associations. While the integration role that refugee women's associations play is not to be forgotten, it must also be recognized that many are concerned that their members should be empowered and to this end they endeavor to equip asylum seeking and refugee women with the four main 'weapons of the powerful': first, information of various types is given to their members (see the list above); second, members are invited to offer opinions in both role play (communication and assertiveness training) and real situations (at association meetings for example); third, members are invited to discuss and set priorities to do with the activities that associations undertake; and fourth, many associations (in particular those that are not highly and formally structured) include as many of their members in decision-making as possible. Given situations of political repression in countries of origin from which asylum seekers and refugees escape and given that women's associations often emerge as a result of the lack of democracy in the male-dominated refugee associations, the majority of refugee women's associations are keen to include, if possible, all members in their democratic functioning.

In addition to the main roles and functions described above, associations also enable asylum seeking and refugee women to deal with different notions of women's status in reception societies, with their aspirations, and how to negotiate a place for themselves within their families and communities. This allows for the construction of a sense of self and control over their lives.

Many associations simply provide a physical space and psychological support, outside the home, for women to meet and talk about their aspirations and gain the confidence to set themselves up independently. Sub-Saharan African women's associations (especially from West and Central Africa) have, over the years, imported networking skills from countries of origin whereby groups of women may pool their human and financial resources in order to set up businesses run on cooperative lines or where financial resources are pooled in order to create small savings and credit unions (*tontines*).[27] *Tontines* have provided numbers of refugee women with exposure to micro-financial methods and helped them to become familiar with banks and other business institutions in Britain and France, as well as created opportunities for self-employment. As *tontines* also have political clout in traditional African communities, the asylum seeking and refugee women involved in them gain personal esteem vis-à-vis family, friends, and community.

Also, while associations do not interfere directly between women and their husbands (barring cases of domestic violence) or family, the strength that is developed by the women through associative activities often puts pressure on male heads of household and communities to rethink their attitudes and practices toward women and girls. Such pressure is further increased when associations gain public recognition for their work and links with public governance institutions.

For asylum seeking and refugee women, the knowledge of having an alternative to support from husbands and family brings a sense of freedom which then pushes them to participate further in the public domain. It develops the idea that they can operate as mothers, volunteers/workers, and political subjects in a number of arenas and consequently reinforces self-identity in a different society.

11.6 Conclusion

The study of refugee women's associations in Britain and France strengthens the conviction that their role and goals deserve to be examined and made visible. If one subscribes to the view that citizenship is as much about becoming part of an active political community as it is about achieving a particular legal status tied to the possession of rights, then refugee women's associations can act as citizenship-builders for some of the most disadvantaged groups of people in European societies. While some of these people may go on to achieve formal rights, a large number of others will not. But through their participation, however, they will have avoided some of the worst aspects of marginalization that asylum seekers and refugee communities face today. They will have come together in networks of solidarity and collective action, gained some sense of their own power, rendered some legitimacy to their concerns, and made some contact with the reception society and its institutions.

This chapter has presented refugee women's associations as significant sites of autonomous action, mediation (between different groups of refugee women; between refugee women and their communities; and between refugee women and reception society), and challenge (to established thinking and practices in their own communities and reception society), and hence as important citizenship-builders. However, it should not leave the reader with the impression that they work in an unproblematic way. Of course, these associations encounter various problems as do most others. Independent discourses and action toward active citizenship-building can give way to discourses and practices that do not suit all its members or that become neutralized and sometimes ineffective as some associations become more heavily involved in formal public governance. Furthermore, these associations are dealing with women of negligible material resources who are often in mental anguish and turmoil. So, while large numbers of refugee women participate politically (in the widest sense), there are vast numbers who cannot think beyond the everyday concerns of finding accommodation, feeding their families, and progressing their asylum applications. Such women are unable to add to the resources of the associations from which they seek help.

The question of the limitations (financial constraints, factionalism, accountability, legitimacy, and so on) of refugee women's associations is one which certainly requires further research.

Notes

1. The author would like to thank the British Academy for financial assistance and participants at the Women's World Congress 2005 (Seoul, June 2005) for their helpful comments. The research presented here forms part of a larger study of asylum seeking and refugee women in Britain and France which will be published by Manchester University Press in 2006.
2. An asylum seeker is defined as someone who has made an application for asylum under the terms of the 1951 Geneva Convention, but who has not received a final decision from the relevant authorities on that application. Also included here in the category 'asylum seekers' are those who claim the right to remain in Britain or France, on humanitarian grounds, under the terms of Article 3 of the European Convention on Human Rights (ECHR) and in France under the terms of the Constitution which supports the right to pursue freedom without persecution (*asile constitutionnel*). Finally, the category 'asylum seekers' also includes those whose asylum claims have failed but who, for one reason or another, have not left the country where their claim was lodged.
3. The term 'refugee' refers to a person who has received a decision on his/her asylum claim which allows him/her to remain (under the terms of the 1951 Geneva Convention) in the country where the claim was lodged. Furthermore, it includes those who have been given leave to remain under the terms of ECHR Article 3 and in France to those who have obtained residence under the terms of *asile constitutionnel*. Finally, it also refers to those who have been given discretionary leave to remain.
4. It should be noted that the term 'refugee' is sometimes used in this chapter in its generic sense as in 'refugee community associations' (that is without the addition of 'and asylum seekers'), and in these instances it covers both categories asylum seekers and refugees as defined in notes 2 and 3.
5. For the purposes of this research, the term association is used to include both registered associations as well as collectives, groups, and networks of women which run on more informal lines, but which have decided for one reason or another not to set themselves up as formally structured or declared associations.
6. It is not suggested here that the issue of citizenship is less relevant to men, but women as a particularly dispossessed section of refugee populations constitute the focus of this chapter.
7. In 2004, 41.5 percent of women who entered France as asylum seekers were married while a further 7.3 percent had partners (OFPRA, 2004: VI 1/1). Although a proportion of these may have entered without husbands/partners and although the statistics provided by OFPRA do not indicate whether these women are primary claimants or dependants, we can assume that a significant number arrive as part of a couple or family group in which they (and any children) are the dependent ones. As far as the United Kingdom is concerned, female dependants made up 53 percent of dependants and of these 26 percent

were over the age of 18. Although UK asylum statistics do not indicate the civil status of dependants, it would be fair to assume that a large number are either women accompanying husbands or partners who are the primary claimants (Heath and Jeffries, 2005: 13).

8. The case of Verah Kachepa is one such to have made recent headlines in Britain. Verah Kachepa and her four children entered Britain, from Malawi, as dependants of her husband in 2001. Following the breakdown of their marriage, Mr Kachepa returned to Malawi. Left in an illegal situation, Verah Kachepa and her children claimed asylum but were turned down, to eventually face deportation. They were deported on 25 August 2005 (Barkham, 2005a, 2005b). In France, the 1993 Nationality Act increased the vulnerability of migrant women whose legal rights depended on the status of the head of household. The law stipulated that residence permits could be revoked if divorce or separation took place within a year of acquiring them. This pushed hundreds of separated or divorced women, previously dependant on husbands, into a situation of illegality. The *sans-papières* ('women without papers'), as they are known, were therefore forced to claim asylum – more often than not without success.

9. Contributory actions motivated by individual responsibility can range from attending building planning application hearings to reporting neighborhood louts to the police, to working to targets set by government (hospital waiting lists, etc.) to scooping dog poop off pavements. Such actions of the new Right's 'good' citizen contrast with the radical activist politics of 'undesirable' or non-citizens.

10. For an endorsement of neo-liberal citizenship see Roche (1992) and Mead (1986). For a Left critique of it, see Plant (1991).

11. See, for example, Dietz (1992), Elshtain (1993), Lister (2003), Mouffe (1992a, 1992b), Pateman (1989), Phillips (1991, 1993), Siim (2000), Vogel (1991), Young (1989, 1990), Yuval-Davis and Werbner (1999).

12. In an attempt to break the recent monopoly of the neo-liberal Right over discourses of civic responsibility, progressive-minded citizenship theorists have put forward political participation, represented by dynamic, collective politics, as a civic obligation. See, for instance, Dietz (1992).

13. Among which are the following: Catani and Palidda (1987), Jenkins (1988), Layton-Henry (1990), Leveau and Withol de Wenden (1991), Rex (1973), Rex and Tomlinson (1979), Rex, Joly and Wilpert (1987), Withol de Wenden (1988, 1992), and Vertovec (1999).

14. Such spaces, outside state and other formalized institutions of governance have been referred to elsewhere in a number of different ways. For a discussion of this, see Cornwell, 2002.

15. In 2004, women made up 30 percent of all principal asylum claimants in the United Kingdom compared with 19 percent in 2000 (Heath and Jeffries, 2005: 10), while 2004 figures for France show that women accounted for 32.9 percent of all asylum seekers (no distinction is made between principal claimants and dependants) (OFPRA, 2004: VI/1) compared with 29.6 percent in 2001 (OFPRA, 2001: VI/1).

16. Dispersal measures were introduced to relieve pressure on London and local authorities in South-east England which were required to house and support

increasing numbers of asylum seekers throughout the 1990s. Hence, other areas in the Midlands, Eastern and Northern England were designated 'cluster' zones for the reception of asylum seekers.

17. Birmingham was the top dispersal city in England from 2001 to the end of 2003. In 2004, it was overtaken by Leeds and Sheffield.

18. Studies (e.g., Goulbourne, 1991; Werbner, 1991) of some of the longer established migrant associations in Britain have challenged the assumption that associations are united and representative of all sections of their communities.

19. For example, two such recently formed groups in Paris are a Congolese women's group, set up with support from Secours Catholique and the Comité des femmes Djiboutiennes contre les viols et l'impunité both of which see themselves as 'groupes de parole et de réflexion' on the events that are taking place in the Congo and the Horn of Africa. Both groups wish to raise awareness about gendered violence in the current conflicts affecting their respective countries of origin.

20. The *sans-papiers* (those without papers) protest movement came to prominence in August 1996 when a group of 300 *sans-papiers* were ejected from a Paris church which they had occupied over a two-month period in protest against a law that had turned them into undocumented migrants. Since then the movement has extended to all of France and even has off-shoots in other EU countries.

21. Refugee women's associations are particularly badly off, relying on irregular and meagre individual subscriptions, small amounts of financial aid from the EU (e.g., the European Refugee Fund or Integration of Third Country Nationals – INTI – program), British and French government sources (for instance, the British government's Time Bank and Invest to Save programs or the French government's *Fonds d'action et de soutien pour l'integration et la lutte contre les discriminations*), and money raised from cultural events. Refugees and asylum seekers constitute the most disadvantaged socio-economic group in EU reception countries.

22. While there is generally insufficient data on the resources that asylum seeking and refugee women bring with them, a 2002 survey of refugee women's skills and qualifications, published by the Greater London Authority, found that 68 percent of refugee women were educated to University level and the same proportion were employed in their respective countries of origin. Of the survey sample, 33 percent had trained and worked as teachers, 32 percent as nurses, and 25 percent as doctors while the rest were students, or had trained and worked in professions as varied as architecture, social work, business, and marketing (Dumper, 2002). A more recent skills audit (Kirk, 2004) gives a breakdown of refugees' qualifications and occupational status in their country of origin according to gender, age, and nationality.

23. RWRP is funded via the NGO Asylum Aid and was set up to provide women asylum seekers and refugees with free legal representation and advice. Since its establishment in 2000, its aims have extended beyond just representation and advice. It now also acts as an umbrella for refugee women and their associations.

24. AFRW, funded mainly through the NGO Refugee Action, is a network bringing together refugee women and their associations across Britain.

25. Large numbers of refugee women are not experienced activists, but nevertheless display high levels of politicization in their ability to see the broader issues at stake in a given conflict situation.
26. The first Intifada, an action of mass civil disobedience and protest against an increasingly brutal Israeli occupation, began in 1987 and lasted until the early 1990s. One of its characteristics was the repeated mass demonstrations by Palestinian women in the refugee camps (of Gaza in particular).
27. In both Britain and France, the most common businesses set up in recent years (mainly by Nigerian and Congolese women) are small grocery stores (often combined with hair-plaiting and beading) and community cafés.

References

Barkham, P., 'Sorry, but We'll Still Deport you, Home Office Tells Family', *Guardian*, 28 July 2005a.
Barkham, P., 'Third Time Unlucky for Kachepa Family', *Guardian*, 26 August 2005b.
Catani, M., and Palidda, S., *Le rôle du mouvement associatif dans l'évolution des communautés immigrées* (Paris: FAS-DPM, 1987).
Cornwell, A., 'Making Spaces, Changing Places: Situating Participation in Development', *IDS Working Paper*, 170 (2002).
Dietz, M., 'Context is all Feminism and Theories of Citizenship', in Mouffe, C. (ed.), *Dimensions of Radical Democracy: Pluralism, Citizenship and Community* (London: Verso, 1992).
Dumper, H., *Missed Opportunities: A Skills Audit of Refugee Women in London from the Teaching, Nursing and Medical Professions* (London: Greater London Authority, 2002).
Elshtain, J., *Public Man, Private Women: Women in Social and Political Thought*, 2nd edn (Princeton, NJ: Princeton University Press, 1993).
Goulbourne, H., 'The Offence of the West Indian Political Leadership and the Communal Option', in Werbner, P., and Anwar, M. (eds), *Black and Ethnic Leaderships in Britain. The Cultural Dimensions of Political Action* (London: Routledge, 1991).
Gould, C., *Rethinking Democracy* (Cambridge: Cambridge University Press, 1988).
Heath, T., and Jeffries, R., *Asylum Statistics United Kingdom 2004* (London: Home Office/Research Development and Statistics Directorate, 2005).
Jenkins, S., *Ethnic Associations and the Welfare State: Services to Immigrants in Five Countries* (New York: Columbia University Press, 1988).
Joly, D., 'Refugee Associations: between Society of Origin and Society of Exile', in Joly, D., *Haven or Hell? Asylum Policies and Refugees in Europe* (Basingstoke: Macmillan, 1996).
Joly, D., 'Refugees and Citizenship in the Framework of the New Asylum Regime', in Leveau, R., Wihtol de Wenden, C., and Mohsen-Finan, K., *Nouvelles citoyennetés: réfugiés et sans-papiers dans l'espace européen* (Paris: IFRI, 2001).
Kirk, R., *Skills Audit of Refugees*, On-line Report 37/04 (London: Home Office/ Research Development and Statistics Directorate, 2004): http://www. homeoffice.gov.uk/rds/pdfs04/rdsolr3704.pdf (accessed 27 July 2005).

Layton-Henry, Z., *The Political Rights of Migrant Workers in Western Europe* (London: Sage, 1990).

Leveau, R., and Withol de Wenden, C. (eds), *Modes d'insertion des populations de culture islamique dans le système politique français* (Paris: MIRE, 1991).

Lister, R., *Citizenship: Feminist Perspectives* (Basingstoke: Palgrave Macmillan, 2003).

Lloyd, G., *The Man of Reason: 'Male' and 'Female' in Western Philosophy* (London: Methuen, 1984).

Lutz, H., 'The Limits of European-ness: Immigrant Women in Fortress Europe', *Feminist Review*, 57 (1997): 93–111.

Marshall, T. H., *Citizenship and Social Class* (Cambridge: Cambridge University Press, 1950).

Marshall, T. H., *Class, Citizenship and Social Development* (New York: Doubleday, 1964).

Mead, L., *Beyond Entitlement: The Social Obligations of Citizenship* (New York: Free Press, 1986).

Mouffe, C., 'L'offensive du néo-conservatisme contre la démocratie', in Jalbert, L., and Lepage, L., *Néo-conservatisme et restructuration de l'État* (Montréal: Presses de l'Université de Québec, 1986).

Mouffe, C., (ed.), *Dimensions of Radical Democracy: Pluralism, Citizenship and Community* (London: Verso, 1992a).

Mouffe, C., 'Feminism, Citizenship and Radical Democratic Politics', in Butler, J., Scott, J. (eds), *Feminist Theories of the Political* (London: Routledge, 1992b).

OFPRA, *Rapport d'activité 2001* (Fontenay-sous-Bois: OFPRA, 2001).

OFPRA, *Rapport d'activité 2004* (Fontenay-sous-Bois: OFPRA, 2004).

Pateman, C., *The Disorder of Women, Democracy, Feminism and Political Theory* (London: Polity Press, 1989).

Phillips, A., *Engendering Democracy* (Cambridge: Polity Press: 1991).

Phillips, A., *Democracy and Difference* (Oxford: Blackwell, 1993).

Plant, R., 'Social Rights and the Reconstruction of Welfare', in Andrews, G. (ed.) *Citizenship* (London: Lawrence & Wishart, 1991).

Rex, J., *Race, Colonialism and the City* (London: Routledge & Kegan Paul, 1973).

Rex, J., Joly, D., and Wilpert, C. (eds), *Immigrant Associations in Europe* (Aldershot: Gower, 1987).

Rex, J., and Tomlinson, S., *Colonial Immigrants in a British City* (London: Routledge & Kegan Paul, 1979).

Roche, M., *Rethinking Citizenship: Welfare, Ideology and Change in Modern Society* (Cambridge: Polity Press, 1992).

Salinas, M., Pritchard, D., and Kibedi, A., 'Refugee Based Organizations: Their Functions and Importance for the Refugee in Britain', *Working Papers on Refugees* (Oxford and London: Refugee Studies Programme and British Refugee Council, 1987).

Siim, B., *Gender and Citizenship: Politics and Agency in France, Britain and Denmark* (Cambridge: Cambridge University Press, 2000).

Vertovec, S., 'Minority Associations, Networks and Public Policies: Reassessing Relationships', *Journal for Migration and Ethnic Studies*, 25:1 (1999): 21–42.

Vogel, U., 'Is Citizenship Gender-Specific?', in Vogel, U., and Moran, M., *The Frontiers of Citizenship* (Basingstoke: Macmillan, 1991).

Wahlbeck O., 'Community Work and Exile Politics: Kurdish Refugee Associations in London', *Journal of Refugee Studies*, 11:3 (1998): 215–230.

Werbner, P., 'The fiction of Unity in Ethnic Politics', in Werbner, P., and Anwar, M. (eds), *Black and Ethnic Leaderships in Britain* (London: Routledge, 1991).

Werbner, P., and Anwar, M. (eds), *Black and Ethnic Leaderships in Britain. The Cultural Dimensions of Political Action* (London: Routledge, 1991).

Wihtol de Wenden, C., 'Associations d'immigrés, une citoyenneté concrète', *Les Cahiers de l'Orient*, 11 (1988): 115–35.

Wihtol de Wenden, C., 'Les Associations "beur" et immigrées, leurs leaders, leurs stratégies', *Les Cahiers de l'Orient*, 178 (1992): 31–44.

Young, I. M., 'Polity and Group Difference: A Critique of the Idea of Universal Citizenship', *Ethics*, 99 (1989): 250–74.

Young, I. M., *Justice and the Politics of Difference* (Princeton, NJ: Princeton University Press, 1990).

Yuval-Davis, N., and Werbner, P., *Women, Citizenship and Difference* (London, New York: Zed Books, 1999).

Zetter, R., and Pearl, M., 'The Minority within the Minority: Refugee Community Based Organizations in the UK and the Impact of Restrictionism', *Journal of Ethnic and Migration Studies*, 26:4 (2000): 675–98.

Postface

Etienne Balibar

The essays assembled in this book seem to me to raise some fundamental questions. They are rooted in the specific history of these two great nation-states of Western Europe, but they also involve global problems which testify for the universal importance of population shifts and the hybridization of cultures in today's world. They demonstrate the strong impact of such social changes on the constitution of our political systems which, in the first years of the twenty-first century, appear much less stable in their legitimacy and much more hesitant in their commitment to equality than we had imagined only a decade ago. It is precisely in order to give the governing institutions a renewed and broader basis, and to associate an increasingly multinational civil society with the ideals of liberty and justice that the European construction was approved by the public opinion of its member states over half a century. It is therefore a test of its achievements and failures to closely scrutinize how the progressive (albeit uneven) integration of such powerful constituencies as France and Britain within the communitarian framework has influenced their own democratic evolution.

I had the great honor of being asked by Christophe Bertossi and his co-authors to contribute to some general reflections on these issues. Relying on their work, I will indicate why I believe that the authors have produced a fine work of clarification, raising what I consider to be 'the good questions', that is, those with no simple, univocal, or ready-made solution. I consider it to be our scientific task that we ceaselessly investigate them, while it is our civic duty to address them practically. I certainly have no pretension to provide final answers myself, not only for reasons of space. But I want once again to draw the attention on the critical importance of institutions and public policies in articulating the fluctuations of collective representations (including racism, xenophobia, sexism) with the hazardous transformations of the historical environment.

As indicated by the title, the key notions at work here are 'discrimination' and 'citizenship'. They seem to readily clash with one another. This comes from the fact that, throughout its history, the concept of citizenship was associated with a strong notion of equality or equal rights (*aequum ius*), a legal rejection of individual and collective discriminations: by definition citizenship *is* antidiscrimination, and discrimination

237

is *anticitizenship*. However this statement of principles was always qualified for two reasons at least, which refer to the fact that 'citizens' exist only in historical *communities*, with an internal distribution of power between 'executive' and 'subaltern' functions, and a common identity based on the distinction of 'interior' and 'exterior'. There never existed anything like a community of citizens with universal political participation of its members and unlimited access to citizen's rights for foreigners and new-comers, although these practical or statutory 'distinctions' considerably varied over time and space, which can be considered an index of the degree of actual democracy achieved by each historical polity. It is on the background of this long and conflictual history that the initiative of the European Union (acting through its quasi-legislative and quasi-governmental organs, and grounded in the *Charter of fundamental rights*, adopted at the end of 2000) to promote 'anti-discrimination policies' in the member states must be valued and interpreted. What it seems to set on the agenda is a new *politics of equality*, even if formulated in a limited and negative manner (but the 'constitutionalization of fundamental rights', to borrow the expression from legal historian Gerald Stourzh, is bound to proceed in the typical form of the suppression of what actually suppresses them). This could be seen as evidence of the fact that the European Union is now on its way to resuming the progress of equality, moving toward an increasingly effective and universalistic concept of citizenship, therefore *overcoming* the intrinsic limits of the nation-states from the point of view of their own democratic exigencies. Or in a more cynical manner it could be seen as a sign of the fact that European states, which are still very far from forming a single constituency (if they will ever go that way), are increasingly using the European institutions as an *ideological* smokescreen to cover their more or less regressive social evolutions and their practice of inequality. This is a dilemma that admits of no simple solution. The previous chapters have offered abundant evidence of the acute contradictions involved here, particularly emphasizing three aspects.

A first aspect crucially concerns the obstacles preventing a 'dialogic' encounter of different political traditions. What makes the comparison of France and Britain particularly interesting in this respect is the strong contrast of their public ideologies, deeply rooted in their rival histories as nations, states, empires, civil societies, intellectual cultures, and con-stantly reinforced by their belonging to heterogeneous ensembles – within and outside Europe – which tend to pit them one against the other. One can observe a strange exchange of postures and languages around such notions as 'migrants' and 'minorities', which easily allow

British intellectuals and politicians to denounce the Gallic rhetoric of universality and its ignorance of historical groups and cultures (including 'races', or 'colours'), whereas their French counterparts warn against Anglo-Saxon communitarianism and protection of collective identities (very often *internally* oppressive and discriminatory themselves) at the expense of individual freedom. This book convincingly argues that the European integration, however partial and formal, together with the now global situation after the end of the Cold War, has considerably reduced the *practical* importance of these antagonisms, in terms of actual antidiscrimination policies. They are often more a question of names than of reality. It remains to be shown, however, if the relative neutralization of the ideological consciousnesses comes from the fact that each political tradition has learned something from the other, in a self-critical manner, or they are simply adding blindness to suppression, competing for the worst as it were. Arguments can be proposed for each side of the dilemma.

No single question is more likely to test the capacity of European nations to address the issue of multiple 'belongings', exclusive or incompatible 'loyalties', the growing uncertainty of boundaries between 'insiders' and 'outsiders' (or, rather, the increasing number of 'citizens' who are neither simply inside nor simply outside), than the status and the importance of *Islam* within the European space. Both Britain and France, owing to their colonial histories, and their postcolonial ties with Africa, South-East Asia, and the Middle-East, have a long experience (meaning acquaintance and prejudice, real knowledge and misperception) of the 'question of Islam' and the coexistence between Westerners and communities of Muslim origin and culture. Neither of them, however, was really prepared to confront the form in which their own public opinion is now increasingly regarding Islam as the reincarnation of an old figure: the 'interior enemy'. Which is not to say that, on different sides of the political spectrum, in different institutions of the public services or the civil society (such as the educational system or the labor market, but also the police, sometimes the army), nothing is done to address the discriminations. This is clearly a fierce, lasting, uncertain struggle. A much desired move toward truly equalitarian citizenship, ranging from work and job opportunities to family life and symbolic status in the public sphere, remains largely paralyzed by very real contradictions. The geopolitical context epitomized by the Israeli-Palestinian conflict, plus the 'War on terror' and its 'Jihadist' counterpart since 9/11, had had a disastrous impact, providing an easy rationale for old forms of xenophobia. Above all there is the fact that Islam is a *religion*, therefore also a *culture* (as Christianity itself), but in situations of discrimination it basically works as a fictitious *race* (or becomes invoked and treated in a racist manner). Islamophobia is the arch example of what some theoreticians for years now have called 'new racism', 'differential racism', or 'cultural racism'. Which in turn leads to the consequence (repeatedly addressed in this book) that the categories of 'individual emancipation' and 'collective recognition' (each of which may justify a rebellion against discrimination, without which there would be hardly any *politics of equality* that would promote citizenship) easily conflict with one another, and become 'double edged swords' (as particularly illustrated by the disturbing fact – discussed here by Estelle Ferrarese – that *to give names and not to give names* of 'origin' to the French or British citizens deemed *others* proves equally discriminatory). But none of these strategies can be sacrificed for the sake of the other. This is indeed true in general, not only in the case of Islam, and it does not only concern women (who typically develop their capacity to claim and recreate citizenship *within and against* Islam as a symbolic name of community). But it takes undoubtedly a more antagonistic form in this case. This is perhaps where the dilemma of specific European politics of equality and deeply rooted Eurocentric forms of neo-racism become particularly conspicuous and perilous.

Finally the book strongly emphasizes a third uncertainty. The terminology of 'discrimination' (and antidiscrimination) can indicate why. As several contributions to this book have clearly demonstrated, there is a permanent oscillation of such terms between a practical and an ideal level, more precisely a reference to statutory rights and obligations within the nation-state, and universal 'human rights'. This is undoubtedly where a new concept of citizenship seems to be needed, not suppressing the distinctions between national and transnational solidarities, but 'dialecticizing' them, or establishing a network of reciprocities between them (instead of creating a system of 'hierarchical citizenship' at the global level, where inequalities within nations and inequalities among nations are adding and reinforcing each other, as Stephen Castles convincingly argues). This will (ideally) involve a *reversed determination* of the dual notions of citizenship and nationality (or 'citizenship qua participation' and 'citizenship qua belonging'), where membership in a national community appears as a *capability* and not an essentialist condition or entitlement. But there seems to be no way of addressing this issue without, at the same time, reflecting again on the interaction of *race and class* in the production of inequalities. Whereas the notion of 'discrimination' apparently matches in a perfect manner the case of racial (or racist) exclusions from rights and statuses (albeit pushing them in the direction of 'natural' phenomena, as it also does for sexist discriminations, discriminations against disabled persons, etc.), it describes very badly the production of class inequalities, if it does not squarely ignore and cover them.

Politically, programs of redistribution and equal opportunities counteracting the extreme forms of class inequality are very unlikely to become included in the range of antidiscrimination norms, especially in a period of seeming triumph of neo-liberal ideologies. This also explain why there is such a resistance to include basic social rights within the realm of 'fundamental rights' protected by constitutional or quasi-constitutional Charters, while cultural rights are more easily recognized – at least verbally. But socially there is a complete overdetermination of class by race, and race by class. The creation of the notion of 'social exclusion', particularly discussed by Carl-Ulrik Schierup in this volume, is a perfect example. It was prepared by the way in which social rights became progressively incorporated into the broader citizenship of the Welfare State (which I would define myself as *national and social* state), and crystallized in its crisis, within the context of economic globalization and labor migrations. Class conditions (especially when it comes to the extreme forms of unstable migrant labor) will directly determine which 'ethnic', 'cultural', 'religious' differences become *racialized* and stigmatized or serve as imaginary characters of the excluded Other. And racial or quasi-racial identifications will become immediate instruments for the reproduction of class differences (what we might call 'classification' toward upper or lower levels) both inside and outside the national territory. As a consequence, a European political agenda for fighting discriminations, while usefully pushing the governments and civil societies of the member states to confront their own dark side, particularly their postcolonial embedded forms of violence, might also divert the attention from the dismantling of social protections of labor and universal welfare, or reinforce the feeling, broadly shared among Europeans from the popular classes, that such a dismantling forms the hidden agenda of the European Union. But, again, this is a double-edged process, and the effect could be in the longer run to make plainly visible the extent to which race and class determinations are actually intertwined, and strengthen the collective demand for a *combined* politics of fighting discriminations, inequalities and exclusions in the new institutional space.

In short, the comparative study of the contradictions of democracy in Britain and France, and the illustration of the extent to which they are no longer independent, but form part of a broader European cultural, social, and political problem, shows that in this part of the world the idea and practices of citizenship have reached a *limit point*. Conflicts call for solutions, which call for institutions, which call for collective forces. Such forces, in turn, are slowly and separately emerging from different corners of the very diverse society in which we are living now (including the apparently most 'marginal' ones: witness the activity of refugee women associations described by Kursheed Wadia). Citizenship has a past, but it also has a future, partially recognizable in the shadow of current contradictions, partially unpredictable. It is the very openness of the situation which makes it such an exciting and vital object of reflection.

Index

Printed in the United States
140646LV00002B/13/A